THE ROLE OF HIGHER EDUCATION IN INITIAL TEACHER TRAINING

THE ROLE OF HIGHER EDUCATION IN INITIAL TEACHER TRAINING

EDITED BY
JOHN FURLONG AND RICHARD SMITH

London • Philadelphia

First published in 1996

Kogan Page Limited
120 Pentonville Road
London N1 9JN

British Library Cataloguing in Publication Data

A CIP record for this book is available from the British Library.

ISBN 0 7494 1619 X

Typeset by JS Typesetting, Wellingborough, Northants.
Printed and bound in Great Britain by Clays Ltd, St Ives plc

CONTENTS

Part 3: Principles Guiding the Future of Higher Education in Initial Teacher Training

NOTES ON THE CONTRIBUTORS

Patricia Ambrose is a Senior Administrator at the Committee of Vice-Chancellors and Principals (CVCP), where she provides policy analysis and advice on many academic areas, including teacher education. She has recently published papers on continuing education and vocational higher education.

Michael Barber is a professor at the London Institute of Education. He has carried out extensive research on aspects of school improvement, urban education and teacher appraisal. His recent books include *The Making of the 1944 Education Act* (Cassell, 1994).

David Bridges is Professor of Education at the University of East Anglia. He was recently Director of the Eastern Region Teacher Education Consortium (ERTEC) in the Employment Department's Enterprise and Higher Education programme. His writing on teacher education includes, co-edited with Trevor Kerry, *Developing Teachers Professionally* (Routledge).

Carole Cox teaches English at Wyggeston Collegiate Sixth Form College in Leicester, where she is also Head of Theatre Studies and Equal Opportunities Co-Ordinator. She recently completed her doctoral thesis on F R Leavis, and has published a number of articles on literary education.

Peter Downes is Head of Hinchingbrooke School, Huntingdon; he was President of the Secondary Heads' Association, 1994–95. He is a regular contributor to periodicals such as *Managing Schools Today* and lectures widely on school budgeting, school governance and the development of financial autonomy for schools.

John Furlong is Professor of Education at the University of Bristol. He is author of a number of books and articles on initial teacher education. His most recent work has been on the role of mentors in supporting student teachers' school-based learning.

Philip Gardner is University Lecturer in Education and Fellow of St Edmund's College, Cambridge. He is currently researching a book on the oral history of teaching in the twentieth century. His previous books include *The Lost Elementary Schools of Victorian England*.

Paul Hirst is Emeritus Professor of Education, University of Cambridge, and Visiting Professor at the University of London Institute of Education. His major writings in philosophy of education concern issues in curriculum planning, moral and aesthetic education and teacher training.

Peter John was Head of Department and Head of Faculty in two large comprehensive schools before entering teacher education in 1989. His research interests include the policy and practice of teacher education, the teaching and learning of history and the role of citizenship in the curriculum.

David McNamara is Professor of Education at the University of Hull. He has researched and published extensively in the fields of teacher education and primary schooling, including the recent *Classroom Pedagogy and Primary Practice* (Routledge, 1994).

Trisha Maynard is lecturer in the Department of Education, University of Swansea. She is co-author (with John Furlong) of *Mentoring Student Teachers: the growth of professional knowledge* (Routledge, 1995).

Richard Pring is Professor of Educational Studies, University of Oxford. His research interests include philosophy of education and changing policies and practice in education and training. Recent publications include *Closing the Gap: Liberal Education and Vocational Preparation* (Hodder & Stoughton, 1995).

Richard Smith is Senior Lecturer in Education and currently Director of Combined Studies in Social Sciences at the University of Durham. He is editor of the *Journal of Philosophy of Education*.

Margaret Wilkin, currently at the Research Unit, Homerton College, Cambridge, specialises in the politics of education, mentoring in initial teacher training and postgraduate education. Her most recent publication, edited with Derek Sankey, is *Collaboration and Transition in Initial Teacher Training* (Kogan Page, 1994).

INTRODUCTION

John Furlong and Richard Smith

One principal difficulty – and in many ways a chief point of interest – in writing about higher education (HE) and the training of teachers is that none of the parts will stand still. For a start, whether teachers are to be *trained* or rather *educated* in the sense of being offered a wider intellectual challenge and enrichment is precisely one point at issue. Nor is it that the training (to concede this term here for the sake of convenience) of teachers is the only contentious variable, as if the schools teachers are being trained for and the higher education that might or might not have a role in that training are stable and known quantities. To take higher education first, what was not long ago an elite and enclosed university system is now moving to one characterised by far greater participation and flexibility. Modularity and credit transfer bring greater possibilities for students to exercise choice in what they study, and the majority of students is now over 21 years of age. Political parties, and students themselves, are prepared to contemplate the 'customers' of higher education paying a direct contribution towards the cost of their education in return for the benefits it confers.

In short, 'universities and colleges are being transformed from sheltered institutions of the pre-modern world to public service organisations in a modern (or, some would say, post-modern) world' (Higher Education Quality Council, 1994, p.313 para. 1000). They are likely to become less the sites for the initiation of youngsters into disciplines of knowledge defined by academics themselves and more places where people go at different points in their lives to update their knowledge, acquire new skills and reorient themselves. Perhaps they will become 'more like a combination of FE college and polytechnic than Oxbridge' (Ball, 1995). Against this background the Secretary of State in November 1994 called for a review of higher education and a re-examination of the question of what it is *for*.

If the nature of higher education is in flux, this is more true still for our society in general. It has become a commonplace that we live in a time of rapid, even unparalleled, change. New technologies introduce new ways of working; thrusting Pacific Rim economies pose a threat to the living standards of the rest of the world. Nations risk being left behind unless they learn to adapt in response. Flexibility, creativity and the abandonment of outmoded practices are all called for. Those in positions of responsibility in education and business above all need skills in the 'management of change'. In future we must all see the acquisition of new skills and knowledge as a challenge and a stimulus rather than as a problem and a barrier. We need to become a 'learning society'; this (see, eg, the White Paper

Competitiveness: Helping Business to Win, 1994) is the state of affairs for which education and industry must find solutions.

The world of the school is itself not unchanging either, despite the impression sometimes conveyed that we now have – and always did have, but for an unhappy interlude of child-centred progressivism – a secure subject-based curriculum, intuitively recognisable from century's beginning to century's end, with little more addition than that of information technology. The last seven years have brought enormous change, particularly in the management of schools and in regimes of assessment and recording. The curriculum too seethes beneath the surface of ordered subjects. The cross-curricular elements (environmental education, health education, education for citizenship) threaten to break through and assert their obvious importance to the world in which we live. There is the whole ethical dimension of education, which politicians hasten to bolt back on whenever mischief is in the news and which every teacher knows cannot be ignored. Our confused and changing times call for personal and social education, the preparation of young people to be flexible and creative, emotionally literate, able and willing to 'learn to learn', and so on. The last decade has brought TVEI and Enterprise Education, as well as the National Curriculum itself, and it would be astonishing if there were not further radical changes to the nature and content of schooling in the next decade.

The extent of change affecting schools, universities and our society in general makes it easier to understand why the preparation of teachers is such a complex issue. It is not a sign of failure if the agencies historically involved in this training (HE, government, schools) do not believe they have already 'got it right' once and for all. It is no criticism of the contributors to this book that they have no simple answers, that they do not articulate a common vision or supply a blueprint for the future.

An understanding of these changes suggests two further points. First, teacher training pioneered many developments now taking place in 'mainstream' higher education: new ways of conceiving academic disciplines responsively to students' needs, close collaboration with organisations (mainly, but not only, schools) in the wider community, a shift from 'teaching' to 'learning' as the emphasis and from 'direction' to 'guidance' as the mode of teaching (cp. HEQC, 1994, p.315, para. 1010). Above all, this arm of higher education challenges the educationally disastrous fantasy that universities are first and foremost transmitters of information, the only difference between past and present being that where once they transmitted information clumsily via the lecture now they will do so dazzlingly and cost-effectively via the Internet and other devices. Teacher training, just as work with trainee or experienced social workers, probation officers, nurses, lawyers or managers, is a standing reminder of the many different educational relationships that take place in universities, in which matters of understanding, values, skills, perspectives, sensibility, maturation and even wisdom – and, crucially, of the sometimes extraordinarily complex interrelationships between these qualities – are at issue, as well as ones simply of knowledge.

The second point is that, in times of rapid and complex change in particular, we cannot afford to neglect any of the resources from which understanding and even inspiration may be drawn. As Barnett (1994) notes, the rationality of our society in one sense may be increasing incrementally, but it tends to be rationality of a limited and one-dimensional kind. Universities' traditional commitment to truth, and the academic freedom which makes this possible, should perhaps be understood largely as the readiness to preserve and develop ideas, languages and ways of thinking which do not necessarily fit the prejudices of the age. Few people on the outside of universities have the expertise or resources to challenge, in the name of truth, either the current received wisdom or the assertions of politicians or those who, more and more in our centralised state, find their roles politicised and compromised.

To insist on the importance of universities' involvement in the preparation of teachers is neither to insist on the *status quo* nor to diminish the importance of the involvement of schools in the process. Clearly that involvement is properly fundamental and extensive, and the recognition that schoolteachers and university tutors meet on this ground as equals, with different and complementary forms of understanding and expertise, is the basis for honest and successful cooperation and partnership. That is one theme of this book: the benefits which a full and vigorous partnership between schools and universities can bring to both trainee and practising teachers *and* to universities themselves. In his re-examination of 'the idea of the university' the American historian Jaroslav Pelikan (1992) writes:

> *When they are performing at their full potential, the professional schools of the university [that is, departments and schools of education, law, medicine and so on] are positioned in a delicate balance between the university and the society, and specifically between the university and the professional constituencies for which the professional schools are responsible. The university protects them from becoming the vassals of the constituency or shaping their course to what the constituency believes at any particular moment to be needed for a true professional in the field, which may be, and usually is, significantly different from what such a professional will need some years down the line. But the constituency, in turn, protects them from becoming mere satellites of the graduate school of arts and sciences. . . . That delicate balance puts the professional schools into their leadership position in the lifelong education that is reshaping the mission of the university as a whole.*

Our purpose here is precisely to try to develop the thinking about the 'full potential' of higher education for the preparation of teachers and so for its other roles in our changing world. Whether the government's alterations to the pattern of the initial training of teachers will prove a stimulus or a set-back to such thinking remains to be seen.

In Part 1, The Changing Context of Higher Education's Contribution to Initial Teacher Education, Pring contrasts the most recent government-led reforms of initial teacher education with the earlier postwar period when the universities were dominant. University domination meant the domination of the 'theory into practice' model of training with students spending substantial amounts of time studying 'the foundation disciplines' of education. How and why was this dominant model challenged? Pring sets out the range of criticisms – many of which he considers have some validity – that in recent years were levelled at the theory-into-practice model of training. He then presents what he sees as the basic principles of effective training: principles built around partnerships between schools and higher education. Effective partnerships are, he suggests, difficult to achieve; moreover the distinctive role of the university in that partnership needs to be argued for. In concluding,

Pring sets out his own view of how that contribution can be justified.

Ambrose provides an account of the campaign by the Committee of Vice Chancellors and Principals (CVCP) to defend the role of higher education in teacher training during the passage of the 1994 Education Act. A central provision of the Act was the establishment of the Teacher Training Agency (TTA) which has formally separated the funding of teacher education in England from the funding of the rest of higher education. As Ambrose explains, both the initial government consultation paper and the subsequent Education Bill were seen by the CVCP as a threat not only to the future involvement of higher education in initial teacher education but to academic freedom and the continuing role of universities in professional and vocational education.

Gardner sets the changing relationship between the systems of higher education and initial teacher education in a broader historical context. At one level, he suggests that the establishment of the TTA may be seen as an interruption to a long-standing and fundamental principle that there should be a necessary and intimate relationship between the two systems, a principle first instituted by the Cross Commission of 1868. However, as Gardner demonstrates, the reality is that the relationship has always been fragile, full of disappointments and lost opportunities as well as successes. From this view, the advent of the TTA does not represent a fundamental break with the past so much as a manifestation of a long-standing weakness in the position of teacher education within higher education.

Bridges takes a different approach to evaluating the development of school-based training in that he starts from a recognition that the whole notion of higher education is currently undergoing radical transformation. Dramatically increased student numbers, the development of more flexible teaching modes, the introduction of modularisation with its consequent undermining of coherent disciplines and levels of study, the development of accreditation of prior and experiential leaning, all these pressures, and many more, are leading to an increasingly diversified system with different aims and different criteria of quality. From this perspective, the development of school-based and even school-led training does not appear particularly radical. Bridges suggests that any debate about the key principles of higher education that should be protected in initial teacher training needs to address the issue of how they are to be maintained within this new and complex context.

The context of change, however, is not merely one that affects higher education: schools too are subject to massive pressures. Barber argues that any serious discussion of the future of teacher education must engage with the complex and unpredictable nature of these changes for they will profoundly affect what sort of teachers we will need in the future. As the new millennium approaches, Barber predicts that society is likely to expect the education service to play an increasingly broad and ambitious role, including improved academic standards and contributions to solving a range of pressing social and ecological problems. While the evidence suggests that the effectiveness of teachers has improved significantly over the last decade, facing the challenges of the future demands that the profession is radically reconstructed. Fewer teachers will be needed but they will have to be far more qualified and higher education must have a central role in that process.

In Part 2, The Complexities of Initial Teacher Education, Downes provides a head teacher's perspective on the strengths and limitations of school-based programmes. While there clearly are, from the school's point of view, a number of disadvantages to the partnership model of training, over all, he concludes that the advantages outweigh them. However, he does suggest that schools are unlikely, in any number, to try to take on complete responsibility for initial training. The responsibility and the expectations are simply too great. No matter how dedicated and well-motivated practising teachers are, they simply do not have the time to read widely in the methodology of their own subject, let alone keep up-to-date on all the wider trends in curriculum development and educational management theory. Functional effectiveness, Downes suggests, is not enough; there needs to be time for reflection and the wider perspective, and this is where the higher education contribution continues to be paramount.

Cox, a secondary English teacher, provides a more detailed rationale for the contribution of higher education in the training of teachers in her own discipline. English teachers are, according to Cox, particularly in need of the contribution that higher education can make to their professional development because of the fundamentally ethical nature of the subject. Studying literature, for example, demands that one wrestle with what characters choose to do and choose not to do and how the writer presents these choices to the readers. Such dimensions, Cox suggests, cannot but bring ethical considerations into play – as such, they provide a significant challenge for English teachers working in a pluralistic society. Yet despite the centrality of ethics in English, first-degree students seldom have the chance systematically to confront such issues yet they are essential for effective schoolteaching. A proper consideration of ethics could never be provided 'on the job' for student teachers and the continued involvement of higher education is, Cox suggests, therefore essential.

The two chapters that follow take a rather different tack in that they present evidence from empirical investigations of different aspects of teacher education programmes. Maynard begins by noting that in the latest government regulations on primary teacher-education school experience is understood in simple terms. Learning to teach is constructed as no more than the acquisition of 'practical skills' and the opportunity to 'apply' subject knowledge. If this is all school-based learning is, Maynard asks 'What possible justification can there be for the involvement of the higher education tutor?' She goes on to report her research which indicates that students' school-based learning is far more complex than the government circular implies. If students are to become professional educators, Maynard argues, then they need to be challenged critically to evaluate their thinking and their practice. Maynard's evidence leads her to suggest that there are profound difficulties in expecting mentors to take on this 'challenging' role; as a result, she argues that it is a task that must continue to be taken on by the higher education tutor.

John reports the results of an in-depth empirical investigation into the work of secondary teacher educators, focusing in particular on the subject-method seminar. From the analysis of extensive interviews, observations and documents, John suggests that subject-method seminars seem to serve five crucial functions: a liberalising role; a collaborating role; an enquiring role; a reconceptualising role; a modelling role. As a result of his analysis, he identifies a number of 'oppositions' between the contribution of schools and higher education in initial training. They are: reflection versus action; scepticism versus direct intervention; theory versus pragmatism; scholarly versus personal justifications; universal versus particularistic experience. He concludes that the seminars offered by subject tutors therefore serve a vital and unique function in the education of prospective teachers.

In the final section, Part 3, Principles Guiding the Future of Higher Education in Initial Teacher Training, Wilkin avowedly directs a polemic at teacher trainers based in higher education. For too long, Wilkin suggests, the response of lecturers to government-imposed changes was merely a political one. That political response is understandable; jobs are threatened and the contribution of the lecturers diminished and demeaned. Nevertheless, such an approach undermines the credibility and stature of higher education. Instead, Wilkin argues that those in higher education should take a broader view and concentrate on the reappraisal of government initiatives in their value for students. If lecturers do this publicly and fairly and then act firmly on their conclusions, it will, Wilkin argues, reaffirm their expertise and strengthen their professionalism.

Furlong begins by exploring the 'sociological' and 'epistemological' challenges to teacher trainers in higher education; their autonomy has been undermined and there is a lack of certainty about the value of their specialised forms of knowledge. However, Furlong emphasises that such challenges are not confined to the field of teacher education – they are endemic throughout higher education. He goes on to argue that much of the practical preparation of student teachers that currently takes place in universities and colleges could, in principle, take place elsewhere. If higher education has a contribution to make in this field, it must be sought in the *essential* nature of higher education itself. That essential nature, Furlong argues, is revealed by students' and lecturers' common commitment to the pursuit of 'truth'. Finally, Furlong discusses the significance of such a commitment to the development of teachers' practical professional knowledge.

In the next chapter, Hirst explores the role of theoretical knowledge in professional development. As he notes, education as an object of study is a highly complex affair; moreover, the practice of education has been subject to sustained study only in relatively recent times. Not surprisingly, the achievements of this work have to date been limited. Even though such achievements are limited, to ignore the complexity, to advocate simplistic and reductionist accounts of goals and procedures with minimal practical training is merely an evasion of the demands that contemporary professionals constantly face. To fail to equip young entrants to the profession with a clear and critical grasp of at least the most defensible goals and practices of education is, Hirst argues, to put them and their pupils at the mercy of prejudice and ill-considered ideology. Some engagement with theory, however partial and inadequate, is therefore essential, yet the relationship between theory and practice is far from straightforward. Hirst reminds us that the rationalist paradigm, which saw practice as the application of theory, has been undermined. Theoretical reason cannot itself, he suggests, provide the basis for generating rational practice, but it can provide crucially important knowledge. Such knowledge sets out the boundaries, the framework within which rational practices can be developed. How best to initiate student teachers into all of this, Hirst suggests, is currently inadequately developed, but it is hard to escape the conclusion that it demands experts – who have a sophisticated and analytical grasp of the different elements of practice. There is a vital and continuing role for a contribution from those in higher education.

In sharp contrast, McNamara argues for a reduction in the role of University Departments of Education (UDEs). He begins by arguing that it is no longer possible to insist that quality in initial teacher education necessarily demands the involvement of higher education: other agencies – schools, Local Education

Authorities (LEAs) and even private consultancies can provide training that is equally good. While much of higher education may continue for the foreseeable future to have a role in the practical training of teachers, it is no longer possible, McNamara suggests, for such training to be at the heart of what UDEs actually do. Instead, he argues that UDEs should focus on what is distinctive in their contribution to the study of education. His central purpose is to explore what that distinctive contribution might be. It is, he suggests, to contribute to the 'world of ideas' about education, with which it may be desirable for students in training to engage, but not essential. In the future, the substantive focus, for what inevitably will be a smaller number of schools of education, should be undergraduate, post-graduate and post-experience teaching and research.

Like Hirst, Smith, in the final chapter, is also concerned with the role of theory in professional preparation but he asserts that traditionally its role has been miscast; as a result much of the practice of teacher education in the last 30 years has been deeply flawed. For Smith, the central difficulty with theory is that it has been seen traditionally as informing *practice* whereas in reality its best role is in supporting, enriching and stimulating *people*. The education of teachers as persons is so central because professional activity centrally involves judgement and 'practical wisdom'; as a result currently fashionable approaches to training which see it as technical activity are simply inadequate. In conclusion, Smith discusses what education in judgement and practical wisdom might involve and what role higher education might play in that process.

References

Ball, C (1995) 'Developing the Learning Society', speech to the North of England Conference, York, January.

Barnett, R (1994) *The Limits of Competence*. Buckingham: Open University/ Society for Research into Higher Education (SRHE).

Higher Education Quality Council (HEQC) (1994) *Choosing To Change: Extending Access, Choice and Mobility in Higher Education*. London: HEQC.

Pelikan, J (1992) *The Idea of the University: A Reexamination*. London: Yale University Press.

PART 1

The Changing Context of Higher Education's Contribution to Initial Teacher Education

CHAPTER 1

JUST DESERT

Richard Pring

The shift from university-led to school-based teacher training was spelt out in the Secretary of State's North of England Conference speech in January, 1992. Kenneth Clarke argued that: the training of teachers should be 80 per cent school-based; schools should be selected for this purpose according to criteria agreed by the Secretary of State (these schools to include independent ones); mentors should be chosen from within these selected schools to supervise the trainees; there should be a closer partnership between schools and colleges in which the schools should take the lead in planning; there should be a reallocation of funding to reflect this change of balance; and the training should be more practical, much less theoretical.

The reasons given for these 'reforms' were three:

- to attract into teaching those who might be put off by the orthodoxies of the past;
- to enable the Council for the Accreditation of Teacher Education (CATE) to achieve its objective of a much more competency-led and school-based training;
- to 'break the dogmas about teaching method and classroom organisation' which (it was claimed) prevailed in training institutions.

My aim is, first, to outline the university role in the heyday of 'theory before practice'; second, to examine the growing disillusion with this university dominated perspective; third, to spell out certain 'first principles' concerning the preparation of teachers; last, in the light of this history and of the criticisms, to outline the distinctive role of universities in the professional preparation of future teachers.

The Historical 'University Role'

The new picture of teacher training might be contrasted with what had developed since 1947. The McNair report of that year recommended that training institutions come under the academic umbrella of university-based institutes of education. This would give an academic respectability to the training of teachers, which too often was lacking, and would ensure intellectual rigour in thinking about teaching. In subsequent years, universities attempted to give this academic respectability. Diploma courses were established; bachelor of education (BEd) degrees (first, three years ordinary, then four years honours) were created as the main route into teaching, particularly for primary teachers; a literature grew in the philosophy, psychology, sociology and history of education which became the basis of masters- and research-degree programmes. These 'foundation disciplines', as philosophy, psychology and sociology came to be called, were celebrated in Tibble's edited book *The Study of Education* (1967), which described the foundation of the 'general theory of education' as distinct from the methodological questions peculiar to the teaching of specific subjects or topics. Such a general theory was felt to be necessary because of what Peters (1977, p.158) referred to as 'the undifferentiated mush' of the theoretical perspective which too often had been the academic background to the profession of teaching.

Thus, philosophy of education drew upon the prevalent tradition in analytic philosophy of a close examination of relevant concepts – those of 'education', 'teaching', 'needs', 'interests', 'subject disciplines', 'learning' – clarifying language, making distinctions where meaning was vague or blurred, pointing to the deeper questions in ethics or the philosophy of mind or epistemology which underlined the everyday practical decisions and arguments of teachers. The sociology of education located the organisation of schooling and of learning in a wider science of society characterised by key concepts such as 'social class', 'equality of opportunity' and 'social norms'. The psychology of education exposed different theoretical positions which underpinned our understanding of children's development and learning: those of the cognitive developmentalists, such as Piaget and Kohlberg, on the one hand; and, on the other, those of the behaviourists, such as Pavlov and Skinner.

The point was that there could be a systematic theoretical position which illuminated the task of getting children to learn. Such a position paid respect to the work of philosophers who were concerned with questions such as:

- What is worth learning?
- What is the logical structure of the knowledge which we seek to teach?
- What is the logical connection between what we perceive and measure and what goes on in the child's mind?

Once established, such a position then sought the empirical evidence, through the social sciences of sociology and psychology, for determining the most appropriate means for reaching those desirable, philosophically delineated, goals.

Such a position is best illustrated by Wilson, Williams and Sugarman (1967). The book, in three parts, first gives an analysis of what is *meant* by 'moral'. It draws upon the work of mainstream moral philosophy, in particular that of Hare in *The Language of Morals* (1952). In clarifying the meaning, the first part sets the stage for the empirical evidence from sociology and psychology in the final two parts. From such a highly developed theoretical position, certain curricular prescriptions followed (Wilson, 1990).

Two aspects of such a theoretical approach need noting: first, there was the assumption that theory both precedes and, in retrospect, illuminates practice. The practising teacher would be practising more effectively, more intelligently, having thus acquired a theoretical perspective. Versed in philosophy, such teachers would have clarified their goals; have a better grounded set of educational aims; and be able to identify more effectively the structure of the subject matters they were to teach; not be fobbed off so easily with ill-founded prescriptions; and be able to talk more intelligently about their educational principles and practice to sceptical parents. They would, in other words, be educational thinkers, not simply trained craftsmen.

Second, such a theoretical perspective underlined the importance of placing the preparation of teachers in the hands of universities and gave a dominant role to those universities, for these were the places where theory was generated, research conducted for the development of that theory, and academic respectability bestowed upon those who were responsible for teaching the next generation.

I feel much sympathy with this position. How our society raises, and educates, the next generation is surely a most important yet difficult issue that any society must address, and it cannot escape the knotty philosophical questions concerning what is a 'worthwhile form of life' to which we want to introduce the next generation. It would seem prima facie plausible that the formation of *thinking* teachers would require systematic thinking *about* teaching and that those who are to form the minds of the next generation should themselves have their minds formed by thinking systematically, rigorously and, on the basis of evidence rather than anecdote, about what they are doing. And yet so much seems to have come unstuck. Why?

Disillusion with Academic Respectability

There are several quite distinct reasons for recent scepticism over the programme which Tibble's contributors outlined so confidently.

The Theoretical Critique of Theory

Perhaps the most vigorous critique of the academic respectability of educational theory is that of O'Connor in *An Introduction to the Philosophy of Education* (1957). The critique is as follows. Theory refers to a set of principles which organise experience in a coherent way. Such theory explains what happens and predicts, in the light of such explanations, what *will* happen in certain circumstances. Sociological theory, for example, should explain why children from certain social backgrounds generally fail and would, in the light of such explanations, predict what would happen to them if certain interventions were made. 'Schools cannot compensate for society', declares Bernstein (1967), but schools could take society into account in determining the purposes of schooling as well as in alleviating some of the consequences of social background.

O'Connor asks, where are these theories which predict with accuracy and precision and which, in the light of the evidence, can be shown to be true or false? It is the absence of any such developing theoretical framework, analogous to developments which are found in the natural sciences, which prompted O'Connor to declare that there is no theory. It is an illusion. It is little more than the emotive preferences of particular power groups – let us say, those in universities in whose interest it is to create theory – dressed up in a language which makes it *seem* academically respectable. According to O'Connor, there are two sorts of statement in so-called educational theory: statements about desirable goals such as happiness, personal growth, social welfare or intellectual excellence, and statements about the means to achieving those goals. The first are ultimately matters of choice rather than rational argument; no theory can disguise the irrational and emotive nature of why certain kinds of goal are chosen in preference to others. The second are matters of empirical fact and require clear, testable, lawlike statements if they are to be theoretically significant. How few and insignificant are the well-tested statements that we have! Is it not apparent that, even in such practically important matters as the effect of class-size, no one can point to well-tested theories upon which policy might be determined or criticised? Hence, educational theory is but a 'courtesy title' given to a miscellany of facts, anecdotes, speculation, feelings and desires, and disconnected theoretical statements drawn from sociology and psychology.

O'Connor's criticism appeared nearly 40 years ago, but it is still significant insofar as it represents a distrust of theory, which resonates with less philosophically minded people who have influenced the shift away from academic respectability to pragmatic common-sense and professional relevance.

Political Scepticism

A second and related critique has been that universities, under the banner of academic respectability, were often peddling theoretically suspect political propaganda. Such bodies as the Centre for Policy Studies assumed that much theory was the promulgation of ideologically committed views about children or about society which have done much harm to individuals and to society as a whole. The aim of creating a more equal society is often quoted as an example. Lord Joseph once accused me of being responsible for all the harm that had befallen our schools – for introducing teachers to the child-centred tradition as developed in the works of John Dewey. The criticism of political bias is linked with O'Connor's critique of educational theory in that theoretically unsound beliefs not only permit nonsense but promote it under the banner of academic respectability.

Theory Before Practice

A third criticism was that, even if there be a respectable theoretical framework, this is not the sort of theory which one first learns and then puts into practice. Theory provides no such clear-cut prescription for practice. Practice is too muddled and complicated, too unpredictable, too dependent upon whim and idiosyncrasy and too much the product of free choice for it to be captured in any theoretical and simplified account of how things work. The tacit knowledge and the intelligent practice are what count. Teachers, or people in general, do not think first and then act; they do not entertain theory and then engage in practice. There is no clear distinction between 'ends' and aims, on the one hand, and 'the means' of getting there, on the other. The rational curriculum planning of Tyler (1949) is not a valid model of human activity: rational behaviour requires intelligent activity, certainly, but not intelligence which *precedes* the activity, not a 'thinking' and then a 'doing', not a 'theory' and then a 'practice'.

This theory/practice dichotomy was one reason why, so it was argued, the training of teachers became increasingly separated from the practice of teaching and why the role of the university needed to be scrutinised critically. Teachers were all but excluded from the formation of teachers; their practical wisdom did not add up to the theoretical knowledge that universities, in positions of power, insisted was necessary.

Such a range of criticism – the philosophical defects of educational theory, the political bias of educational theorists, and the irrelevance of theoretical training to professional practice, provided the basis for a practical critique of the university contribution.

The result of that critique has been the gradual undermining of the distinctive university contribution in several ways, and the Secretary of State's North of England speech simply reflected what was already happening. First, there was the weakening of the autonomy of the university in what should be considered an academically respectable training. University departments attempted to maintain the myths that they are autonomous in the organisation of their teaching programmes, that they are the custodians of an educational tradition which respects the freedom of thought based on scholarship and research; that such a tradition should be protected by not external constraints but internal conditions of academic critique and corroboration; matters of truth and validity, of enquiry and scholarship should not be matters of government decision; such matters arise from within a tradition of research and are protected by free intellectual enquiry, sustained by institutions dedicated to that purpose. Such autonomy was not obviously so necessary to those who pay the money and are responsible for the supply of teachers. Once such autonomy in socially sensitive areas is massively dependent upon government funding, then it is difficult to justify. CATE was an instrument of government interference in the erstwhile autonomy of university departments. Courses had to comply with what the government, advised by its own politically selected advisers, thought were the competences that made for successful teaching. Universities could, of course, ignore such prescriptions; they could preserve their autonomy and appeal to academic respectability, critiquing (often with research-based justification) the government-prescribed competences. If they were to do so, however, the products of their courses would not be recognised as professionally qualified. In practice, the autonomy of professional studies in education, as in social work, was severely questioned.

More recently, the shift of funds for teacher training from the University Funding Council to the new TTA removed at one stroke the buffer between government funding and university autonomy – the protection against government interference in the freedom of enquiry and of teaching.

I want to be both supportive and critical of these developments: supportive because the autonomy of universities can not be unconditional, critical because something very important is in danger of being lost.

The autonomy of universities can never be unconditional because freedom of enquiry can be abused. Furthermore, that abuse is less easy to tolerate when those university activities are geared to preparing professional people for public service in medicine, teaching and social work. Wider social considerations need to be taken into account by the otherwise autonomous university departments, such that, if they are not taken into account, then others, protecting the interests of the 'consumer', will feel obliged to intervene. Do, for example, university departments, exercising their freedom, produce the competent teaching force which they are paid to deliver?

The problem is threefold, bearing in mind the criticisms already outlined. The critique of educational theory initiated by O'Connor has been continued ever since by different voices, including those who teach and who can see no sense in theory. It is hard to protect the autonomy of an academic discipline when the academic status of that discipline is seriously questioned. The criticism of O'Connor needed to be taken seriously; although those criticisms reflected a too limited and philosophically questionable 'theory of theory', they nonetheless raised the questions to which we must constantly return if universities are to justify their autonomy in the pursuit of educational theory. Are the theoretical claims argued for, O'Connor would ask, with sufficient clarity and precision that we would know what would count as evidence against them?

- Are the theories part of a sustained and developing body of knowledge which is thoroughly corroborated through critical enquiry?
- Are correct predictions made as a result of theory?
- Does the discussion about educational ends meet the criteria found acceptable within a wider tradition of philosophical criticism?

Second, lacking a firm, well-corroborated theoretical position, lacking a respectable and coherent tradition of intellectual enquiry and peopled often by lecturers of weak academic credentials, the academic world of education did produce much dross – a literature much of which could not be taken seriously by teachers, parents, policy-makers, the wider public and academics from other disciplines. This state of affairs is reflected in the current research-assessment exercise where some institutions are paying publishers to publish work otherwise found unacceptable, where new journals are established to publish articles rejected from elsewhere, where academics with poor publishing records spent weekends in jacuzzi-style hotels to produce collected papers to be edited and published by members of their own department. In preparation for the deadline of 31 March 1966, universities are proliferating professorships of education to seduce those who have 'serious' publications so that departmental ratings may be boosted. This is not confined to educational studies, but affects all university departments in this ill-conceived exercise. How can such risible behaviour be treated seriously by those who, outside the 'academic' world, look for the standards of academic rigour and seriousness? How can teachers and parents respect the claims to academic respectability, as departments of education are forced to take part in the inflationary exercise of moving the publications around to the highest bidder? No increase in quality, only in quantity and price.

Last, there was the exclusion of those who teach from the world of those who teach about teaching – institutionalised through different salary scales, career paths, titles and status. This is but one aspect of that dualism between theory and practice, thinking and doing, 'knowing that' and 'knowing how'.

It is reflected in the justified criticism by many teachers of the university lecturers, charged with the training of teachers but drawing upon past experience only dimly remembered and never critiqued. Are not the real experts of the *practice* of teaching in the schools? Has not the myth been wrongly promoted that those most distant from the practice are the ones who have the superior knowledge from which to advise and to criticise?

These interconnected criticisms – the poor state of theory, the all-too-often peddling of *personal* values from a *public* position on the basis of theoretically questionable authority, and the consequent separation of that theory and these values from the world of practice – are what sustained the polemical writings of Lawlor (1990) and O'Hear (1988) as they criticise the past arrangements for teacher education, infiltrate agencies such as CATE and the TTA and influence government policy, shifting it towards a much more school-based, school-dominated apprenticeship model. Nor is the position of higher education helped by those who, seeing which way the wind is blowing, suddenly and uncritically embrace school-based teacher education, talk enthusiastically about partnership, 'scatter their students to the schools' but collect the fees and write about schools instead. One college of higher education was allocated a large cohort of secondary students even though the college had no experience of secondary training, no research or scholarship in this area. The students were put into schools, in recognition of the new school-based nature of the teacher training, an ex-teacher was appointed to organise the activity and to collect from elsewhere reading lists and material (the Open University came in useful) and the college collected the fees. Why preserve the pretence of a university activity? Unless university departments can justify a distinctive university role – not simply orchestrate a school-based scheme or concentrate upon writing yet more discredited theory – then they should be closed down.

There have always been those who doubt that universities are the proper place for professional preparation. John Stuart Mill in his inaugural lecture at St Andrews in 1867 wrote (p.133):

> *There is a tolerably general agreement about what a university is not. It is not a place of professional education. Universities are not intended to teach the knowledge required to fit men for some special mode of gaining their livelihood. Their objective is not to make skilful lawyers, or physicians or engineers, but capable and cultivated human beings.*

Such a sentiment is widely shared, and reinforced where the ultimate responsibility for professional training resides outside the university in professional bodies or in the government which must provide the public services that the professions serve. It is reinforced further where the theory is not sufficiently refined as to produce 'capable and cultivated human beings'.

Yet, sympathetic though I am to those criticisms, I am not wholly convinced. I believe (and argue later, under 'University Role') that there remains a distinctive role for universities, that such a role is essential if the profession of teaching is to be preserved but that it is a role which must take account of these criticisms.

Principles

We must consider the principles from which to begin any consideration of how teachers should be prepared; only then might we be clear about the distinctive role of universities. In establishing such principles, I refer particularly to the work of Donald McIntyre whose research over many years sustains a view of teacher education that respects the distinctive contribution of teachers (Brown and McIntyre, 1993; McIntyre, 1989, 1991). McIntyre quotes Alexander (1984):

> *Learning to teach must be a continual process of hypothesis-testing framed by detailed analysis of the values and practical constraints fundamental to teaching. The 'theory' for teacher education should therefore incorporate (i) speculative theory, (ii) the findings of empirical research, (iii) the craft knowledge of practising teachers, but none should be presented as having prescriptive implication for practice; instead, students should be encouraged to approach their own practice with the intention of testing hypothetical principles drawn from the consideration of these different types of knowledge.*

The reason why 'none should be presented as having prescriptive implications for practice' is that 'there is not, nor can there be, *any* systematic corpus of theoretical knowledge from which prescriptive principles for teaching can be generated' (McIntyre, 1989).

In other words, there is a deep suspicion of the 'from theory to practice' approach; in the absence of a 'corpus of theoretical knowledge' no general prescription for practice can be put forward. In that respect, there is sympathy with the philosophical criticism of O'Connor. Instead, there is a recognition of the 'tacit knowledge' which underpins successful practice. Most people recognise the good teacher – the teacher who works intelligently, imaginatively, sensitively, displaying knowledge of subject and of the many and varied ways in which that subject might be represented in an intelligible and fruitful mode. Such a teacher displays an understanding not only of the individual's learning pattern but of how that pattern fits into the mosaic of learning patterns within the larger group. That understanding is implicit within classroom management, but such knowledge is implicit, tacit, practical. There is a 'knowing how' which cannot be captured within the 'knowing that' of theory. The question then is: how can one give the trainee teacher access to that tacit or craft knowledge of the teacher? Moreover, if such knowledge can be given, why should it be the job of the university teacher, removed from practice, rather than that of the schoolteacher, who has the craft knowledge? Furthermore, how is that access possible when trainee teachers come with their own conceptions of teaching – and own agenda for learning based on those conceptions – derived from models of teaching in their own school experience? For example, trainees whose experience of teaching has been that of a formal grammar school might find the dominant ideas of teaching within their own experience too strong to enable them to avail of themselves of the craft knowledge of the successful but less formal approach of the comprehensive school mentor.

The consequence seems to be that:

- the trainee must be placed in a situation where preconceptions of how to teach may be challenged
- such a challenge is made where there is access to practical or tacit knowledge, possibly with different values and beliefs
- such a challenge is accompanied by the encouragement within a framework where fresh ideas might be hypothesised, put to the test and evaluated.

The trainee teacher needs to *develop* a knowledge of successful practice – a knowledge drawn from access to others' practical knowledge, from a process of hypothesising, testing and evaluating performance, from a critical examination of educational aims and values and from relevant research. The lack of a clear corpus of theoretical knowledge entails the process of creating *personal* knowledge, but it must be created within a *public* context of criticism, evaluation and research. Such a process needs to be learned; it requires both intellectual skills and intellectual virtues, developed within a context in which the skills or virtues are respected. It requires a context in which the uncertainties with which conclusions are reached might be recognised, but in which such uncertainties can be embraced with confidence – if the conclusions reached are the product of deliberation, reflection, evaluation, criticism and relevant knowledge.

The consequences of this for teacher education are:

1. There should be 'training schools' in which trainee teachers are exposed to the craft knowledge of successful teachers, but in which there is the supportive context wherein that practice, in the light of pupils' learning, can be examined critically, adapted, tested and evaluated.
2. There should be a prolonged attachment of the trainee to that school so that the thinking about specific practice is firmly embedded within the broader context of school life – embracing conflicting educational aims and values.

3. Teaching styles and values should be explored within a group of other trainees and teaching mentors, who can, from different perspectives, help challenge received assumptions, but also provide encouragement and support.
4. Analysis should be focused on the subject matter to be taught and on the mode through which it might be made intelligible to learners at various stages of development.
5. There should be a stage-by-stage initiation into teaching, eschewing the 'in-the-deep-end' approach, as skills are acquired, confidence built up, knowledge gained, evaluation developed, criticism engaged in, values questioned and formed.
6. Alternative styles and values should be shown, such that received assumptions can be challenged and new approaches put to the test.
7. When relevant, a wider critical debate and research should be introduced about the very matter which the trainee teacher is confronting at the school.
8. A systematic and diagnostic feedback should be given to trainee teachers on how their performance is perceived in terms of pupils' learning, professional qualities, and quality of thinking about teaching and the wider context.

These general principles do go against the grain of traditional teacher training, but in no way can they be seen as implying a simple apprenticeship model. Such a model, though implicit in some government recommendations, in many of the school-based developments and in the practice of departments of educational studies as they unthinkingly embrace school-based approaches, runs counter to what is essential to an academically respectable preparation for the profession of teaching. The apprenticeship model fails, on the whole, to establish training schools, schools which are geared to *teacher* learning as much as they are to pupil learning. Such schools should be learning institutions in which, first, the process of learning is explored and teaching is a problematic activity to be examined, researched into and treated experimentally; second, a framework of support is provided for the initiate to explore what will or will not work in the light of evidence and criticism; third, alternative aims and values are explored within the context of particular cases; fourth, there is focused examination of the structure of the subject in relation to children's learning; fifth, there is a graduated, carefully monitored initiation into the complex skills and tacit knowledge of teaching; and, sixth, there is exposure to a wider critical debate and wider research.

The experience of the Oxford internship scheme, now well researched in terms of trainee teachers' learning and mentors' development (see Benton, 1990; Davies, 1989; Pendry, 1990) demonstrates how difficult this task is and how inadequate are the simplistic models of apprenticeship, on the one hand, and university-dominated training, on the other. There is a need for partnership, but the distinctive role of the university in that partnership needs to be argued for.

University Role

Universities ought to be places of research, scholarship and critical though informed deliberation. Such deliberation need not be immediately practical, but indirectly it must be so in that any practice participates in a world of ideas and is affected by the shifts and changes within that world of ideas. The so-called child-centred practices do themselves embody theories of learning and of child development, of ethical standards and of human nature which are the product of deeper philosophical considerations. The failure to recognise this leads to the trivial rejection of child-centred education by politicians and chief inspectors; they fail to make relevant distinctions or understand the ideas which, implicitly, underpin the complex practices of the child-centred teacher.

For schools to be centres in which trainee teachers become professionals, intelligently exploring the ideas beneath the practices to which they are being introduced, rather than blindly apprenticed to existing practice (however bad that is), they need to be plugged into a wider network of intellectual life where critical enquiry, deliberation, questioning, speculation and research are central rather than peripheral activities. Universities at their best provide the framework and the stimulus for such a network. They ensure a critical tradition, a tradition which is indispensable where education rather than mere training is being fostered and which is constantly endangered by those who wish to make teachers subservient to politically determined values and goals. The profession rather than the craft of teaching requires institutions whose job is to nurture and to protect independent criticism and enquiry.

Hence, the role of universities in the training of teachers is fivefold.

1. They are places where the analysis of the subject matter to be taught is related to the mode of understanding of those who are to learn. Clearly, the initiates to teaching, frequently already well-versed in their own particular subjects, have given little thought to the philosophy of the subjects – to the key ideas, principles, concepts and skills which need to structure the process of learning. Understanding one's expertise in these terms is a necessary prerequisite to good teaching; it rarely occurs in undergraduate studies; it needs time set aside in a place set apart where such analysis can be conducted. This is true as much of the preparation of primary teachers as it is of specialist subject teachers at secondary level.
2. In an increasingly fragmented world of schools (following the creation of grant-maintained schools and city technical colleges and the

enfeeblement of local education authorities) there is a need for centres of expertise which can be put to the service of schools (eg, in special educational needs or in equal opportunities or in assessment or in the teaching of particular subjects). Such expertise does exist in the schools, but it does so unequally over the 25,000 schools of England and Wales.

3. The training of teachers must take place against a background of relevant and systematic research. I am not thinking here of the fundamental research in sociology or in psychology – surely the job of the university departments of those names. I am thinking rather of the kind of research, informed no doubt by sociological, psychological or philosophical perspectives, which arises out of the questions raised in schools about method, organisation, motivation, purposes or assessment and which feeds directly back into those practical realities. Research is systematic thinking – systematic identification of problems, formulating possible solutions, seeking evidence and testing answers. Why should that be anathema to those who say they are concerned with standards?
4. The creation of 'training schools' and the development in such schools of the intellectual and research-based framework within which there can be the exploration and testing of ideas essential to professional preparation require support from those who exemplify such activities. The Oxford internship scheme at its best shows how that interconnection between university and schools, in which the university tutors work in the schools and the school mentors and professional tutors work together in the university, produces the integration between practice and theoretical reflection upon practice conducive to the intellectual development required of professionals rather than craftsmen.
5. Most important, the training of teachers must take place within the context of a critical tradition. Educational studies are eclectic (so are most university subjects), but they do contain a literature, a 'critical conversation' involving the most intractable problems of ethics and the philosophy of mind; they draw upon research and systematic enquiry. Teachers participate more or less consciously and critically within that context. The more consciously they participate, then the more effectively do they 'think' as well as 'act' and become professionals rather than operatives or technicians. One can see how those who want to control from afar and who are dominated by notions of efficiency might be frightened of teachers being prepared within such a tradition.

The defence of university involvement, therefore, lies in the presence within their departments of that expertise, that relevant research and that critical tradition, in which teachers participate. If that is destroyed, then a key element in sustaining teaching as a profession will also be destroyed. Why is that so very urgent today?

The Secretary of State marginalised Her Majesty's Inspectorate (HMI), that century-old body of independent advisers and critics upon which previous governments depended for professional advice. He emasculated local education authorities with the expertise and local knowledge which they contain. He even removed senior civil servants whose advice he did not like. He instead surrounded himself with unrepresentative advisers, who know little about schools and who have had no experience of teacher training. There is now nothing between the Secretary of State (with detailed powers to say what should be taught and with control over funding used in a most discriminating way to ensure compliance) and the fragmented 24,000 small businesses, once called schools – except the universities which preserve some measure of independence. One can see why those surrounding the Secretary of State want these university departments diminished, if not destroyed. Everyone, especially those who see teaching as a profession, should recognise what this means – and should be fearful.

Nonetheless, the universities need to justify themselves as institutions where there is a vibrant critical tradition, where that tradition through drawing upon relevant academic disciplines is securely founded in the practice of teachers and where there is competently conducted but practically relevant research. Such a marriage between academic respectability and professional relevance is rare indeed, but where it occurs the *professional* preparation of teachers is enhanced.

It is not clear how many university departments can meet these strict conditions. Teacher education in universities is notable for its lack of thinking about how teachers, especially new teachers, learn – even in some institutions most famous for educational research and most prolific in the production of teachers. No amount of claims to 'partnership' with schools, or books written about mentoring, can disguise that most partnerships are a sham or that most books on mentoring are written by people who have had little experience of it or conducted little relevant research.

No one should be fooled by the rush to publication to meet the 'research exercise' deadline. The integration of theory and practice, university and schools, thinking and doing, academic respectability and professional relevance, 'knowing that' and 'knowing how' is a long and difficult path which few are prepared to tread.

References

Alexander, RJ (1984) 'Innovation and continuity in the initial teacher education curriculum', in Alexander, RJ *et al.* (eds) *Change in Teacher Education: Context and Provision since Robbins*. London: Holt, Rinehart & Winston.

Benton, P. (ed) (1990) *The Oxford Internship Scheme*. London: Gulbenkian.

Bernstein (1967) 'Open Schools, Open Society', *New Society*, 14th April.

Brown, S and McIntyre, D (1993) *Making Sense of Teaching*. Buckingham: Open University Press.

Davies, C (1989) 'The conflicting subject philosophies of English', *British Journal of Educational Studies*, **37** (4).
Hare, RM (1952) *The Language of Morals*. Oxford University Press.
Lawlor, S (1990) *Teachers Mistaught*. London: Centre for Policy Studies.
McIntyre, D (1989) 'The contribution of research to quality in teacher education', *South Pacific Journal of Education*, **81**.
McIntyre, D (1991) 'The Oxford University model of teacher education', *South Pacific Journal of Teacher Education*, **19** (2).
Mill, John Stuart (1867) 'Inaugural Lecture at the University of St Andrews', in *James and John Stuart Mill on Education*, Cavanagh, FA (ed) Cambridge: Cambridge University Press.
O'Connor, DJ (1957) *Introduction to the Philosophy of Education*, London: Routledge.
O'Hear, A (1988) *Who Teaches the Teachers?* Research Report no. 10. London: Social Affairs Unit.
Pendry, A (1990) 'Dilemmas for history teacher educators', *British Journal of Educational Studies*, **38**(1).
Peters, RS (1977) *Education and the Education of Teachers*. London: Routledge.
Tibble, JW (ed) (1967) *The Study of Education*. London: Routledge.
Tyler, RW (1949) *Basic Principles of Curriculum and Instruction*. Chicago, IL: University of Chicago Press.
Wilson, J (1990) *A New Introduction to Moral Education*. London: Cassell.
Wilson, J, Williams, N and Sugarman, B (1967) *An Introduction to Moral Education*. London: Penguin.

CHAPTER 2

MODEST PROPOSALS? TEACHER EDUCATION AND THE EDUCATION ACT 1994

Patricia Ambrose

The focus of my chapter is the campaign by the Committee of Vice Chancellors and Principals (CVCP represents the executive heads of all UK universities and exists to promote, encourage and develop UK universities) to defend the important role of higher education (HE) in teacher education during the passage of the Education Act 1994. Both the initial government consultation paper (DFE, 1993a), and Part I of the subsequent Education Bill were seen by universities as a threat to the future involvement of HE in teacher education and, in broader terms, as a challenge to academic freedom and to the continuing role of universities in professional and vocational education.

The Vocational Challenge

Higher education in the United Kingdom is undergoing a period of profound cultural change. The move towards a mass system of HE, with increasing emphasis on lifelong learning, presents universities and other higher education institutions (HEIs) with a range of opportunities and challenges. Factors that have some bearing on the future role of HE in professional and vocational education include:

- the well-established history of vocational education within HE (eg, medicine, law, teaching, engineering etc) and the relationship between HEIs and professional bodies/institutions
- the growing expectation by government and business that HE has a role in economic regeneration, in preparing people for work and in

continuing education (CE) and continuing professional development (CPD) through specifically vocational courses or through more broadly vocational programmes and the development of personal, transferable skills
- the development of the framework of National Vocational Qualifications (NVQs) and their Scottish equivalents (SVQs) which may be seen both as a threat to HE's traditional domination of higher level qualifications and also as presenting a range of further opportunities for HE to become more vocationally relevant and to build links with a complementary framework of new qualifications.

The recent changes to teacher education represent one major strand in the general challenge which HE faces from the development of new forms of high-level qualifications such as NVQs/SVQs. As education is seen increasingly as a means of improving national competitiveness (Department of Trade and Industry, 1994; Confederation of British Industry, 1994), so government wishes to intervene more actively to see its expectations fulfilled. If HE does not take up the challenge and also fight to preserve its distinctive role in vocational education, then it will be increasingly marginalised. Teacher education is peculiarly vulnerable as the government already has extensive control over its content through the Secretary of State for Education's criteria for initial teacher training (ITT) courses; there is a sense that what happens today in teacher education may well happen tomorrow in other professional areas.

The Government's Proposals for the Reform of Initial Teacher Training

The government's consultation document on teacher education (DFE, 1993a) set the scene for the major debate which was to ensue during the passage of the 1993 Education Bill. It included the following proposals:

- the establishment of a Teacher Training Agency (TTA) to allocate funding for all initial teacher training (ITT) and much educational research in England (removing this function from the Higher Education Funding Council for England (HEFCE)); a central part of the Agency's remit would be to encourage the development of school-centred initial teacher training (SCITT) courses
- the abolition of the Council for the Accreditation of Teacher Education (CATE) which advised the Secretary of State on teaching matters
- some alternative approaches on quality assurance to ensure that courses would meet the Secretary of State's published criteria.

Proposals for Wales differed in that the Higher Education Funding Council for Wales would remain responsible for funding of ITT; its powers would be extended to enable it to fund SCITT provision. Similar quality options were outlined, but with the Secretary of State for Wales having responsibility for criteria.

The proposed establishment of a TTA for England and the disbanding of CATE indicated government desire for further centralisation of power over teacher education. While CATE was never a substitute for an independent General Teaching Council (GTC), with its abolition the Secretary of State would no longer even draw on the professional expertise of a standing body. Teaching would become one of the most unprotected of the professions.

Despite widespread opposition to the government's proposals for teacher education from bodies representing HE, schools, parents and governors associations, Part I of the 1993 Education Bill contained the majority of these proposals and was introduced to the House of Lords in November 1993.

The CVCP Response

Members of CVCP expressed fundamental opposition to the proposals outlined in the government consultation document and in the subsequent Bill. Their response affirmed their commitment to the vital contribution of universities to teacher education at initial, advanced and research levels. The government's proposals were seen as a serious threat to quality and likely to lead to an increase in political control over teacher education which would be incompatible with the concept of a university education. The proposals would affect not only ITT, as the title of the consultation document suggested, but provision of teacher education at all levels. They would seriously undermine the independence of educational research. The CVCP response (1993) outlined the view that universities and other HEIs, with their tradition of independent enquiry and presentation of best practice, should continue to play a leading role in teacher education. Their continuing role would be essential to maintain and improve the quality of such education and to ensure the protection of an independent teaching profession.

In formulating its response, CVCP stressed its support for the concept of partnership between HEIs and schools in ITT. CVCP recognised the many benefits in developing partnerships between HEIs and schools, with a larger proportion of trainee teachers' time being spent in schools. There was little evidence, however, to suggest that the majority of schools wished to play the leading role in the provision of ITT. In a survey by Newcastle University of over 400 headteachers of primary schools, only 6 per cent had expressed dissatisfaction with the current system of ITT and 90 per cent believed that HE should retain overall responsibility for the welfare, development and assessment of trainee teachers (Carrington and Tymms, 1993).

A subsequent, and much wider, survey by the Standing Conference of Principals (SCOP, the representative body for Principals of Colleges and Institutions of Higher Education) revealed similar conclusions. The SCOP survey of 1,202 primary headteachers indicated that only 12 wished to take the major share of responsibility for the intellectual and pedagogical development of the trainee teacher (SCOP, 1994).

An HE environment was judged to be the best place for rigorous intellectual and academic subject development and for exposure to, and interaction with, other academic disciplines. Teaching is a complex activity and cannot simply be reduced to the acquisition of a limited range of competencies; trainees need the opportunity to acquire breadth and contextual knowledge, to be able to reflect critically upon their experience and to lay the foundations for their future professional development.

The CVCP response to the government's consultation paper and the subsequent Education Bill focused on:

- objection in principle to the creation of a new and separate agency (the proposed TTA) to fund teacher education and research
- the damage to the quality and independence of educational research if its funding were to be separated from the rest of HE research
- the key role of universities in teacher education
- the need for a statutory body, such as a General Teaching Council (GTC), to provide independent, professional advice to the Secretary of State and to enhance the professional status of teaching.

Teacher Training Agency (TTA)

Within HE it was believed that the proposed Teacher Training Agency would set a precedent for the future fragmentation of HE provision of professional and vocational education. There was also concern that the TTA would be responsible for dispensing large sums of public money without any requirement for it to consult or be accountable to those affected by its decisions. It would be yet another example of the proliferation by government of appointed and unaccountable bodies with its membership personally selected by the Secretary of State for Education. The existing system of funding through the HEFCE had had to operate within a system of checks and balances (including peer review of research) which would be missing in the proposed TTA. In fact, the TTA would simply create another bureaucratic layer; it would have to duplicate HEFCE procedures and would need to rely on HEFCE to provide advice on the quality of research.

CVCP could not see in the government's proposals any logical arguments to support the creation of a separate agency to fund teacher education in England; its view was that funding should remain with the HEFCE. In fact, the proposals for Wales, whereby funding would remain with the Higher Education Funding Council for Wales (HEFCW), demonstrate that the creation of another agency was unnecessary. Moreover, the system of funding through the various national HEFCs for England, Wales and Scotland, had only been established as the result of the 1992 Further and Higher Education Act and had yet to be fully tested and evaluated. CVCP did, however, recognise that the HEFCE procedure for funding could and should be improved and set out its own alternative funding proposals for ITT.

CVCP's alternative was to propose the establishment of a committee of the HEFCE which would provide specialist advice on the allocation of student numbers and funds for ITT. The funding of higher degrees, research in education and the non-ITT courses within the Education Academic Subject Category (ASC 11) would continue through the existing HEFCE mechanisms. This alternative would ensure that funding for ITT in England remained part of the unified HE system. It would do away with the need to establish yet another agency, with the inevitable duplication of effort and resources this would entail.

> *The Government's implied preference for 'school-centred' training [cf. DFE, 1993a, ch. 3, paras, 8–9] raised serious questions about the ability of a TTA to give balanced support to HE-based training. At the Second Reading of the Education Bill in the House of Lords on 7 December 1993, the Minister for Education, Baroness Blatch, emphasised the role of the new Agency as being to 'encourage diversity by supporting courses run by schools as well as Higher Education'*. (*Hansard*, 7.12.1993, col. 820)

The concerns of universities and other HEIs included:

- that the TTA would concentrate on SCITT, which most schools did not wish to provide, to the detriment of courses provided by HE and schools in partnership
- that a profound shift in ITT practice was being advocated before there had been any evaluation of the pilot SCITT schemes by the Office for Standards in Education (OFSTED).

An earlier evaluation of the articled teacher scheme had demonstrated that school-based ITT was more expensive, made more quality assessment demands and did not lead to higher quality training. This HMI report (OFSTED, 1992) had concluded that:

> *Higher Education institutions provide an academic and professional expertise which is crucial in the support both of individual students and of schools. They are also*

responsible for the resourcing of initial training and the awarding of qualifications to students. Given the scale of initial training, no straightforward and cost-effective way of devolving these functions successfully to a large number of schools is apparent. (p.4)

Key Role of HE in Teacher Education

The government's proposals and the Education Bill focused on the training of teachers only in the narrowest sense. The CVCP response emphasises that the teaching profession was built upon a body of knowledge and skills best provided by HE and schools in partnership. The implementation of the proposals would put at risk the particular contribution made by universities to ITT: namely, a high quality subject-based element and a recognition of the rigorous intellectual preparation required for intending teachers. The OFSTED survey (1993), found that levels of new teacher satisfaction in these aspects of their training were very high. It was felt that the government should build on this success and not plan to remove the delivery and validation of these areas from HE. A major part of ITT should continue to take place in institutions where a broad range of academic disciplines were taught. While ITT should certainly equip teachers with the skills and competencies necessary to perform successfully in schools, it was vital that new teachers also developed the ability to adapt to future changes in educational practice and to new developments within their own subject areas.

The government's proposals risked damaging the status of teaching as a graduate-level profession and re-iterated the government's desire to move towards shorter first-degree courses in education. The CVCP view was that a reduction in course length was unlikely to lead to any improvement in the quality of ITT. The government also claimed that the development of a wide range of routes to qualified teacher status would help to broaden access to the profession. While the broadening of access to teacher training may be seen as desirable, the view within HE was that this should not be at the expense of the quality of academic study and professional training. Cutting off teacher education from the mainstream education of other professions would also weaken its status and deter high-calibre applicants.

The National Commission on Education (1993) highlights concerns at the need for teaching to attract high-calibre applicants and has put forward proposals for a continuum of education and training spanning initial training, induction and continuing professional development. The Commission states that 'There seems to be no doubt that the most successful teacher training occurs when there is a genuine partnership between school and Higher Education institution, each playing a distinctive part according to strength.' (p.214).

The distinctive role for HE, according to the Commission (1993, p.215), involves:

- operating admissions to ITT, assessing and supporting students, administering and validating qualifications to ensure quality across the system
- providing a breadth of perspective which goes beyond the individual circumstances of particular schools and giving access to the full range of educational research
- developing knowledge and understanding, especially in the areas of children's learning, assessment, management, equal opportunities and cultural awareness
- allowing economies of scale in information technology, libraries and staff expertise
- initiating student profiles
- providing support and training for mentors in schools
- providing consultancy, critical perspective, advanced degrees and continuing professional development courses for teachers, and educational research.

The need for an improved system of CPD for teachers and the particular benefits of higher degrees within this were ignored in the government's initial consultation paper and led to concerns within universities that the profession would be further 'de-skilled' by any new arrangements. There was little confidence within HE that the government recognised the importance of continuing professional development for serving teachers. This same government had already taken the retrograde step of abolishing the probationary year for new teachers from 1 September 1992.

Research

The proposed separation of educational research from other HE research was, similarly, believed to set a dangerous precedent and to pose a threat to academic freedom. Any attempt to influence research funding by criteria other than peer-reviewed quality assessments would be resisted by universities. The separation of educational research would have serious consequences:

- Research in education would be arbitrarily separated from the continuum of research across many academic disciplines. Collaborative initiatives with other disciplines would be more difficult to arrange, with a consequent loss of cross-fertilisation. The TTA's remit would have to extend far beyond research carried out in ITT-specific departments
- It would lead to a narrow, less critical focus. Under the existing system, education competed on an equal basis with other social science research ensuring standards and rigour were maintained

- The separation of funding would occur at a time when universities were seeking to ensure that research in all subject areas was developed under a comparable basis of quality. Such a separation could only be damaging to the quality and reputation of educational research
- Academic freedom would be threatened; centralisation in a specialist executive agency would remove safeguards to scholarship and research.

Universities were not complacent about the quality of educational research and recognised that, as in all research areas, further improvements could be made. Handing funding to the TTA, however, was not likely of itself to bring about any improvement. Educationalists acknowledged that there was 'much critical debate about the quality, credibility and impact of educational research' (Bassey, 1994) but also that, in many cases, insufficient credit was given to the UK's achievements in this area. CVCP felt it was important to focus on the high quality and international reputation of much current educational research. Its response drew on the work of British universities on school effectiveness and school improvement and emphasised the international recognition this has received (eg, the pioneering work of the Hatton Board of Education in Canada, which based its Effective Schools Project on British research). The involvement of universities in educational research ensured that national and international good practice was properly recognised and developed.

A General Teaching Council

Teaching is one of the few major professions without its own statutory professional body. With the abolition of CATE under the provisions of the 1993 Education Bill there was a clear need for a body to advise the Secretary of State for Education on the criteria for ITT courses. In making its case, CVCP drew on the Scottish precedent and invited comparison between teaching and other major professions such as medicine. Scotland has had a GTC since 1965, with elected, appointed and nominated members, while the medical profession has the General Medical Council (GMC) to promote the standards of medical education. Teachers in England and Wales also needed a statutory framework which recognised their professionalism and gave them some control over their own standards. The Dearing Report (DFE, 1993b) emphasised the importance of the professional judgement of teachers in the development of a more effective education system.

> *I believe that a policy which trusts more to teachers' professional judgement and which cuts back on administration to free time for teaching will, coupled with an acceptance that schools are accountable to parents and society for their stewardship, produce the results we need. (p.27)*

CVCP's view was that it was crucial for the standards and effectiveness of the teaching profession that a professional body be created to provide independent advice and to accord teaching the professional standing it deserved.

Media Attention

The campaign against the proposals for teacher education in Part I of the 1993 Bill was hampered from the outset because the Bill also contained separate provisions on student unions (Part II of the Bill). These proposals received widespread coverage and condemnation in the press and other media and tended to overshadow the debate on the future of teacher education. CVCP's position was to treat the two parts of the Bill as separate entities and to campaign strongly against both sets of proposals; there were to be no trade-offs or concessions.

Media coverage of Part I of the Bill was not representative of the scale of opposition to the proposals both from bodies representing educational interests and from peers in the House of Lords. An analysis of the speakers during the Second Reading debate on 7 December revealed that of the 28 speakers against the Bill, 17 spoke mainly or solely on the proposals for teacher education.

Why were the proposals on teacher education not given wider or more positive coverage in the press? Probably because, for the present government, teachers, and their trainers, remain an easy target for 'bashing', a convenient scapegoat for society's ills. In an article in the *Times Educational Supplement* (1994) Christopher Price stated, 'Headlines bashing rowdy students, trendy teachers and yobbo schools bring cumulative dividends from a certain sort of voter. It matters not that the legislation in question has no impact on these issues.'

Successes and Failures

As with much recent educational legislation, the only realistic chance of substantial amendment to the proposals occurred in the House of Lords. The most significant Lords' amendment was to Clause 12 of the Bill which dealt with the conditions under which courses of ITT could be provided. These were changed to ensure that schools could not 'go it alone' in the provision of ITT; all courses should be provided in partnership with, and accredited by, an institution of higher education. This amendment was narrowly carried in the Lords and subsequently reversed when the Bill reached the Committee Stage in the Commons in June 1994. The CVCP stated that 'the news was "highly regrettable" but inevitable given the Government's built-in majority on the committee' (Tysome,

1994). The Lords staged a further protest when the Bill returned to them for consideration of the Commons' amendments, but this was not carried.

There were also unsuccessful attempts during the Bill's passage through the Lords to amend Clause 1 so that the functions of the proposed TTA would revert to the HEFCE and to bring about the establishment of a General Teaching Council, a professional body for teachers. While both proposals generated much support, they were not carried.

There were, however, other major changes to the original Bill which did survive passage through the Commons. These included amendments to clarify that SCITT courses could only be undertaken by graduates and, importantly for the universities, that the majority of research funding for education would remain with the HEFCE. So, while unsuccessful in its campaign against the establishment of the TTA and the ability of schools to provide SCITT courses without HE involvement, there was some qualified success in modifying the extent of the changes.

The Future

The 1993 Education Bill received its Royal Assent on 21 July 1994 and the TTA was subsequently established and has allocated its first tranche of funding for ITT for 1995/96 (adapting the former HEFCE methodology for the short term). The new agency appears to be proceeding cautiously and to be wary of alienating HE providers unnecessarily. A range of consultations have taken place, including one on the institutional accreditation of ITT providers. Further consultation is expected later in 1995 on the development of a new funding methodology for ITT.

One reason for caution so far as the TTA is concerned may be the sound of chickens coming home to roost. As those who campaigned against the Bill grew tired of saying, the vast majority of schools does not want to take the lead in the provision of ITT, and many are also dropping out of the new partnership arrangements for training when the high levels of commitment required are becoming apparent. A survey by the Universities Council for the Education of Teachers (UCET) shows that

> *Schools and specially trained mentors are dropping out of training . . . leaving teacher trainers unable to find the crucial work placements for students. . . . In some popular institutions this has actually restricted recruitment, with shortage subjects like science, maths and modern languages suffering worst.* (Pyke, 1995a)

Evidence is also mounting to suggest that the pilot SCITT schemes are producing results ranging from poor to average in evaluations by OFSTED. Concerns were highlighted by Pyke (1995b), who notes that:

> *HM Inspectors have reported on all SCITT projects, but individual reports will not be released. Instead, a summary report is expected in late spring. There is speculation that ministers barred the publication of individual reports as these would have highlighted specific failures at a very early stage.*

It appears that, for the present at least, teacher training cannot survive in a credible form without the continued involvement of HEIs. Universities and other HEIs must not, however, take their position for granted, but must continue to argue their case for playing a full role in ITT, as part of their contribution to the higher level professional and vocational education and training which the UK needs. The former Employment Department (1995) recognised that any future, national framework of high-level qualifications would rely on effective partnership between HE, statutory and professional bodies, and employers. There is an opportunity for HE to be a major influence in the definition of high-level education and training and to secure its role as the major provider of courses designed to develop knowledge, understanding and critical skills within a national framework. The battle is not yet over, either for teacher education or for other areas of professional and vocational education.

References

Bassey, M (1994) 'Why Lord Skidelsky is so wrong', *Times Educational Supplement*, 21 January, p.18.

Carrington, B and Tymms, P (1993) *For Primary Heads, Mum's Not the Word!* London: NUT.

Committee of Vice Chancellors and Principals (1993) CVCP Response to the Government's Proposals for the Reform of Initial Teacher Education. Paper N/93/220 (unpublished).

Confederation of British Industry (1994) *Thinking Ahead*. London: CBI.

Department for Education (DFE) (1993a) *The Government's Proposals for the Reform of Initial Teacher Training*. London: HMSO.

DFE (1993b) *The National Curriculum and its Assessment*. The Dearing Report. London: HMSO.

Department of Trade and Industry (1994) White Paper on *Competitiveness*. London: HMSO.

Education Bill 1993. London: HMSO.

Education Act 1994. London: HMSO.

Employment Department (1995) *A Vision for Higher Level Vocational Qualifications*. London: HMSO.

Hansard (1993) House of Lords Second Reading Debate, 7 December, columns 819–822.

National Commission on Education (1993) *Learning To Succeed*. London: Heinemann.

Office for Standards in Education (OFSTED) (1992) *School-based Initial Teacher Training in England and Wales*. London: HMSO.

OFSTED (1993) *The New Teacher in School.* London: HMSO.
Price, C (1994) 'A new vice anglaise', *Times Educational Supplement*, 14 January, p.19.
Pyke, N (1995a) 'Staffing shortage "caused by reforms"', *Times Educational Supplement*, 20 January, p.1.
Pyke, N (1995b) 'Inspectors cast doubt on in-school training', *Times Educational Supplement*, 10 March, p.1.
Standing Conference of Principals (1994) Press Release. Training Teachers: the Schools' View (unpublished).
Tysome, T (1994) 'Teacher training link broken', *Times Higher Educational Supplement*, 17 June, p.48.

CHAPTER 3

HIGHER EDUCATION AND TEACHER TRAINING: A CENTURY OF PROGRESS AND PROMISE

Philip Gardner

The inauguration of the Teacher Training Agency (TTA) in 1994 is surely a timely moment at which to reflect on the nature of the relation between higher education and the initial training of teachers (ITT). If such reflection is to be properly conceived and carefully judged, we would do well to give some thought to the parameters within which it should be set. In a period when the pace of educational reform has seemed both unprecedented and unrelenting,[1] it is too easy to think of this relation only within a contemporary policy context – a context dominated by an ideologically driven, centralising administration, by increasingly apprehensive and defensive institutions of higher education (HE) and by correspondingly ambitious and innovative senior managements in the schools. Certainly, this is a legitimate and important perspective from which to read the changing landscape of professional training at the close of the twentieth century. But on its own, it is not enough. The nature of the policy initiatives we have witnessed in recent years, together with the responses which they have raised among teachers and teacher educators need to be understood in a much longer time frame.

If we concentrate analysis not just on the last decade but widen our focus to range further into the past, we may begin to see that the establishment of the TTA represents something more than just another short-term policy adjustment. Rather, it might be seen as a token of an intellectual break with a fundamental article of intent which has, to a periodically greater or lesser degree, informed more than a hundred years of development in the initial training of teachers. This principle is a simple one. It proclaims that there should be a necessary and intimate relationship between the nation's institutions of higher education (HEIs) and the arrangements it makes for the training of new generations of schoolteachers. Here, the principle was earlier enunciated by Canon Warburton, a witness before the Cross Commission of 1886–88 – the agency first to stimulate the translation of principle into practice.

> *I hope to see a closer approximation of our training college system with the liberal culture of the universities, so that all that is best and highest in modern education may be brought within the reach of those to whom the teaching of the great mass of the children of this and coming generations will be entrusted.* (Cross Commission, 1886, p.xxv, quoted in Dobson, 1973)

The application of this high principle from its inception in 1890, however, has been far from straightforward. The nobility of the idea, in practice, has been ravaged on many sides – by the combined effects of inherited inequalities in the structure of education, institutional ambivalence, professional jealousy and political pusillanimity. As a result, the successive links which, over the years, were forged between the world of teacher training and the world of higher education have often turned out to be weaker and more uncertain in implementation than they had promised to be in prospect. I might add, however, that until now this was a tendency which, though pervasive and well-understood, has often been possible for educational historians to underplay (Dent, 1977). So long as the principle of linkage between training and higher education retained its long hegemony in some form, it was always possible to cast failures or disappointments in practice as tolerable – as regrettable yet bearable setbacks in a slow but always fundamentally progressive journey of forward movement.

Certainly there has always been much to celebrate and to admire in the history of teacher training conventionally portrayed as incremental advance and steady progress. Two reasons for this are: first, because advances, if only slowly achieved, have unquestionably been real and important in improving the quality of the nation's teachers in the twentieth century; and, second, because progress in teacher training always had to be painfully won. The story of teacher training over the last hundred years tells, in one respect, of a journey from rags to riches (Roach, 1966, p.13). No other element of our education system has had to travel so far from such humble beginnings and to overcome so many obstacles. First conceived in the educational poverty of the early nineteenth-century elementary school, the long-term prospects for formal teacher training did not initially look inspiring. But driven in part by the widening of new educational opportunities, in part by the aid of sympathetic supporters outside the profession and in part by powerful ambitions within it, teacher training moved forward, winning its greatest triumph in the 1970s with the achievement of all-graduate professional status – a goal which, to the teachers themselves, had first began to seem attainable fully half a century before (Board of Education, 1925, p.23; NUT, 1939, pp.149–65).

If there is legitimacy in an approach which traces the long upward trajectory of teacher training from pupil-teachership to graduate status, there are also serious limitations. To the extent that we accept that the best metaphor in the history of teacher training is that of steady progress along a road clearly signposted by the great official reports of successive generations – the Cross Commission of 1886, the Departmental Committee Report of 1925 and the reports of McNair (1944) and Robbins (1963) – we are likely to underestimate the powerful and potentially destructive ambivalences and atavisms which always lurked along the route. These centre upon questions which, if in rather different contexts, would have been quite as familiar to educationists at the start of this century as they are at its end. Fundamentally, they are questions which arise from basic uncertainties about what the business of teacher training should properly involve, about where it should be done and about who should control it. From the first, these have been deeply contested issues, within as well as between, the many groups with a vested interest in the training process – central government, local government, the voluntary bodies, the long-established training colleges, the universities, teacher trainers and the teachers themselves. As a result, detailed policy agreement, in contrast to the statement of general principles, was always elusive, as the McNair Committee of 1944 was to find.

> *Our witnesses have almost without exception, been in favour of closer connection between training and universities. They have desired that somehow it should be brought about, but they have not always been successful in suggesting practicable means to it.* (Niblett *et al.*, 1975, pp.28–9)

The existence of an established and enduring framework of mutual disagreement and distrust helps to explain why the promise which the association with higher education has held out to teacher training for more than a century has always seemed greater than the reality of its achievement. It may also help us to see why now, with the historic linkage with higher education so explicitly challenged, the natural support of the professional constituency in the schools – the teachers – upon which, above all others, HEI's might have expected to count, is muted and uncertain. The universities have had a full century to establish a presence in the teacher-training process so indelible that colleagues in the schools could never have countenanced any threat against it. To understand why they have not, so far, succeeded in achieving such a place, we should look back to the beginning of the story – to the new regulations of the Elementary Education Code of 1890. (Committee of Council on Education, 1890; Aldrich 1990.)

In its training provisions, the 1890 Code offered a direct response to the recommendations of the Cross Commission of 1886–88, set up to enquire into the operation of an elementary education system which had been revolutionised by the Act of 1870 and subsequent measures. One of the first effects of this legislation had been to expose the impossible demands which, in a rapidly expanding system, now came to bear on the existing channels of teacher supply. Over the half century following the Act of 1870, the national total of adult teachers in elementary schools rose elevenfold from 14,500 to 160,000 (Board of Education, 1925). Moreover, once the great urban school boards began to organise their ambitious development plans, it became evident that it was not merely the quantity but the quality of teacher supply that was in question. Increasingly, critical attention was focused on the twin pillars of Victorian teacher training – the pupil-teacher system and the established denominational training colleges. The first was criticised for its reduction of teaching to a set of mechanical techniques and for its assumption that professional preparation could effectively begin at the precocious age of 14 (Board of Education, 1907); the second was challenged for its intellectual and denominational narrowness, for its spartan and restrictive residential regime and above all, for its effective isolation from the world of higher education (Board of Education, 1914). What the 1890 Code sought to offer was a wholly new variety of training which would address some of these weaknesses and revitalise a tired and deficient pattern of professional preparation. Alongside the old residential colleges there would henceforth be a new species of day-training colleges established in connection with the universities and the university colleges. It is to this moment that we can trace the origins of what were ultimately to become our university departments of education (Thomas, 1990a). A third category of training college – those operated by local education authorities – came into existence as a result of the 1902 Education Act. A generation after the appearance of the new day-training colleges, the influential 1925 Departmental Committee on the Training of Teachers could look back to 1890 and declare that 'At that point, for the first time, the arrangements for the education and training of Elementary School teachers touch the main current of higher education, and the long period of separate development is seen to be drawing to a close' (Board of Education, 1925, p.124). This was a judgement echoed a few years later by the notable historian of teacher training R W Rich. 'The institution of the day training college', he wrote, 'is one of the most important points in the history of teachers' training in England' (Rich, 1933, p.227).

If the universities decried traditional teacher training for much the same flaws and failings as Dickens describes in the character of Mr M'Choakumchild – who, together with, 'some hundred and forty other schoolmasters had been lately turned at the same time, in the same factory, on the same principles, like so many pianoforte legs' – they were nevertheless eager to embrace the opportunities which the 1890 regulations afforded them. One reason for this was undoubtedly the useful source of guaranteed fee-income which was promised against relatively modest increases in staffing costs. Another was the opportunity to establish the study of Education as a significant academic discipline – as it was on the Continent and in Scotland – in a way that was beyond the resources and the ambition of the existing training colleges (Tibble, 1966; Thomas, 1990b; Simon, 1985). In the words of Rich (1933),

> *the greatest significance of the development of the day training colleges lies not so much in the mere technique of teachers' training, as in the status of the study of education in popular estimation . . . the universities refused to look upon education merely as the training of the teacher, or the study of the art of school-keeping. They saw in it a subject of vast significance and with great possibilities, a subject susceptible of scientific, philosophical and historical treatment, which they had neglected in the past, and they proceeded to render it worthy of university status.* (p.231)

Both the purpose and the regime of the day-training colleges were conceived in very different circumstances from those of their older, austere forebears where students had been attuned to 'perform with effect the drudgery of teaching' (Edinburgh Review, 1861, quoted in Joint Standing Committee, 1939). With the standards and expectations of the elementary sector pushing upwards, particularly in the form of the urban higher grade schools, there was growing demand for a new kind of elementary school teacher – better-educated, flexible, unaffected by denominational narrowness and responsive to educational innovation. The day-training college was one key part of the policy response to this demand. The other, instituted by Robert Morant, the charismatic Permanent Secretary at the Board of Education in the first decade of the twentieth century, was the substitution of the old pupil-teacher apprenticeship with a new preliminary route, offering scholarship entry to grammar school and a full course of liberal education to the age of 17 and latterly to 18. Both reforms had as their aim not only the raising of the academic standing of the elementary teaching force but, equally important, the diminution of its traditional pattern of recruitment from among the working class. The profession was to move upmarket as well as to shed its old, enclosed caste status; a process,

> *by which teachers in Public Elementary Schools would be recruited much more freely from the middle classes. . . . It was hoped that, if intending teachers were instructed in Secondary Schools, they would no longer be set apart at too early an age as a separate class, but would join freely in both the intellectual and the social life of other pupils of the same age as themselves, but destined for different professions.* (Board of Education, 1907, pp.14-15)

The day-training college, with its prestigious university connection and a gathering emphasis on scholarship, research and theory which was to lift education from, 'its amateur and empiric stage' (Meiklejohn, quoted in Tibble, 1966, p.6) presented a challenge to which the residential colleges were obliged to respond. After 1890, they had continually to strive to keep up with the model set by the pacemaking newcomers (Gardner, 1993). But if the day-training colleges acted as a motor driving up the academic standards and status of the old colleges, this was often at the expense of that traditional focus of nineteenth-century courses of training – practical school experience. The concentration on rectifying one profound weakness in the old training courses tended to mean that the steep decline in school-based work – resulting from the phasing out of the pupil-teacher system and its short-lived successor, the student-teacher scheme – was overlooked. This was a matter of regret for many older teachers who had gone through long and arduous apprenticeships as pupil-teachers and who continued to see their work predominantly as craft skills rather than professional expertise (Rich, 1933; Widdowson, 1980). More important, it was widely deprecated by the new generation of teachers in training in the decade following the First World War.

Current research into the recollections of survivors from this generation makes it clear that though the recruits from these years certainly applauded and valued the sense that their training was being drawn closer to the orbit of higher education, they also questioned their progressive loss of contact with work in the schools.[2] The memories of these former teachers are full of disjunctions between academic work – however personally valued – done in college and the experience of practical work in schools. In the absence of any partnership in the modern sense between school and college, students made their own sense of the contact between these two sets of experiences. When such contacts were not made, we begin to learn of a moment of professional disorientation and to recognise the seeds of what, over the coming years, was to become a common refrain of the classroom teacher recalling his or her college training – interesting but not always relevant; valuable but often out of touch (Patrick, 1986).

The nature and extent of school-based experience did not return substantially to the policy agenda until the early years of the Second World War, when the wholesale reform of secondary education was being planned. As part of those discussions, S H Wood, head of the Board's Teacher Training Branch pressed the argument that it was 'undesirable to launch a student on the schools as a fully trained teacher at the age of 20 or 21 without ever having been anything but a student and without any real experience of teaching except while on school practice' (Niblett *et al.*, 1975, p.83). In so doing, he was reopening the wider question of the balance of theory and practice in teacher training – a question which, if it was to remain a vexed issue over the next 50 years, had certainly not seemed so problematical 20 years before, when the drift away from practice was at its height. Students leaving college by the mid-1920s increasingly had but a tiny fraction of the classroom experience of their counterparts a generation earlier (Gardner, 1993). To this extent, the reform of teacher education during the interwar years is a story of opportunities missed as well as seized.

Instead of taking as a goal the search for a model of effective training for new teachers in which the elements of training were appropriately balanced, reform was based on a liberal-academic deficit model of the old colleges against the new. In effect, this was to measure the quality of teacher training less by its practical outcomes and more by its changing status in an education system traditionally understood as a hierarchy of separated sectors (Simon, 1987). In short, the world of teacher education was primarily concerned with consolidating and developing its academic bona fides and raising its standing in the public eye. In this respect, it was not hard to associate the professional and practical aspects of training with the recently departed, bad old days of apprenticeship and learning on the job. The coming of the day-training colleges held out a very different and more elevated promise – a promise which the Board of Education was pleased to celebrate:

> *The great need of the system before 1890 had been a supply of teachers who should have a wide knowledge of their subjects, and who would kindle intellectual enthusiasm and stimulate power of thought rather than aim merely at securing passes at an examination. As was anticipated, this need was met to a great extent by the recognition of Day Training Colleges attached to places of higher education. The students in these Colleges were brought into contact with teachers who were men of eminence in their subjects. They were also free to follow their own bent in studying under these teachers.* (Board of Education, 1914, p.31)

Also entangled with the problem of the lowly academic status of the traditional colleges against the newcomers was the much wider question of contemporary perceptions of the gendered character of the teaching profession. From the late nineteenth century, elementary teaching was numerically dominated by women (Bergen, 1988). Women were, however, paid considerably less than men, their promotion opportunities were considerably more limited and, in most authorities, they were obliged to resign on marriage (Oram, 1987). Because of these associations, for many male teachers the dominance of women in the profession was seen as a barrier to the achievement of higher social and professional status (Partington, 1976). As a result, it was not difficult for the issue of the status distinctions between the newer training departments associated with the universities and the older residential colleges to become implicated in the broader gender question (Heward, 1993).

We can see this particularly clearly expressed in an exchange between R H Tawney and Winifred Mercier, Principal of Whitelands Training College, which took place in 1923 at a meeting between the Training Colleges Association and the authors of a Labour Party/TUC pamphlet, 'The Training of Teachers'. This document argued the radical line – an increasingly logical development of the 1890 reforms – 'that the education of the teacher should be "higher" education of that type which it is the function of the university to supply' (quoted, Niblett *et al.*, 1975, p.24). Tawney insisted that the effective training of teachers demanded the highest academic, as well as professional, standards. His chosen model for all teacher training was a consecutive one – three years' undergraduate study, followed by one-year postgraduate training. For many in the traditional women's colleges, such a model seemed to strike at the established principles of concurrency and early contact with the professional aspects of teaching. Mercier responded:

> *In my experience a large number of girls leave school at 18 and do not wish to study. The school course has so far satisfied them. They are anxious to get to work and fond of children. They are willing to go on studying when they see the incidence of it on their work* (quoted, Niblett *et al.*, 1975, pp.25–6).

Tawney ignored the implication of the male domination of the universities and persisted with the intellectually powerful argument for the university connection as the necessary and inevitable way towards an effective teaching force for the future. The gender implications of this policy – whatever its justification in either professional or class terms – emerge as strongly, if less self-consciously, in his words as they had done in Mercier's.

> *Perhaps they've chosen this career at too early an age. Your real argument is that you have for an elementary teacher the type of person who would not profit by a university education. That is not a fit state of things. It means you draw on a small stock. You take a third rate of quality. In the coming years you will get a superior type of man and we shall have to adapt our training and education to that. As the pool widens so you can raise the demands on the teacher. Has the time not come to start?* (quoted in Niblett *et al.*, 1975, p.26)

If the advent of the day-training colleges was profoundly important in helping to challenge and reorder many of the fundamental priorities of the teacher-training community, in one particular respect we can also identify a specific and very significant policy consequence. The day-training colleges enjoyed a relative autonomy denied to the older colleges in the area of syllabus and examinations. The academic element of the day-training college course was set and examined under the auspices of the parent university, rather than – as for the residential colleges – by the Board of Education itself (Board of Education, 1914); this had important results. When, in 1926, the Board took the decision to relinquish its control over the examination process in the traditional colleges as well, it was able to pass this responsibility to the universities as the senior partners in newly formed Joint Boards of Universities and Training Colleges which linked each university with a regional cluster of colleges. The examination of practical teaching ability remained centrally regulated through HMI. The significance of this decision – stemming from the recommendations of the 1925 Departmental Committee – was twofold: first, it signalled a critical shift in thinking about the appropriate relation of the state to the form and content of teacher-training programmes. These were matters which the government now perceived as properly falling to the hands of the profession itself, through the independent agency of the universities (Humphreys, 1965). In the words of the then President of the Board of Education, Lord Eustace Percy,

> *The Board's policy in regard to the training of teachers is to enable the Training Colleges to take their proper place in the general educational provision of this country in co-operation with the Universities and to give them the freedom and the right to exercise their academic judgement in regard to the education they give to teachers and candidates for the teaching profession.* (Humphreys, 1965, p.19)

This policy shift was endorsed in the 1944 McNair Report and more widely in the years following the Second World War, when expectations of general social advance were at their height.

Second, the new policy formalised an institutional relationship between training colleges and their regional universities. However half-heartedly this new arrangement was engaged by the universities – and, initially, by some of the colleges – it established a foundation upon which the more ambitious integrative machinery of the Institutes of Education could be built after the Second World War.

The new association with higher education established by the Joint Boards did not signal the start of the process of organic convergence for which some members of the 1925 Departmental Committee had hoped (Niblett *et al.*, 1975). In part this was due to the residual feelings of distrust – and sometimes of contempt – that many university representatives held for the colleges. Nearly 20 years on from the Departmental Committee, as the McNair Committee began its search for new ways of revivifying a stalled relationship, S H Wood reminded the other committee members of the unpropitious background to their task. 'It is no good pretending that the training colleges are regarded as centres of light and learning. On the contrary, some of them are despised as educational institutions' (quoted in Niblett *et al.*, 1975, p.89). Such perceptions cannot be explained only as inherited suspicions or prejudices. They also stem in part from important changes of direction which the day-training colleges themselves had undergone in the years just before the First World War and which, within 30 years of their inception, had carried them away from their key function as the pacemakers of progress in the mainstream two-year training course for elementary school-teachers (Dent, 1977).

Because they were permitted to organise their own courses of subject study for their students, it was natural for the day-training colleges to arrange for their more able students to undertake their academic work in the classes of the parent university or university college (Humphreys, 1976). Moreover, Education Department regulations were immediately provided for a third year of study which would allow the most gifted of students to work concurrently for a degree and their teachers' certificate. Though the three-year concurrent course grew in popularity, its concentrated demands on student time were clearly excessive, and in 1911, the Board of Education introduced a new four-year consecutive course.

Four-year students were to complete a full undergraduate course before proceeding to a final year of professional training – an early model for the current Postgraduate Certificate in Education. The inception of the academically rigorous four-year course offered the day-training colleges the opportunity to consolidate their status as legitimate university departments of education (Humphreys, 1976; Dixon, 1959). In consequence the synergy between the university departments and the residential colleges began to run down. In most of the former, the two-year course disappeared altogether in the 1920s, establishing the familiar pattern of postgraduate training in the universities, with the old two-year course confined to the colleges. The process of continued professional convergence around the principle of effective training – a goal which was to be readdressed by the McNair Committee – was dissipated. Godfrey Thompson, Head of the Durham Department of Education in the early 1920s, and himself a former pupil-teacher, was aware that a development which benefited his own department in its relation with its parent institution was also likely to damage the coherence of the profession as a whole.

> *The non-graduating students were gradually being squeezed out by the increase in numbers of those qualified to graduate . . . I think myself that it was a mistake to let this happen, but the college was helpless . . . the better qualified students who wished to graduate could not be rejected in favour of candidates who only wanted a two-year course. . . . We had had both kinds under one roof . . . and the separation was a retrograde step.* (quoted in Tyson and Tuck, 1971, pp.60–61)

A parallel factor which further separated the nation's training institutions was the concentration on training for secondary teaching which accompanied the shift towards postgraduate training. Three years before the arrival of the four-year course, the Board of Education had for the first time made grants available to support training for secondary teachers. This represented another significant opportunity for university departments for, with the rapid expansion of secondary schooling that followed the 1902 Education Act, the demand for trained secondary teachers was beginning to rise quickly. As a result, departments began increasingly to turn to a concentration on secondary work to match the new emphasis on graduate training.

If the intellectual influence of the university departments upon the training colleges continued to be extensive during the 1920s and 1930s, particularly in encouraging a pedagogy that was child-centred rather than subject-centred, then the gulf between the two types of institution in terms of professional status was at its widest. Teachers preparing for the elementary and secondary sectors knew themselves to be destined for different educational worlds. Eileen Traynor, for example, recalls that, having completed her degree at Birmingham University in 1924, she chose to take her training year at Oxford because alongside its postgraduate training, Birmingham continued to offer the traditional two-year course.

> *I think there was a little bit of snobbism because I think Birmingham was mixed up with the people doing elementary teaching, and I think there may have been a sort of feeling, you know – better to go somewhere else.*[3]

From the other side of the fence, the perceptions of trained elementary teachers of their secondary colleagues was equally distant:

> *We had very little contact with anybody else. They rather despised us you see. We were the lower grade according to them.*[4]

If the early years of the day-training college experiment had brought high expectations across the profession (Tropp 1957) then the interwar years – the Joint Board years – saw the promise of higher education beginning to wear thin. There was disillusion among practitioners and policy-makers alike (Niblett *et al.*, 1975). In the McNair Report of 1944, we see the promise, if much debated in the detail of its form, rejuvenated. There were a number of reasons for this. The Butler Act of 1944 marked the opening of a new educational epoch celebrating equality of opportunity and a secondary school place for all; 'putting an end to the socially divisive and poverty-ridden elementary education code' (Niblett *et al.*, 1975, p.87). And if the frustrated expectations of educational reformers in the interwar years seemed about to be answered in the schools, then it was recognised that they would also have to be reflected in the form of a newly conceived and cohesive teaching force with the highest standards of education and training (Roach, 1966). The achievement of such standards, together with the promise of an end to the divisive and damaging dual-track character of professional preparation in the past could be guaranteed only by securing the whole enterprise of teacher training under the aegis of the universities.

As the Second World War was drawing to a close, the investment of teacher training in the universities seemed particularly important for another reason. With the excesses of corporatist and totalitarian regimes still freshly etched in popular consciousness, there was little enthusiasm to look to the state for renewed control over the form and content of the training of those who would be the teachers of the nation's children. For a new era in which the values of democracy and active citizenship would carry a special importance, control over teacher training required a particular sensitivity. In this respect, it was not just the intellectual leadership and the high academic status of the universities that was sought but the advocacy of their traditional values of truth in scholarship and independence in thought and expression. This was a moment when teacher educators from all institutional backgrounds could come together to voice their collective agreement.

> *At this critical turning point in English education it is essential for the proper development of the teaching profession that immediate steps should be taken to establish a close and integral association with the universities, through whom alone*

> *the standards, status and freedom of the profession can be assured.* (Executive Committee of the Association of Teachers in Colleges and Departments of Education, May 1944, quoted, Niblett *et al.*, 1975, p.116)

This was to look to the universities for a new sense of leadership and a broadening of vision in their national role which, in the prewar years, seemed a long way off.

The McNair Report presented two ways forward:

- The first proposal, Scheme A, provided for the close partnership of colleges with the universities and for the universities constitutionally to take responsibility for all varieties of teacher training through the establishment of Area Training Organisations in the form of Institutes of Education.
- The second, Scheme B, did not put the universities at the apex of the enterprise but instead envisaged a development of the Joint Board organisation in which the work of all training colleges and departments would be governed by the creation of regional bodies with administrative and organisational responsibility, but no direct role in the process of training itself.

In the postwar climate of opinion, it was the university-led Scheme A which commended itself more strongly and by 1951, of the 16 new Area Training Organisations, 13 were of this character (Dent, 1977). The long period of organic growth and successful regional development which was to follow grew from the implementation of the basic principle that the intimate association of teacher training with higher education was the most professionally appropriate one. Whatever the genuine achievements and future promise of this association in the postwar years, there was also, as we have seen, a longer history of disappointment and disillusionment to be drawn upon as the particular concerns of the postwar mood faded. It was the legacy of this longer history which could be invoked when, in a period of very different political priorities, new training regulations in 1975 saw the removal of area responsibilities from the institutes, and the beginning of the process which would lead ultimately to the Council for the Accreditation of Teacher Education and, latterly, to the Teacher Training Agency. This part of the story can be traced in terms of the practical pressures of demographic change and political expediency. It can also be read in another way, as the fading of a faith in the principle of that necessary link between the teaching profession and higher education which had seen its first expression in the 1890 training regulations. The dissipation of this faith can be seen in the failure to implement the 1963 Robbins recommendation for the strengthening of the higher education connection as it had developed since McNair (Taylor, 1989), and, reversing the trend of half a century, in the 1972 James Report's questioning of the place of theory in teacher training (Gosden, 1990; James, 1972).

At a time when the state is fast reclaiming the ground in teacher training that it once gladly relinquished to higher education as the more appropriate agent, it is worth remembering that this is possible, in part, because the universities and the teachers have not, over more than a century, been able to achieve a partnership capable of dissolving historic mutual suspicions and uncertainties. However unfavourable the political environment in which it now has to exist, the promise of higher education in such a partnership nevertheless remains as rich as it has ever done. The degree to which it will ultimately be realised will depend very much on the lessons we draw from our professional past.

In summarising some of the observations made before the McNair Committee by representatives of the National Union of Teachers, D W Humphreys observed that 'The unwillingness of the universities to shoulder the problem of training teachers had been a hindrance in the past. Also the teaching world itself had been alternately attracted and repelled by the university connection' (Niblett *et al.*, 1975, p.91). The legacy of such ambivalent and misconceived professional manoeuvrings from the past continues to weigh heavily on our present dilemmas; but if we can begin to learn from our collective history over the last 100 years, then the promise which has burned bright before could do so again.

Notes

1. Such a judgement is of course a relative one. In the history of teacher education, change has often appeared as elemental to the successive generations who have had to accommodate it. The words with which Jeffreys began his 1961 volume, could, with dates suitably modified, legitimately serve as an introduction to the experience of each such generation; 'When the history of education in the twentieth century comes to be written, the middle years (from the 1940s to the 1970s) will stand out as a time of remarkably rapid and far-reaching change, not least in the field of teacher-training.' (p.v)
2. 'Professional identity and school-based training in the early twentieth century', a three-year research project funded by the Leverhulme Trust, co-directed by Peter Cunningham and Philip Gardner.
3. b. 1903, Birmingham; father: civil servant; mother: home; private school followed by grammar school and a French degree from Birmingham University. Diploma from Oxford University, followed by a grammar school teaching career.
4. Venee Blatch; b.1909, Liverpool; father: clerk; mother: governess until marriage; church elementary school. Scholarship to grammar school. Student-teacher. Bangor Normal College 1927-9. Then teaching in

Liverpool elementary schools. Resigned on marriage in 1939. Returned in 1949; retired 1972 as Head of Science in a Liverpool comprehensive school.

References

Aldrich, P (1990) 'The evolution of teacher education', in NJ Graves (ed) *Initial Teacher Education: Policies and Progress.* London: Kogan Page.

Bergen, B (1988) 'Only a schoolmaster: Gender, class and the effort to professionalise elementary teaching in England 1870–1910', in J Ozga (ed) *Approaches to the Labour Process of Teaching.* Open University Press.

Board of Education (1907) Circular 573, Memorandum on the History and Prospects of the Pupil-Teacher System.

Board of Education (1914) *Report of the Board of Education for the Year 1912–13.* London: HMSO.

Board of Education (1925) *Report of the Departmental Committee on the Training of Teachers for Public Elementary Schools.* London: HMSO.

Browne, J (1979) *Teachers of Teachers: A History of the Association of Teachers in Colleges and Departments of Education.* Sevenoaks: Hodder & Stoughton.

Committee of Council on Education (1890) *Report 1889–90.* London: HMSO.

Dent, HC (1977) *The Training of Teachers in England and Wales 1800–1975.* Sevenoaks: Hodder & Stoughton.

Dixon, W (1959) 'The relation of teacher training colleges of England to the universities', *The Year Book of Education 1959: Higher Education.* London: Evans Bros.

Dobson, JL (1973) 'The training colleges and their successors 1920–1970', in TG Cook (ed) *Education and the Professions.* London: Methuen.

Gardner, P (1993) 'The early history of school-based training', in D MacIntyre, H Hagger and M Wilkin (eds) *Mentoring: Perspectives on School-Based Teacher Education.* London: Kogan Page.

Gosden, P (1990) 'The James Report and recent history', in JB Thomas (ed), *op. cit.*

Heward, C (1993) 'Men and women and the rise of professional society: the intriguing history of teacher educators', *History of Education,* 22(1).

Humphreys, DW (1965) *The Relationship between the Training Colleges and the Universities before McNair.* University of Bristol Institute of Education.

Humphreys, DW (1976) *The University of Bristol and the Education and Training of Teachers.* University of Bristol.

James, Lord (1972) 'The education and training of teachers', in International Council for the Education of Teachers, *Innovation Now! International Perspectives in Teacher Education.* Washington DC: ICET.

Jeffreys, MVC (1961) (ed) *Revolution in Teacher Training.* London: Pitman.

Joint Standing Committee of the Training College Association and Council of Principals (1939) *Memorandum on the Training of Teachers.* London: University of London Press.

National Union of Teachers (1939) *The Training of Teachers and Grants to Intending Teachers.* London: NUT.

Niblett, WR *et al.* (1975) *The University Connection*. Windsor: NFER.

Oram, A (1987) 'Inequalities in the teaching profession: The effect on teachers and pupils', in F Hunt (ed) *Lessons for Life: The Schooling of Girls and Women 1850–1950*. Oxford: Blackwell.

Partington, G (1976) *Women Teachers in the Twentieth Century*. Windsor: NFER.

Patrick, H (1986) 'From Cross to CATE: The universities and teacher education over the past century', *Oxford Review of Education*, **12**(3), pp.243–61.

Rich, RW (1933) *The Training of Teachers in England and Wales during the Nineteenth Century*. Cambridge: Cambridge University Press.

Roach, JPC (1966) *The Teaching Profession: Some Reflections on a Century of Development*. University of Sheffield.

Simon, B (1985) *Does Education Matter?* London: Lawrence & Wishart.

Simon, B (1987) 'Systematisation and segmentation in education: the case of England', in DK Muller, F Ringer and B Simon (eds) *The Rise of the Modern Educational System: Structural Change and Social Reproduction 1870–1902*. Cambridge: Cambridge University Press.

Taylor, W (1988) 'Robbins and the Education of Teachers', *Oxford Review of Education*, **14**(1), pp.49–58.

Thomas, JB (1990a) 'Victorian beginnings', in JB Thomas (ed), *British Universities and Teacher Education: A Century of Change*. Basingstoke: Falmer.

Thomas, JB (1990b) 'Day training college to department of education', in JB Thomas, *op. cit.*

Tibble, JW (1966) 'The development of the study of education', in JW Tibble (ed) *The Study of Education*. London: Routledge.

Tropp, A (1957) *The School Teachers*. London: Heinemann.

Tyson, JC and Tuck, JP (1971) *The Origins and Development of the Training of Teachers in the University of Newcastle upon Tyne*. University of Newcastle Department of Education.

Widdowson, F (1980) *Going Up into the Next Class: Women and Elementary Teacher Training 1840–1914*. London: WRRC.

CHAPTER 4

INITIAL TEACHER EDUCATION AND THE RECONSTRUCTION OF THE UNIVERSITY

David Bridges

The introduction in England and Wales of government measures providing for the extension of the period of school-based training in all initial teacher training (ITT) courses and the development of some courses which are entirely school-based have provoked fresh consideration and debate about the distinctiveness or otherwise of the contribution of the universities to initial teacher education, a debate which is richly reflected in this volume.

The Role of Universities in the Education of Teachers

Arguments in defence of the universities' continuing central role rest on a mixture of pragmatism and principle with, no doubt, an element of self-interest on the part of university departments determined to hang on to one of their central functions and schools either hungry for new authority in professional training and the resources that this might bring or dismayed at the prospect of yet further responsibilities being added to their already considerable burden.

Pragmatically, it can be argued that the local or regional coordination of admission, training and assessment of relatively large numbers of students by a university is more efficient than delegating these functions to smaller units of individual schools or school consortia and that it provides for more consistent standards, quality assurance and accountability. As unit costs are pushed down, university-based training also allows for economies of scale in parts of the training which few schools can match.

Happily, however, the debate has not just been couched in terms of organisational efficiency. All parties have made reference to educational and other related principles to do with:

- the kind of learning involved in the development of teaching competence and the conditions under which this takes place;
- the nature of teachers' professionalism and how this is best cultivated;
- the place of research and reflection in the education of teachers and the conditions under which these are developed;
- academic freedom and government control in the professional formation of teachers and the circumstances under which the former is best protected from the latter.

Central in these arguments has been a realisation by the universities and teachers that if the continuing role of the universities in initial teacher education is to be defended, then it has to be shown that (apart from being a convenient administrative centre) there is something distinctive which the university contributes to initial teacher education which the school or school consortia cannot adequately emulate.

Richard Pring has been prominent among those articulating a principled case for the role of the university in teacher education (Pring, 1994; see his contribution to this collection). Crucial to his argument is a characterisation of universities and of those who teach in them:

> *Universities are places of advanced learning and teaching. It is difficult to see how these two functions can be separated. One is able to teach well at an advanced level only if one is engaged in learning – either through research or through scholarship. To be a teacher in a university should signify that one is 'expert' in a particular area of public knowledge such that others will respect (even if they disagree with) one's writings, pronouncements, reasoning in that area.* (Pring, 1994, p.2)

On Pring's account university departments are *centres of expertise* or relevant knowledge underpinned by a theoretical perspective; *centres of research and scholarship* in which systematic enquiry provides the basis for improved professional practice and for teaching about that practice; and (especially important at a time of intensive government interference in educational matters) *centres for the maintenance of a critical tradition*,

> *enjoying the freedom to challenge received assumptions, initiating the next generation of teachers into such a tradition, ensuring that it and thus the future schools are 'learning societies' where both the ends and the means of education are the subject matter of investigation and questioning (p.3)*

It is this kind of characterisation of the nature of the university, linked to a view of the nature of the professionalism exercised by teachers, which provides the basis for the claim that the initial education of teachers should rest substantially in the hands of the universities and the basis for resistance to the development of, in particular, entirely school-based training, but also the development of patterns of training which leave university departments only a minimal coordinating role in what is largely school-based provision.

By implication (and Pring has been vocal in making this point) a university department of education which endorses, validates or enters into complicity with the development of school-based initial training is in a sense betraying its trust or its historic mission as a constituent part of the university. Is he right?

I do not think that we can begin to answer that question without looking a little more widely at what has been happening to schools, university departments of education and universities in recent years. My main unease about Pring's proposition is its apparent lack of grounding in or reference to the changing realities of both schools and university departments and their context of the contemporary reconstruction of the university.

It is this last development that I am most interested in pursuing in this chapter. It seems to me that the notion of a university is itself undergoing radical change (and not all of it for the worse) and that it is interesting to review the case for the role of the university in teacher education in the light of the current reconstruction of what a university represents educationally. There may and, I hope, will still be a place in this scenario for the perspective which Pring advances, but I doubt if it is quite as simple as he suggests.

Before we turn to universities more widely, however, let us note a few features of schools and university departments of education.

Scholarship, Research and Critical Independence in Departments of Education and in Schools

Is it so clear that universities have such an exclusive reservoir of the highest expertise (including expertise in the area of educational theory and scholarship) on educational matters or at least a significantly higher corpus of such expertise than is found in schools?

If this was ever so, the position has been substantially eroded both ways round. The universities have been instrumental in developing the expertise of large numbers of teachers in schools who have taken their MAs and PhDs over the last 10 to 15 years. Many are better qualified than were contemporary university department staff when they entered their university teaching posts. One thing which has changed in recent years is that with the collapse of local inspectorates and LEAs, the cut-backs in HMI and the contraction of many departments of education, well-qualified and experienced teachers are increasingly obliged to remain within the school system rather than making career moves outside. Some who are prominent in school-based training have PhDs and experience in contributing to advanced in-service courses which exceed the qualifications of relatively junior staff or some 'old stagers' from the former colleges of education who are teaching in university departments.

At the same time the salaries offered by universities at lecturer and even senior lecturer level compare unfavourably with those available to senior teachers in schools, and university departments are increasingly having to appoint relatively junior teaching staff and 'grow them on' in terms of research and qualifications within the university environment. The research ratings of many university departments of education (let us say any scoring 3 or below on the research-selectivity exercise) reveal that a significant proportion of their staff are not engaged in research or writing of any significance (though one would have to acknowledge that few if any schools would appear anywhere in such comparisons, even if occasional individuals might merit recognition). Under pressure from research selectivity, reduced funding for initial training and deteriorating staff/student ratios some university staff are effectively being moved to or appointed to teaching-only duties. Even in university departments of education which enjoy a high research reputation this tends to be built up by people who contribute little more than the occasional visiting lecture to PGCE or BEd courses. The teaching, pastoral and administrative work associated with an initial training function in a university department make it extremely difficult for those tutors with a substantial commitment to this area of work to maintain a serious research role as well. The real picture of the distribution of expertise, scholarship and research on educational matters between schools and university departments is, then, by no means as simple as Pring would portray it. What about critical independence?

Universities have long prided themselves on their academic independence, including in particular their capacity for and commitment to teaching, writing and research which is independent and critical of government. State schools have stood in a different and more subservient relationship to both local and central government, and recent legislation has hugely increased the powers of the Secretary of State to regulate the work of schools even without further reference back to parliament. Is, then, the continuing role of the universities in initial teacher education an important safeguard of the intellectual independence of the next generation of teachers?

Perhaps so, but again let us not delude ourselves that the issue is entirely simple. In both school-based and 'partnership' training schemes the government controls (partly through the Teacher Training Agency, which is appointed by the Secretary of State) the conditions of entry into teacher education, the number and allocation of places in teacher training, the accreditation of teacher-training institutions (and until recently individual programmes), the definition of the competencies which programmes are expected to secure in qualified teachers and the funding of teacher training. This is backed up by a system of inspection, which universities now have to accept as a condition of accreditation. (University departments of education were the first to experience erosion of the principle that universities were self-monitoring and excluded from inspection by Her Majesty's Inspectorate.)

Nor is the research role of universities so independent of government control. Universities and university departments of education compete with increasing intensity for research contracts (on which many staff rely for their livelihood) and are increasingly prepared to accept contracts from government departments and agencies (including significantly the National Curriculum Council and SCA) carrying the kind of prohibitions on the independent publication of research findings which might be attached to research into germ warfare but which are entirely unwarranted in the context of the development of public education. In the meantime, too, university staff have been obliged progressively to surrender the tenured employment which was earlier defended as the guarantor of academic independence in favour of less secure contracts, some linked to performance-related pay. Up to a third of staff in some university departments are now on temporary contracts, so if independence of voice is supposed to be linked to security of employment, we might expect to find it more strongly represented in schools than in university departments at the moment.

Teachers' independence has itself been curtailed in recent years by, in particular, anti-union legislation, the introduction of the national curriculum and assessment, more frequent inspection, enhanced powers for governors and elements of market conditions which have to some extent set school against school. There was nevertheless a significant and heartening flutter of opposition against the overweening power of the state when teachers, backed on the whole by parents and governors, fought a campaign of civil disobedience against the government's overcumbersome arrangements for testing pupil performance. This opposition seems to have been successfully bought off, however, with a few pragmatic concessions from government and, at the time of writing, we were reassured (if reassurance it is) that good relations and understanding have been established between the teachers' unions and the Secretary of State.

Add to all this a diminished national inspectorate suffocated under a mountain of inspections, LEAs divested of nearly all their former powers and a political opposition apparently competing with government for credit for the same educational policies and the prospects for serious critical purchase on educational policy do not look too good whichever way you turn. Again, the question as to where *in fact* we may look for independent and critical purchase on educational issues does not admit quite the simple answer that Pring proposes, though I would be the first to agree that the universities *should* be among the most reliable sources.

Departments of Education and Their Status in the Universities

For many years, and in particular in the 'old' university sector, departments of education stood in an uneasy relationship with their parent universities and were often regarded as having inferior status in them. There were readily understandable reasons for this: the BEd degree was a hybrid of educational studies (variously interpreted), teaching practice and main subject study appeared to sacrifice depth for breadth; unusually, one of the conditions for the award of the degree was the assessment of practical teaching competence and not just academic work; the students admitted to such courses often (but by no means always) entered on the basis of A-level grades lower than those required in other areas of the university; the departments and their staff were often constituted from former colleges of education which were regarded by the university as low-status institutions; research was barely visible and, in many eyes, of dubious progeny. The PGCE course was accepted by most universities as a convenient channel through which its graduates could proceed into teaching (if they really insisted that the degree in itself was an insufficient preparation), but no one attached serious academic credentials to the teaching which this course demanded.

Many able people teaching in departments of education had constantly to battle in their universities to gain recognition for the academic quality of their work as well as its professional significance and legitimacy as a function of the university. However, four factors have, I believe, contributed to the achievement of this recognition in most universities.

1. Many of those inside university departments have as it were joined the university on its own terms – upgrading their own academic qualifications when necessary, establishing a serious research commitment and developing publications and entering the university-committee structure, often very successfully because many had managerial experience in the school, LEA or college sector to bring as well as their academic and wider professional skills.
2. The sheer numbers of staff and students in departments of education in some universities have made them a powerful and influential force to be reckoned with and crucial to the prosperity of the university.
3. Teacher education was always better regarded in the old polytechnic sector than in the old university sector. It sat more comfortably with the more vocationally oriented programmes to which the polytechnics were accustomed, and often the former colleges of education provided the polytechnics with some of their more prestigious new campuses. As the polytechnics became universities and underwent rapid expansion their influence on the sector increased rapidly and, with it, the influence of the departments of education.

4. The relationship between departments of education, with their hitherto rather idiosyncratic professional training courses, and the rest of their universities changed as the universities, more generally, expanded, needed to attract new students, entered new professional and vocational fields, become more client-oriented, gave greater priority to teaching and learning, reconsidered curriculum organisation and assessment and developed more flexible learning systems. In all of this the experience and expertise to be found in their departments of education took on new significance. In the reconstruction of the university, some departments of education found themselves shifted from last to first in meeting the university's new priorities.

All this renders problematic what should be the priorities of departments of education in standing for 'the university' in their response to initiatives like school-based training. Departments have to decide whether, broadly speaking, they are going to go along with these changes or, more strongly, take the opportunity that their particular professional expertise affords to provide leadership and support in these changes or whether they are going to attempt to resist or subvert them in the interest of defending the traditional practice of the university. More particularly, they must consider whether their response to initiatives like school-based training will reflect the assumptions of the reconstructed or the unreconstructed idea of the university.

Before returning to these issues let me expand a little on the ways in which universities are being transformed, and, consequently, the idea of the university is being reconstructed in England and Wales.

The Reconstruction of the University

A report of the Higher Education Quality Council (HEQC) describes the pressures for fundamental change in the higher education system in these terms (HEQC, 1994, p.313):

> *It is apparent that universities, in the United Kingdom and internationally, are being faced with unprecedented demands. Governments no longer appear prepared to spend significant proportions of the GDP on a relatively privileged sector; the accountability of institutions and their members is being emphasised by Governments and the general public; students continue to demand places in universities as the best means of securing lifetime benefits; and higher education is expected to continue to improve the well-being of individuals, society and State. In short, universities and colleges are being transformed from sheltered institutions of the pre-modern world to public service organisations in a modern (or, some would say, post-modern) world.*

In a report to the Committee of Vice Chancellors and Principals (CVCP) Williams and Fry (1994, p.8) capture something of the turbulence of change which these kinds of imperative are generating:

> *The meaning of the terms 'higher education' and 'university' have broadened. The radical changes of the past decade are causing fundamental reappraisal of concepts, attitudes, values and prejudices. The tensions between continuity and change are sharper than ever. What must be preserved, what can be jettisoned and what should be reformed are becoming matters of day to day concern . . . Even amongst people who are well informed there is disagreement and confusion about what higher education is doing and what it ought to be doing.*

There are many different but interconnected ingredients to the change which is referred to here. Let me indicate at least some of these.

Students

The sheer number of students has expanded dramatically. Expressed as an age-cohort participation rate the undergraduate population rose from 6 per cent in 1961 to 13 per cent in 1980, 19 per cent in 1990 and 31 per cent in 1993 (Davies, 1994). The period 1985 to 1995 will have seen a decrease in the cohort of 18-year-olds from 778,000 to 551,000 (Ball, 1990), but an increase in the number of these entering higher education from about 109,000 in 1985 to about 175,000 in 1995. The Department for Education (DFE) continues to assert its commitment to a 33 per cent participation rate by the year 2000, though the Confederation of British Industry continues to call for at least 40 per cent as a condition of Britain's commercial and industrial success in the future (CBI, 1994).

At the same time the character of the student body has changed. In 1992–93, 24 per cent of undergraduates were admitted to institutions with qualifications other than A levels. The number of mature first-year students increased by 77 per cent between 1980 and 1990 and, according to a DFE report, 'In 1990 there were more mature students entering higher education than young students' (DFE, 1993, p.36) Slowly too there has been an increase in the number of students from ethnic minorities, especially in some city universities, like Leicester, South Bank and North London, closest to the concentration of ethnic minority populations.

These changes begin to challenge the traditional relations between university staff and students. There was a time, perhaps, when university staff could confidently (if not entirely accurately) assume some superiority over their fresh-faced undergraduates in their life-experience as well as their academic expertise – but no longer. The new generation of students bring a richness of life-experience, including its tragedies, before which the average university tutor must stand in some awe. Some prefer to ignore the change; the best draw on the experience which is in the group as a powerful new resource for learning.

Teaching and Learning

Of all undergraduates in 1992–93, 32 per cent were studying part-time. Indeed by far the largest higher education institution was the Open University with 107,000 part-time students mainly studying through distance learning, but 37 other institutions had more than 30 per cent of their students studying on a part-time basis (HEFCE, 1994). Even Cambridge University has now agreed to admit part-time students to its master's programme (an initiative led, incidentally, by its newly incorporated Institute of Education).

The increase in the number of mature and part-time students and the expansion of higher education more generally has been facilitated by but also created increased demand for different patterns of course provision. In particular, part-time modes, distance learning, flexible study arrangements and the modularisation of degrees (with the facility to accumulate credits over a period of time) eroded the notion of higher education as something which takes place at a particular location, in face-to-face contact with a particular set of tutors over a fixed period of time. 'Teaching' in a university in the past meant some combination of lecturing, conducting seminars and supervisions with individual students – all face-to-face contact. Today it may involve preparing distance-learning materials and putting in place support structures hundreds and thousands of miles away from the university centre. It might involve designing an interactive video to be made available at resource centres in and around the university so that students can access them at any time. It might involve telephone- or video-conferencing across several sites. It might involve responding to work sent via E-mail or fax from anywhere in the world. It might involve helping other organisations to design learning systems suited to the needs of their employees in the workplace. In a sense, though of course the two matters are complementary, the question of how students might best learn has taken precedence over the question of how university tutors might best teach.

Modularisation and Credits

One change which supports part-time and interrupted study, allows for curricula more closely tailored to the interests of individual students and permits some other initiatives to which I shall shortly proceed is the development of modularised programmes and credit systems, now adopted by the majority of universities.

What appears at first sight to be merely a convenient and flexible form of curriculum organisation carries, however, more profoundly disturbing implications:

> *The creation of small units of knowledge and the almost infinite number of ways in which they can be assembled encourages analysis of the scope and nature of knowledge in any discipline, its relationship to other disciplines and sub-disciplines, and the ways*

> *in which this knowledge can best be acquired and its levels of attainment assessed. However, once knowledge has been deconstructed in this way the essential arbitrariness of the degree qualification becomes apparent.* (Williams and Fry, 1994, p.71)

The HEQC report on credit accumulation and transfer points similarly to indications that this development represents the first stages of a move towards 'a credit culture' involving a shift in taxonomies of knowledge, a rewriting of the undergraduate curriculum and 'the reconstruction of the institution itself' (HEQC, 1994, p.316).

Modularisation and credit systems not only challenge the integrity of the traditional disciplines but throw into question the very notion of levels of study. Especially, as the same modules are taken by students at different stages in their academic and professional lives pursuing different paths through 'a complex multidimensional world of learning' (NIACE, 1993, p.23). For some students the module on The Pre-Raphaelites may be a stepping-stone towards their single honours first-degree course in Art History taken perhaps in their second year of undergraduate study. For another, recently retired after years in academia, the same course may be an opportunity to pursue an intense interest which she or he had previously followed only as a hobby. Another student in the same group may be taking it as part of a combined degree in Victorian Studies and another as an add-on to an applied art programme; perhaps two more, museum curators, are picking it up in connection with a professional diploma in museology. Questions of the level of the course become intensely problematic: isn't this something to do with what these different students are able to make of it? and is this properly described as 'adult', 'continuing', 'further' or 'higher' education, and is it indeed 'education' or 'training'? Traditional categories are readily eroded.

Validation and Accreditation

One way in which undergraduate and other forms of university study have been made available to a wider section of the population is through universities working in partnership with other agencies and with each other to provide for the delivery and recognition of university-level study. The recent initiatives in this area include:

- the franchising of elements of degree courses for delivery by colleges, including sixth-form colleges, in, for example, the University of Hertfordshire, and by overseas educational institutions;
- the validation of courses provided by other institutions so that they lead to the degree of the university;
- the accreditation of other institutions, which permits them to take responsibility for courses leading to the degree of the university;

- credit accumulation and transfer arrangements, which allow students to build up credits towards a degree or diploma on the basis of modules of study provided by different higher education institutions (HEIs). The report by the HEQC records that most higher education institutions now have some experience of credit-based systems and proposed 'a national credit framework'. (HEQC, 1994, p.18)

Whatever the controls exercised by an individual university in these procedures, they clearly erode the ownership by one institution of the student and of the degree and they begin to redefine the university as an institution at the centre of the learning network rather than as the exclusive location of that learning.

The Accreditation of Prior and Experiential Learning

The accreditation of prior and experiential learning is taken a stage further as universities accredit not only the learning that issues from relatively conventional courses which they have licensed out to other providers but other forms of learning, for example:

- the accreditation of prior learning (APL) associated with taught courses or training programmes put on independently (ie, outside any franchising or approval mechanism of the university) by another organisation;
- the accreditation of prior experiential learning (APEL) arising out of practice, for example, in the workplace (perhaps developing particular technical skills or managerial insight) or in the home (perhaps developing understanding of child care).

These developments potentially set no boundaries on the context of learning or the source of that learning. The single concern of the university for this purpose is with what learning has actually taken place and how far this satisfies the university's requirements in relation to the criteria to be satisfied for the award of a degree or, more typically, in practice, the award of a certain amount of credit towards a degree or diploma.

The same developments also add to the problematising of the nature of knowledge which is recognised as part of a degree (cf. the preceding comments on modularisation), because much experiential learning is in the form of tacit knowledge or skill. It is craft knowledge rather than intellectualised knowledge and rarely presented in the forms, notably the written essay or research report, to which universities are accustomed. The accreditation of prior experiential learning raises questions, therefore, about how knowledge has to be represented, how evidenced and whether all forms of learning have to be expressed as written assignments to merit recognition by the university.

University Staff

All of these developments have far-reaching implications for the staffing of universities – especially when it is remembered that the rapid expansion in student numbers was in no way matched by a parallel increase in resources or staff. A DFE report (1993) indicated the following 'efficiency gains' (a form of rhetoric which my own university's senate has prohibited its officers from employing) based on the relation between expenditure in real terms and FTE students in HEFCE funded-institutions between 1989–90 and 1993–94:

1989–90	*1990–91*	*1991–92*	*1992–93*	*1993–94*
100	*92*	*85*	*80*	*78*

Nor can cuts of this kind be met simply by piling more and different kinds of students into larger groups and assuming that learning will go on as before.

Williams and Fry (1994, p.5) paint a picture of a developing staff structure in universities, whose beginnings I think we can already observe, in particular in departments of education:

> *There is likely to be . . . more part-time staff combining professional and managerial practice with teaching in higher education, and more mobility between academic work and other professional occupations. . . . The university of 2004 will be evolving towards one with a small core of high quality full-time staff, more formally specialised than at present in terms of teaching and research skills, undertaking core teaching themselves, but also acting as creators and facilitators of high technology learning materials and forming the nodes of networks for part-time staff.*

This is very much the picture of 'the shamrock organisation' and the flexible work force described as part of a more general prognostication of working life in Charles Handy's *The Age of Unreason* (1989). It renders membership of the academy or the senior common-room much more permeable than it has been in the past and locates its membership outside as well as inside the ivory tower – a prospect which gives a certain credence to Kerr's definition of the modern university as 'a series of individual faculty entrepreneurs held together by a common grievance over parking' (Kerr, 1973, p.16).

The Reconstructed University and School-based Training

The cumulative effect of all these interconnected changes on the identity and character of the university is far-reaching. Of course, their effect is not the same everywhere. There is increasing reference in the literature on higher education to the diversification of the system whose institutions have some very different histories and traditions. The Royal Society Study Group (1993, pp.6, 305), for example, suggests:

> *In a diverse system some institutions will wish to pursue a mission of broad access for students, exploiting the opportunities presented by new students, exploiting the opportunities presented by new student groups and novel course structures; others will continue to recruit from the more traditionally prepared student groups; yet others may concentrate on postgraduate and/or post-experience courses. . . . Not all institutions can carry out effectively the tasks which the system as a whole needs to accomplish.*

Christopher Ball (1991, p.103) was among those who for some years have been arguing that the expansion of higher education requires a diversity of forms of higher education provision: 'A diversity of functions requires a variety of qualities. Higher education has a diversity of functions. It must start to recognise a variety of qualities: not *quality* but *qualities*.'

In practice, I believe few if any universities will be able to stand aloof from the kinds of changes which I have outlined. Rightly or wrongly there is a remarkable consensus among political parties, among departments of state (the Employment Department has had a major role through its Enterprise in Higher Education project and other initiatives in promoting these developments), among employers and among a sufficient proportion of the expanded student body to give them political durability. Besides which they fit together in a way that makes it difficult to disentangle one element without having to unpick a lot more.

Whether we anticipate a university system increasingly shaped by these developments or a variety of universities responding differently to them, this setting begins to make the development of school-based training in a variety of forms of partnership with universities (and so far only one such scheme has been developed entirely independently of a university) more or less consistent with the changing character and orientation of universities themselves. Here, after all, we find elements of franchising and accreditation, elements of 'work-based learning', and the extension of the university staff to include school-based mentors, many of them receiving training in their role from university tutors. We find (eg, in the Essex Coastal Consortium) groups of schools providing access to initial teacher training in areas which the university they approached had told them was too distant for it to use for its own 'partnership' training programme.

The decision as to whether to participate in these developments (insofar as there is any choice in the matter) is not difficult for many departments of education. For many such departments the developments in initial teacher education are entirely at one with the developments that their university is actively promoting. They provide an opportunity for the department to collect a new kind of esteem in some sectors of the university for being at the forefront in shaping its new identity rather than at the rear in fulfilling its old view of its priorities and purpose.

In any case, for many in education there are features of the changing ideology of higher education that must appeal to some of the rather confused assortment of unreconstructed egalitarian, democratic and 'progressive' values that they have often been accused of harbouring since the 1960s: wider access for disenfranchised sections of society, experiential learning, flexible learning, closer association between the academy and the outside world (so that as Peter Scott [1990, p.16] puts it 'ideas as well as institutions would . . . become outward-bound') and the critical challenge to the traditional concept of the university. All these express educational principles likely to find favour in many sections of the educational community, independently of their political inexorability.

None of this means that the values which Pring wanted to associate with and safeguard through the university – the maintenance of the critical tradition and the linking of teaching to expertise or, by extension, to scholarship and research (though interestingly neither Newman nor Ortega y Gasset, two classical sources for the traditional idea of the university, saw this latter conjunction as either necessary or desirable) – must or should be abandoned. Rather the task is to work out how they are to be protected and developed in a new environment which itself challenges (as I have indicated) the nature of the teaching task, the kind of knowledge which is within the province of the university and the geographical, temporal and human boundaries of the university community itself.

Viewed from this perspective, the issue of school-based training appears as a relatively minor feature of a transformed educational landscape.

References

Allen, M (1988) *The Goals of Universities*. Milton Keynes: SRHE/The Open University.

Ball, C (1990) *More Means Different: Widening Access to Higher Education*. London: Royal Society for the Arts, Manufactures and Commerce (RSA).

Ball, C (1991) 'Quality and qualities: An overview', in Schuller, T (ed) *The Future of Higher Education*. London: Open University Press/SRHE.

Committee of Vice Chancellors and Principals (1985) *Report of the Steering Committee for Efficiency Studies in Universities (The Jarratt Report)*. London: CVCP.

Confederation of British Industry (1994) *Thinking Ahead: Ensuring the Expansion of Higher Education into the 21st Century*. London: CBI.

Cmnd 114 (1987) *Higher Education – Meeting the Challenge*. London: HMSO.

Cmnd 9524 (1985) *The Development of Higher Education into the 1990s*. London: HMSO.

Davies, G (1994) *An Overview of Recent Developments in Higher Education*. Bristol: HEFCE.

Department for Education (1993) 'Student Numbers in Higher Education in Great Britain 1981–82 to 1991–92', *Statistical Bulletin*, 17(93).

Eggins, H (ed) (1987) *Restructuring Higher Education.* London: Open University Press/SRHE.

Handy, C (1989) *The Age of Unreason*. London: Business Books.

Higher Education Funding Council for England (1994) *Building on Strength: Annual Report 1993–94.* Bristol: HEFCE.

Higher Education Quality Council (1994) *Choosing To Change: Extending Access, Choice and Mobility in Higher Education*. London: HEQC.

Kerr, C (1973) *The Uses of the University*. Cambridge, MA: Harvard University Press.

National Institute for Adult and Continuing Education (1993) *An Adult Higher Education: A Vision*. Leicester: NIACE.

Newman, JH (1852) *The Idea of a University.* London: Longman Green.

Ortega y Gasset, J (1946) *The Mission of the University.* London: Routledge.

Pring, R (1994) Universities and Educational Studies. Paper presented to Universities Council for the Education of Teachers Conference, Coventry, November 1994 (mimeo).

Royal Society Study Group (1993) *Higher Education Futures.* London: The Royal Society.

Schuller, T (1991) *The Future of Higher Education.* London: Open University Press/SRHE.

Scott, P (1990) 'The power of ideas', in Ball, C and Eggins, H (eds) *Higher Education into the 1990s*. London: SRHE.

Society for Research into Higher Education (1983) *Excellence in Diversity: Towards a New Strategy for Higher Education*. London: SRHE.

Williams, G and Fry, H (1994) *Longer Term Prospects for British Higher Education: A Report to the Committee of Vice Chancellors and Principals.* London: University of London Institute of Education.

Wright, P (1987) 'Rethinking the Aims of Higher Education', in Eggins, H (ed) *Restructuring Higher Education.* London: Open University Press/SRHE

CHAPTER 5

THE ROLE OF UNIVERSITY DEPARTMENTS OF EDUCATION IN IMPROVING EDUCATIONAL STANDARDS

Michael Barber

For most of this century work evolved slowly. Someone did a job. When they moved on or retired, they were replaced. The same job was done by a different person. There is virtually no sphere of work where this holds true in the mid-1990s. The nature of work and of any specific job changes constantly. Over the last decade many secretaries have shifted from typing to word-processing and from word-processing to desk-top publishing. Now the results of a study in one computer file can be merged directly into the text in another. Through modems these files might belong to people in different continents. As the technology continues to change at an ever-increasing pace, who knows what may be possible five or ten years from now? The point to establish here is that nobody *replaces* anybody any longer. The nature of the work changes; so does the nature of the product. Word-processing is not an alternative, more economical route to the same academic paper; the outcome is a different, perhaps better, paper.

In any chapter where speculation about the future is required, the author is taking risks. Most of what he or she writes will turn out to be inaccurate. Predicting the future has become a great deal more difficult as the pace of change has increased, especially since change now is not incremental but discontinuous. This means that successful analysis of the future depends less on the study of trends and more on the exercise of the imagination. A Nobel prize-winning scientist claimed last year that he gained more inspiration for the future direction of his work from writers of science fiction than from the learned papers of his colleagues. It seems an appropriate comment on the decade ahead which has tremendous potential for transformation in education while being dangerously unpredictable.

In much of what follows, predictions about the future are made with a confidence designed to be provocative, although in reality I feel the same hesitancy I felt when I (wrongly) predicted that Bulgaria would play Sweden in the 1994 World Cup Final.

First, I draw on chaos theory in an attempt to describe the likely nature of change in the next decade. Next, I look at underlying trends which are likely to impact on the education service over the same period. Then, I examine the implications of all this for the profession and, finally, I look at what it means for the role of universities in teacher education.

In case there is any doubt, I assert at this stage that in my view there is a rich and varied task ahead for universities in teacher education. Nothing however is inevitable. As Brecht said in another context a rosy dawn does not necessarily follow a night of sleep. That task is not there waiting for the universities; it has to be created through their decisions and actions and through their energy, commitment and imagination.

The Chaotic Nature of Change

In 1961, A J P Taylor, Britain's greatest historian since the war, concluded his controversial study *The Origins of the Second World War* with: 'Hitler may have projected a great war all along: yet it seems from the record that he became involved in war through launching on 29 August a diplomatic manoeuvre which he ought to have launched on 28 August.' He provoked a storm of controversy. In the 1960s and 1970s, the fashion in historical explanation was to point to deep underlying forces or systems: nationalism, class conflict or economic determinism. Taylor's predilection for chance, accident and the intervention of the individual was thus considered misplaced.

Now, however, his approach has become mainstream. Simon Schama (1989) wrote in the introduction to his study of the French Revolution: 'The Revolution was a haphazard and chaotic event and much more the product of human agency that structural conditioning.' The trend in history over 30 years is thus from systems to chaos.

In science a similar intellectual trend is evident. For 300 years, as Thomas Gleick put it, 'the search for regularity in experiment has been fundamental. . . . But that means disregarding those bits of messiness that interfere with a neat picture.' This was the scientific approach that ensured that those of us at school had to tackle endless maths problems which began 'Assume a perfectly smooth slope . . .'. To satisfy our teachers and our examiners we suspended disbelief though we knew no such thing existed. Since the 1970s, a scientific revolution has occurred. Scientists began to study the irregularities. Once they began to look for them they turned out to be both everywhere and important. Science discovered what became known as *chaos*. One of its key principles is that tiny differences in input can be overwhelming differences in output: a phenomenon which Gleick describes as 'sensitive dependence on initial conditions'.

In the study of the weather this is known as 'The Butterfly Effect': a butterfly flapping its wings over Beijing can cause a storm over New York a week later. The similarity between this idea and A J P Taylor's explanation of the outbreak of war is uncanny. Science too, it seems, shifted from systems to chaos.

A similar trend is identifiable in management. Here there is no need to go beyond the titles of popular management books: from F W Taylor's *Scientific Management* (1947) and H Mintzberg's *The Structuring of Organisations* (1979) to T Peters's *Thriving on Chaos* (1988) and *Liberation Management: Necessary Disorganisation for the Nanosecond Nineties* (1992).

Here too is the shift from systems to chaos. Yet, as this trend becomes evident across the intellectual spectrum, in education we are in danger of becoming obsessed with systems. At the 1994 American Education Research Association Conference, there were 37 sessions on systemic reform. In the UK almost every debate has been dominated by conflicting views of central government's latest system reform.

If we threw off the shackles of introversion that so often dominate education debate, we would see that we have discovered 'systemic reform' just in time to write its obituary. Systemic reform is dead. Or, put more modestly, systemic reform on its own is not the answer to our problems. Waiting for the next battery of centrally determined change is not the solution. We need not wait for solutions at all. They are already here. As the scientists who discovered chaos found, it is simply a matter of knowing where to look. In Birmingham, Tim Brighouse and his colleagues are bringing about marked improvement through changing not the structure but the culture. In Nottingham, nine primary schools in a GEST-funded scheme have re-examined the grouping of children, found a new balance in pedagogy which gives the teacher a more directive role and developed a creative educational role for classroom assistants. Through rigorous monitoring of pupil outcomes they know it is working.

The educational cutting edge is to be found not in the systems but in the chaos. It would be possible, of course, to exaggerate the point. Clearly some systemic issues to do with the distribution of money and power are important. However, the greater danger is that through an obsession with these factors we miss the tremendous potential that exists here and now in the swirl of change that is education today.

I am sure I was not alone in the last year or two in describing the education service as chaotic. What never occurred to me until I read Gleick's book was that this might be a compliment. As Brian Goodwin, Professor of Biology at the Open University put it: 'The edge of chaos is a good place to be in a constantly changing world because from there you can always explore the patterns of order that are available. . . . What you do not want to do is get stuck in one particular state of order' (1994). This notion of change would seem particularly appropriate for universities, which over the last decade diversified their funding base and established a degree of room for manoeuvre barely dreamt of a decade ago.

External Pressures

The previous section may somewhat exaggerate the state of affairs, but it seems nevertheless likely that the pressure for change will largely come from forces outside of government, though government will no doubt mediate them and sometimes act as their advocate. In short it seems safe to assert that the five years of stability promised by government provide a tremendous opportunity for successful change. At least eight important pressures for change can be identified; in the context of this brief chapter, it is possible to do little more than identify and provide a brief explanation of each of them.

A Fiercely Competitive Economic Climate

Few dispute that international competitiveness is a major concern for the British economy. Certainly politicians from Major to Blair, Heseltine to Ashdown, believe it is. The results of this belief will be a constant demand from politicians for evidence of improved performance from the education service. The social and economic consequences of a fiercely competitive market – above all the need for constant learning and the likelihood of job insecurity – will also lead individuals to demand a great deal from the education service. To some extent these demands will be contradictory (eg, a firm grounding for education throughout life yet preparation for whatever the job market holds when any given individual leaves full-time education). Either way these pressures will ensure dissatisfaction with the *status quo*.

The Nature of Work

The nature of work will change ever more rapidly. Most jobs will demand ever higher levels of skill but also ever-changing skills. Few jobs will have the security associated with public service jobs in the 1970s and 1980s. The pattern of people's working lives is also changing with many people working much harder for a more concentrated part of their lives, but retiring earlier. There will also be unemployment. Some of this will be the inevitable but temporary consequence of the process of change. Some will be the result of educational failure and the continued existence of low-paid, insecure, unskilled and often part-time work.

This will affect schools themselves as employers. It is possible to imagine, for example, that, where in the early 1990s it was the catering or grounds-maintenance contract that was put out to tender, in the late 1990s it might be the science-teaching contract. Schools too will become increasingly important sources of employment in local communities as the number of non-teaching staff increases as a proportion of overall staffing.

The chief impact on schools, however, will be in the relationship between education and work. The experiment beginning in 1995, under SCAA's auspices, of GNVQs for 14–16-year-olds is a portentous one. If successful it could provide a spur to motivation and higher achievement; if not it could result in a second-rate pathway to a highly uncertain employment future. Meanwhile there will be a need to bring coherence to confusion at post-16 level.

Standards

There will without doubt be continued pressure from industry, government and society for ever higher educational standards. It is clear that the economy will increasingly depend on the skills, knowledge and imagination of the workforce. When it can be said, as it was recently, of Microsoft that its only asset is 'the human imagination', it is evident that a paradigm shift has taken place (Peters, 1992). Pressure from industry on government will ensure that, whoever wins the elections between now and the end of the century, politicians will be leading the drive for higher standards.

The revised National Education and Training Targets, for example, include one which states that 85 per cent of young people should achieve five higher-grade GCSEs (or the equivalent) by the end of the century. The young people expected to achieve this target started secondary school in the Autumn of 1995. In other words it is not some distant snow-capped peak but an immediate challenge facing every secondary teacher.

To some in education the target seems ludicrously difficult to achieve. Although there has been on average a 3 per cent improvement per year in performance at GCSE since 1988, each further 3 per cent is clearly more difficult than the last as teachers face raising the performance of those who, on the basis of Keele's database of pupil attitudes, might be described as the 30–40 per cent of young people who are disappointed or disaffected.

The pressure to achieve the target will place a premium on any pedagogical or technological innovations which appear to have the power to motivate. It will also ensure emphasis on that small but significant second half of the phrase, 'five higher-grade GCSEs or the equivalent'. This in turn will place still more emphasis on the need to establish GNVQs for 14–16-year-olds and successfully bring further change to the post-16 qualifications framework.

Diversity

The extent of diversity in British society, whether in race, religion or lifestyle, grew dramatically since the Second World War. The 1944 Education Act was designed and placed on the statute book at what was perhaps the high point of homogeneity in the twentieth century. Racial and religious diversity (except within the narrow bounds of Christianity) was not a factor in R A Butler's deliberations while, during the war, even the class divisions which had characterised the 1920s and 1930s were, at least temporarily, forgotten.

By the 1980s all that had changed. One strand running through the conflicts of the 1980s was the tension between an essentially uniform education service and an increasingly diverse society. Normally these played themselves out under the banner headings of differing interpretations of equal opportunities. Whether the reforms of the late 1980s with their combination of centralisation and delegation reduced those tensions still remains to be seen.

Social diversity seems certain to continue to grow and this is likely to include growing wealth differentials as well as other forms of diversity. Whether these developments will contribute to a need for further system reform, they will undoubtedly continue to present extraordinary professional challenges for many teachers since growing numbers of parents may question the legitimacy of the publicly provided service unless it is responsive. At the same time, a large minority of pupils brought up in disadvantaged circumstances are likely to prove hard to motivate.

Information and Communications Technology

Occasionally, one reads a sentence so startling that it seems to leap off the page. On 22 January 1995 in the *Sunday Times* there was a review of a serious book entitled *The Physics of Immortality* by a serious scientist, Frank J Tipler. It includes the following sentence: 'In about thirty years, Tipler predicts, it will be possible to regard computers as persons.' Whether this turns out to be true, it says something about the rapid pace of technological development that a serious scientist can believe it to be the case.

Technology is transforming work, as we have seen. It will also transform the learning process and therefore pedagogy, which as yet it has not. This is largely a result of a lack not of the relevant technology but of the failure to invest in teachers' skills and confidence. Research in its early stages at Keele suggests that effective use of information technology not only acts as a motivational force among pupils, it also helps them learn more quickly, more effectively and more independently. It also suggests teachers would like to use IT much more, but lack either the skills or the confidence or both.

The Extent and the Limits of Funding

It may be true in 1995 that the recession is over, but the recovery is slow and the potential for higher taxes negligible, even if there is a change of government. If this is hardly positive from the perspective of the public services in general and education in particular, it is also clear that across the political spectrum there is a recognition of the growing importance of the role of education in a learning society. Ultimately this will be reflected in the relative levels of funding between public services. It is interesting, for example, that in 1995 though education expenditure has been tightly constrained it has nevertheless been constrained less than some other areas of public expenditure.

Thus in the medium term it is possible, assuming the recovery continues, to predict real growth in education expenditure at least in line with the rate of growth. Education expenditure as a proportion of government expenditure is likely to rise too.

In addition, a growing amount of investment in education will come from non-governmental sources. Increasingly industry and commerce are investing directly or indirectly in education and training. During the recent recession, for the first time in history, companies spent proportionately more on training rather than less. They are also increasingly committed to working with the publicly provided education system when it suits their needs. Thus, especially in the FE and HE sectors, institutions are far less dependent than they were on traditional government funding. For Keele University, for example, traditional government funding of students provides only about 40 per cent of total income, the rest coming from research grants and cooperative ventures with both private and public sector organisations and other sources.

Furthermore, private individuals are increasingly prepared to invest in their own education. This is evident, not least among teachers, increasing numbers of whom are prepared to pay their own fees for diploma and MA courses. What this means is that growth in education can be anticipated both in real expenditure and as a percentage of GDP. The growth, however, is unlikely to come entirely from government.

Within the overall growth there are likely to be major shifts, which will squeeze some areas while others expand rapidly. In relation to statutory schooling, where overall the potential for raising private finance is limited (though growing), dependence on government funding is likely to remain decisive. Given the growing consensus in favour of a redistribution of funds in favour of primary and nursery education, the prospects for secondary education in particular would appear to be constrained regardless of which party wins the next election. As a result the effective management of existing funds in the school sector and the continuing development of cooperative relationships with, for example, TECs, universities and education-business partnerships will become decisive. Whether government does provide real growth in the schools sector will depend on the extent of public pressure for them to do so. This in turn depends on public perceptions of the effectiveness and importance of the education service. The governors' revolt early in 1995 is evidence that governments which fail to invest properly in education are likely to find themselves on the defensive, perhaps more than ever before.

A Wider Agenda

Perceptions will depend on the role expected of schools by society. There has been, rightly, a high degree of concern about the need to raise levels of academic achievement in recent years. This will undoubtedly continue because, in spite of the improvement during the early 1990s, absolute levels of performance remain well below what a healthy twenty-first-century democracy and economy will demand.

This academic purpose will be only one of a number on the agenda. There is, for example, growing cross-party concern about crime, the failure of the family and social dislocation especially in urban areas. Already each of these concerns leads politicians to turn to the schools, at least in part, for solutions. Hence the emphasis on drugs education and John Patten's ignorant (but heartfelt) outbursts about schools as 'value-free zones'.

While the evidence suggests that schools are playing this ethical role effectively – although often very much against the odds – the emphasis on it is likely to continue. Tony Blair, with his focus on 'community' and the collective power of society being exercised in support of individuals, can be expected to emphasise the wider role of schools in society, and the Conservative Party will inevitably respond.

As if this agenda was not enough, it can be anticipated that within the next five years schools will also be expected to contribute to solving the most fundamental problems facing humanity: population, the greenhouse effect, bio-diversity and the future of the planet. As David Orr said in his prophetic Schumacher lecture in 1992: 'For the most part we are still educating the young as if there were no planetary emergency.' This will surely have to change as the challenges become increasingly explicit and the choices more stark.

Future Alliances

Thus, overall it can be seen that, as the new millennium approaches, society is likely to expect the education service to play an increasingly broad and ambitious role, including improved academic standards, contributions to solving a range of pressing social problems and, beyond that, to helping ensure the continued existence of the planet.

Yet there is no sign that resources will increase proportionately, though some growth can be anticipated. Thus the school system will either fail –

measured against this broader agenda – or become significantly more effective. It is this that makes the huge strides in understanding of school effectiveness and school improvement over the last decade so important. It is also why the school system will need to build effective working relationships with those outside education: business, social services, health, housing and so on.

Finally, and in respect of the theme of this chapter, most important, it is this that makes teacher effectiveness such a vital educational issue. Teachers, individually and collectively, have played an important social role for generations. The evidence suggests that the effectiveness of their contribution improved significantly over the last decade. This climb to the foothills has been controversial and often exhausting; now, without time to pause for breath, it is time to scale the mountains ahead. To do that will require a reconstruction of the teaching profession more radical than any in its history.

The Reconstruction of the Profession

Little more needs to be said in justifying the need for a complete reconstruction of the teaching profession. However, one point needs emphasising. After almost a decade of constant centrally directed legislative change, there is now support across a wide spectrum for the view that teaching and learning, and pedagogy, need to move to centre stage. In January 1994 at a conference organised by the School Curriculum and Assessment Authority (SCAA), Anthea Millett, then Director of Inspection at OFSTED, called for 'methodology for the millennium'. During 1994 at conferences such as the Secondary Heads' Association the message was taken up. In January 1995, in his provocative annual lecture at the RSA, Her Majesty's Chief Inspector made the same point in more colourful language (Woodhead, 1995). He quoted David Hargreaves's recent Demos pamphlet:

> *The main barrier to change may be the professional culture of teachers. . . . Professional and institutional structures and cultures are resilient; they withstand many an assault and have powerful capacities to maintain and reproduce themselves despite surface changes.*

Woodhead takes the argument a step forward:

> *The problem is not merely resistance to change. It is, as I say, a commitment to particular beliefs about the purposes and conduct of education; beliefs which constitute the real impediment to the development of a better education system and which lie, of course, far beyond the legislative ambitions of even the most interventionist of governments.*

Whether one agrees with the pejorative tone of Chris Woodhead's argument, the broader point, that in spite of the most extensive reorganisation of the education service in history classroom practice has been relatively little changed, is surely a powerful one.

The question for policy-makers is how to create the circumstances which encourage the development of a profession enthusiastic for change and innovation and determined to base pedagogical and professional decisions on evidence rather than received wisdom? It is possible, even at this stage in the argument, to glimpse a vital role for higher education in bringing about a questioning professional culture. However, the issue goes far wider than the role of higher education; it will involve first of all removing the barriers to professional change and second establishing a vision of a reconstructed teaching profession. The barriers to change can be rapidly identified.

1. There has been the political approach to education which involved not just systemic reform, much of which has been beneficial, but endless tinkering. In addition, the critical, high-handed and sometimes arrogant statements made by ministers and their minions, far from opening up the possibility of change, in fact drove the profession back into its circle of wagons.
2. Leaders of the profession have often become blinded by the politics of educational change, instead of setting out a vision for the future of the profession. Even now, after the soothing new tone of Gillian Shephard brought a fragile peace, there remains a yawning gap where the professional vision should be. Worse still the profession's leaders have often given priority to the divisions among them rather than building on the common interests of the profession. Ironically, the one true market in education is the competition among unions for members and this market, like many other British markets, causes its participants to focus on the short term.
3. Simply the lack of time teachers have in which to develop their pedagogical skill. Overwhelmed by full timetables, diverse classes and extensive bureaucracy, teachers' own learning often slides down this list of priorities. To misquote Elizabeth Cady Stanton, given the choice teachers often choose self-sacrifice rather than self-development.
4. The absence of a forum in which the future of the profession can be debated openly and constructively bedevils the issue. If the unions are divided, so too is the governance of the profession. Responsibility for regulating the profession is divided uneasily among four quangos (SCAA, OFSTED, the School Teachers' Review Body and the TTA) and one government department. Given the politicisation of appointments at quango level, it is not surprising to discover that none of the four quangos has a long-term agenda either. The date of a general election may also be the end of the line for many of their members and even some of their staff.

None of these barriers is inevitable or permanent. All are within the power of government or profession to change. What is missing, for the moment, is the will. However, the new circumstances brought about by the astute pragmatism of Gillian Shephard and the conscious emphasis on standards of David Blunkett, the Opposition Spokesperson on Education, opens up a new possibility for tearing these barriers down. Whether that will happen remains to be seen. Unless an agenda for the future is set out there would be little point in doing so. It is to an outline of a possible agenda that I now turn. Again constraints of space prevent more than the briefest of explanations of each of the following headings.

A Respect for Research

Increasingly teachers will need to draw on research and undertake research in their own organisations to find effective ways forward amid the chaotic change around them. They will need to adopt a practical 'what works' approach and link action to evaluation and to further action in a constant cycle. This requires teachers to acquire skills, time and confidence they do not yet have.

Teacher Education

The three phases of teacher education – initial, induction and continuing – identified as long ago as 1972 in the James Report, have never been coherently overhauled. The reforms of the late 1980s and early 1990s served only to muddy the waters since the development of the teaching profession as a whole was not on the agenda – sadly – of either government or the profession.

Clearly it is necessary in the next five years to consider the three phases of development coherently. The new Teacher Training Agency has already put this on its agenda. How effectively it is able to develop and implement new thinking will depend above all on the quality of the relationship it establishes with the teaching profession.

Administration

All the surveys of teachers' workload – whether from unions or the School Teachers' Review Body – suggest that teachers have taken an increasingly large administrative burden. Given the argument above about the need for greatly increased effectiveness in a period of constrained resources, this is patently absurd. It is clearly essential to free some time to enable teachers to engage in their own development and research and to focus, more than they have been able to do in the past, on developments in pedagogy. More administrative staff will become essential. If used properly they should not be seen as a drain on resources, but as enabling teacher time and other resources to be used more efficiently.

Teaching Assistants and Associates

The challenges facing education seem to me so daunting that teachers cannot take them on alone. Governors will be a source of support; administrators will too, but neither group provides assistance in the classroom, where the challenge becomes direct and sharply focused. For this reason Tim Brighouse and I (1992) argued that teachers need increasingly to look to two sources of support in their work with children and young people. First, classroom assistants, laboratory technicians, librarians and others need to be thought of as a serious paraprofessional grouping involved in planning, training and school development. These numbers ought to increase as the traditional model of learning involving a teacher, a room and 30 children becomes only one of a number of organisational strategies. Increasingly, it will be necessary to think about pupil-adult ratios rather than pupil-teacher ones.

Second, increasing numbers of adults will be involved in the provision of education in a range of different capacities. It may be, for example, that science-research students will spend time assisting schools in keeping up with the frontiers of their fields. Or perhaps business people will act as mentors to pupils. Secondments from industry increasingly play a part in schools in a wide variety of ways. Means need to be found of recognising their contribution and making it more effective. Tim Brighouse and I suggested describing such people as teaching associates and a project funded by the Paul Hamlyn Foundation is currently exploring how this role might best be constructed and enhanced.

The result might be, in the long run, schools with far more adults than at present but also perhaps fewer teachers.

Teachers Who Learn

If this vision comes to pass it will offer teachers the opportunity to give much more time to their own professional development. They will need to take it because in those well-staffed schools their curriculum, pedagogical and classroom-management skills will be at a premium. This will demand, in turn, the profession defining its own standards for professional development. Tentatively, I would suggest this should involve a professional development interview with peers every five years for all teachers. Remaining in the profession would depend on teachers demonstrating in that interview what they had achieved in professional development terms over the past five years and how that had impacted on their pedagogy and the schools in which they worked and what their plans for the next five years might be.

Further, it would be valuable if the concept of 'lead teachers' was developed. These would be promoted posts, with appointments made on the basis of the best equal-opportunities practice, filled by leading pedagogues who had chosen to have a successful career in the classroom rather than in school management.

Vouchers

Finally, if the current HEADLAMP scheme, which provides newly appointed heads with the right to funded training, is successful, the idea of professional development vouchers ought to be extended to other sectors within the profession: newly qualified teachers, for example, or those newly appointed to posts of responsibility in either management or the classroom.

Whether any of the items on this agenda comes to pass depends to a large extent on the teaching profession itself. The only certainty is that the status quo will become increasingly untenable. The choice for the profession is to set its own agenda or respond to one imposed from elsewhere.

The Implications for Universities

The role of the universities in teacher education has, it sometimes seems, been under threat for many years. The late 1980s and early 1990s saw a number of explicit attacks by government and its supporters on the university contribution to teacher education. Their contribution was caricatured as peddling an outdated and dangerous ideology of progressivism which had infected the teaching profession and undermined standards in the nation's schools. This view was expressed by the Prime Minister in his speech to the Centre for Policy Studies (Major, 1991). There was, he argued, 'a canker in our education system which spread from the sixties, and deprived great cohorts of our children of the opportunities they deserved.'

In practice, the government's reforms have been much more pragmatic than its rhetoric might have implied. In 1984 and 1989 criteria which all initial training courses had to meet were introduced through the Council for the Accreditation of Teacher Education (CATE). In 1992 and 1993 these were tightened with the emphasis on shifting more responsibility for training teachers into the schools. For a brief period it seemed government might attempt to shift all of initial teacher education out of universities but it stepped back from the brink. The 1994 Education Act established the TTA with powers to fund and promote teacher education based wholly in schools. Nevertheless, the government emphasised throughout the passage of the bill that it sees a continuing role for universities in initial teacher education. It seems to have accepted, de facto, that this will be a substantial role for HE, working in partnership with schools.

If this role appears to be secure, it does not follow that all universities will want to continue as providers in what is an uncertain and bureaucratised field. Moreover, the enhanced role of schools in initial training involves a transfer of resources to them. The resource framework in universities has become more restricted as a consequence. While many universities will no doubt maintain their commitment to initial training the message to all of them, particularly given the wider context of chaotic change, would seem to be that they should diversify.

Many have chosen to do so by extending the depth and breadth of their partnership with schools. Schools ceased to be merely places in which students do teaching practice. Instead they contribute fully to course development and to the selection and assessment of students. Partnerships also in many cases take in research, consultancy and the provision of inservice education. Assuming these partnerships maintain a degree of flexibility and that governments do not put ideology before effectiveness the model may thrive through to the end of the century. If it does, then organic links between schools, universities and sometimes LEAs could become a creative feature of British education with practice informing research and research guiding practice.

If the preparation of teachers in this form is likely to remain a function of universities, there is likely nevertheless to be a shift in emphasis towards other areas of work. A number of universities are, for example, already contributing to the training of specialist teaching assistants under the government's pilot programme. The training of the paraprofessional workforce in schools is likely to become a higher profile concern. There are those who believe this is not a role for universities. This view, however, is unlikely to survive, not least because in other fields – medicine and law, for example – universities have not seen any difficulty in contributing to paraprofessional development.

Less controversial, and perhaps even more significant, will be a growing role for universities in teachers' professional development. The growth of part-time and distance-learning MAs and MBAs and of taught doctorates is likely to continue, at least for some years. At the same time the growing emphasis on schools as learning organisations – over 1,000 schools are already involved in Investors in People – suggests there will be a growing demand for consultancy and short-course input from universities though this will only be the case if their research profile covers areas which are of interest to schools committed to improvement.

Increasingly where they do have a profile in this area universities will be able to create networks involving schools and sometimes LEAs and colleges, committed to promoting school improvement. The London Institute of Education has already established a School Improvement Network on a national basis. Newcastle University provides analysis of examination results to schools across the country, while the Centre for Successful Schools at Keele offers analysis of pupil and parent attitudes and other school-improvement consultancy on a similar basis. A Cambridge-based school-improvement scheme has both a regional and national profile in promoting school improvement.

Many other universities are developing this role on a more limited basis. The School of Education at Cardiff is, for example, working with all the grant maintained schools in Wales on a school-improvement programme. Keele University's research for OFSTED last year showed that out of 60 urban school-improvement initiatives across the country, higher education was involved in almost half. This role with schools will drive, as well as be driven by, a university's research profile.

Keele's involvement in the local Two Towns project, for example, led to significant national research contracts in the field of urban education. As the university role declines in initial teacher education it can be anticipated that the research profile of those which choose to remain in education will rise correspondingly. Some of this research will be of the traditional variety funded by research councils but much will be short- or medium-term and fall across the borders among research, advice, evaluation and consultancy. Even the ESRC gives increasing priority to the potential practical use of research work. Some purists may see this trend as threatening. In the medium to long term it is, however, likely to be highly beneficial: the more policy-makers and practitioners become aware of the importance and relevance of research, the greater the potential for it to be funded. Put another way, the research purists live in a territory whose boundaries are defended by more pragmatic policy-focused colleagues, on whom the size of the territory as a whole depends.

Three particular aspects of research are likely to become increasingly important:

- policy analysis, which uses both theory and research funds to provide a critique of specific policy ideas and processes to develop refined policy proposals;
- futures analysis, through which analysts and researchers attempt to anticipate trends and underlying shifts affecting education, contributing significantly to current debate;
- universities using their research knowledge and experience to promote innovation which will, without doubt, be essential to the success of the education service.

Finally, university education departments ought to be able to contribute to raising standards of teaching throughout a university. Various models for doing this are already in operation. The growing emphasis on quality in teaching is helping to drive it. Some universities will also provide qualifications for teachers and managers in FE.

It is unlikely that any given university could play a leading part in all the types of activity discussed in the foregoing paragraphs. Nevertheless, the agenda set out in them are full of promise for universities prepared to be flexible, entrepreneurial and bold. When leadership at departmental or university level lacks this kind of ambition, the future will be uncertain and possibly bleak. Universities that drift in the hope of returning some time to the more comfortable world of a decade or so ago would soon find themselves passing through a fools' paradise on the route to oblivion.

Those who take a more positive approach can advance from the old model of teacher education into this uncertain but exciting world with optimism if not absolute confidence. Decisions largely in their hands will decide the extent of their activity. External forces such as the Teacher Training Agency can adjust the rules of the game, with significant consequences for individual universities. Nevertheless, it will be the universities which convince (or otherwise) the government and society that the game is worth playing.

References

Barber, M and Brighouse, T (1992) *Enhancing the Teaching Profession.* London: IPPR.

Barber, M *et al.* (1994) Urban Education Initiatives: The National Pattern. A Report for OFSTED, Keele University.

Gleick, T (1988) *Chaos.* Harmondsworth: Penguin.

Goodwin, B (1994) *Daily Telegraph*, 10 September.

Major, J (1991) Speech to the Centre for Policy Studies. London: Cafe Royal.

Orr, D (1992) Schumacher Lecture. Reprinted in *Resurgence*, Autumn 1993.

Peters, T (1992) *Liberation Management.* London: MacMillan.

Schama, S (1989) *Citizens.* Harmondsworth: Penguin.

Taylor, A J P (1961) *The Origins of the Second World War.* Harmondsworth: Penguin.

Woodhead, C (1995) Annual Lecture of Her Majesty's Chief Inspector of Schools. London: Royal Society of the Arts, 1995.

PART 2

The Complexities of Initial Teacher Education

CHAPTER 6

THE CHANGING BALANCE IN INITIAL TEACHER EDUCATION: A SCHOOL PERSPECTIVE

Peter Downes

This whole book bears witness to the turmoil in initial teacher training (ITT) and the radical questioning it has provoked. It hardly seems credible that, only a few years ago, the traditional pattern of teacher training was solidly in place over most of the country.

How It Used To Be . . .

The responsibilities of schools and higher education (HE) in the training of new teachers were neatly compartmentalised. In the minds of the teachers in schools, higher education taught the theory, history, philosophy and sociology of education while the schools taught them how to deliver the goods in the classroom. For PGCE students, the pattern of the second term spent teaching in schools was well-established and scarcely questioned within schools. I can never remember any member of staff complaining about having to have a student teacher.

Long before contracts and 1,265 hours of directed time were thought of, it was assumed that this was part of the job of teaching. Obviously a host school had to make sure that there were not too many students at the same time for fear of overloading the pupils with untrained teachers but, other than that unwritten constraint, everybody accepted it as normal. Shameful though it may be to admit it, many teachers welcomed having a student teacher attached to them because it gave them a break in the second term and eased their workload. Those who did not have a student felt deprived.

Student teachers applying for a first post, usually in May or June as there was once a convention that no unqualified teachers were recruited before Easter, would typically say in interview that the most useful part of their PGCE year had been the teaching-practice term and the rest was rather dry and irrelevant. I cannot recall many complaining that the theory lectures had been subversive or anti-establishment, and yet it is in the folk memory that the 1960s and 1970s teacher-education world was peopled with closet or even overt Communists who were seeking to undermine civilisation as we know it.

The world I have described in deliberately oversimplified terms has been disappearing with increasing speed over the last 10 years, but it is important to be reminded that the memory of it colours the thinking of many of those now in schools who are being asked to take on a much greater role. From the school's perspective, the change happened incrementally. First, we were asked to contribute to the first term's work by sending teachers, or heads, as guest lecturers, to make the 'theory' more relevant by presenting to students situations faced in schools from which the philosophical implications could be drawn out. Then the partnership developed further when we were asked to release a teacher for a term or even a whole year in exchange for a higher education lecturer who was needing recent and relevant experience. This brought schools and HE closer, enriching both by the exchange of experience and expertise, notwithstanding the occasional practical difficulties encountered when the departing teacher had other whole school pastoral or departmental roles which the incoming lecturer could not conveniently fill. Nor, of course, could the schoolteacher in the higher education institution (HEI) fulfil easily any wider administrative responsibilities of the lecturer on exchange. Even then, the cost was not counted and the exchange was accepted as part of the unspoken professional bond which links, or used to link, all members of the teaching profession. Next, we started to have students in school in the Autumn term for observation and an initial tentative teaching experience, but still the lead was taken by higher education, the programme directed by higher education and the student teachers felt themselves to be part of a higher education establishment.

The breakthrough to a fuller and more genuine partnership did not happen simultaneously across the country. Once upon a time there was an era when education was less centrally directed and visionary professors of education, directors of education and headteachers could actually come together and create new ways of working, driven by their own initiative. The concept of partnership brought schools in on a more equal footing, with students thinking of themselves as predominantly attached to a school but withdrawn from it back to HE to reflect upon what they were seeing and doing out in the real world of the classroom. The early versions of the partnership/internship schemes often hid funding in the form of training of mentor teachers, supply cover to enable teachers to attend meetings and the input to schools of HE lecturers, but the overriding emphasis was on shared professional development and high quality, relevant training for the novice teachers.

The recent formalisation of partnership schemes as the statutory way of providing ITT, and the recognition of the greater role of schools by the payment of fees to the schools, challenged some of our basic assumptions and caused us all to reconsider exactly what are the benefits to schools of a substantial involvement in teacher training, what practical problems have to be faced, and the extent to which schools could or could not provide the input previously made by HE. Looking to a longer-term future, we shall have to consider whether new patterns of relationship between schools and HE will emerge to bring together not just ITT but also research, INSET and inspection.

What's in It for Us?

A side-effect of the reforms of the last decade or so has been to make us all focus more on the impact on us and our establishments of workload, effort, cost and time. The fragmentation of the education service (school against school in the league tables, grant maintained schools (GMS) versus locally managed schools (LMS), services provided through semi-independent agencies within or outside LEAs, the client-provider mentality, the incorporation of further education (FE) colleges) has made us more sensitive to the effect on ourselves, wherever we are in the system, of centrally imposed changes.

At school level there are, I believe, a number of specific and tangible benefits to a school hosting novice teachers:

- Their sheer physical presence increases the number of adults in the building and this helps to reduce the risk of misbehaviour. Their inclusion on the duty rota and their attachment to a tutor-group helps to relieve the pressure on staff.
- They improve the pupil-teacher ratio in the classroom: pupils receive more adult attention and are surrounded by more adult role-models.
- Their presence stimulates higher performance from other teachers who do not want to be embarrassed by appearing to teach inadequately.

- They bring in new ideas on teaching methodology, often being more willing to experiment and having more time to prepare new materials which, increasingly, shift the emphasis from what is taught to what is learned.
- Their need to perform well to succeed raises their preparation, classroom performance and marking to a level which (some) established teachers need to be reminded of.
- Being (generally) younger, fitter and emotionally less battle-scarred, they give a fresh impetus to extracurricular life, provided that the host school remembers to include this in the range of activities expected of the novice teachers.
- They provide a pool of potential new teachers for the school. Many successful novice teachers go on to get their first full-time post in the school where they did a teaching practice.
- Their closeness in age to the pupils/students can, in certain circumstances, provide an added pastoral resource.

The presence of novice teachers in a school adds a dimension of vibrancy, enthusiasm and dedication which, ideally, rejuvenates the whole staff. Therefore, there is much to be gained by a school from joining in a partnership.

The Problems for Schools

The idealised picture painted above needs to be tempered by reality. Having novice teachers in schools causes difficulties as well as bringing benefits:

1. Their presence puts pressure on the physical space in the staff room and in departmental bases.
2. Their presence, far from stimulating experienced teachers in the way indicated, can actually increase the psychological pressure on older staff and cause them to perform less well, especially when they know that they compare unfavourably with the new teacher they are supposed to be training.
3. In these days of increased public accountability through the league tables and through greater parental involvement, the work of novice teachers can be seen by some parents as detrimental to their children's chances of exam success. Parents are fearful, and sometimes with justification, that their child's unique life chances may be damaged by exposure to teachers still in training. Very few parents have the longer perspective of seeing the need for the profession to be renewed by the influx of new teachers – what they have been persuaded to expect is the maximum yield for their own children now.
4. Novice teachers generally use up precious resources (reprographics, ohp transparencies, videos, etc) more rapidly than experienced

teachers because they are being encouraged to try out a range of teaching techniques.
5. They increase the unquantifiable but nonetheless real pressure on teachers who do take their role as model and mentor seriously. It is a considerable responsibility to take on a major role in the training of a new teacher and if, in a minority of cases, it is necessary to be part of a decision to fail that potential teacher, there is a considerable burden of worry.
6. On any strict costing of time expended against income received, the school is 'paying' for having novice teachers. The level of payment to schools varies across the country but the general perception from the school perspective is that they are losing out financially, even allowing for the previous unquantified goodwill referred to in the opening of this chapter. That would not perhaps have mattered when schools were under less financial pressure but it is becoming a more contentious issue as budgets decrease, bringing increased class sizes and decreased non-contact time.

These negative pressures seem all the greater when the whole education system is creaking under innovation overload. The recent series of disruptions to established practices, probably very desirable in isolation, has used up the spare capacity on many teachers' mental processors. The warning signs ('the disk is full') are clearly to be seen in greater staff absence, more early retirements on health grounds, declining willingness to take part in extracurricular activities and a firmer determination to do only what is strictly required (given that the requirements are much more specific than ever before). Not surprisingly, some teachers simply refuse to take part in a partnership scheme, not because their brains reject it or their logic denies the need for the training of new members of the profession but simply because they have reached a level of emotional exhaustion which overrides rationality.

When you overlay general budget restrictions (virtually 4 per cent per annum cut over each of the next three years) on that already tense climate of low staff morale, it is understandable that more and more schools will find excuses for not receiving novice teachers in their schools.

A Balanced Partnership

Heads and governors must weigh up the advantages and problems outlined and come to their own conclusion about participation in ITT. My instinctive reaction is that most will feel that the benefits outweigh the drawbacks and that the deep-rooted commitment to the development of the profession *as a whole* will overcome the worries associated with the impact on the individual school.

In some areas of the country the School-Centred Initial Teacher Training (SCITT) model, with novice teachers being totally attached to schools with full funding and schools buying in HE expertise as needed, has been introduced and first evaluations are coming through. On the positive side, SCITT proves to be particularly appreciated by those schools not traditionally involved in ITT because they were too far away from university towns and some practitioners from the schools have reported positively on their experience. Evaluation from HMI is said to question its effectiveness, angering training schools by making unfavourable comparisons with courses run by established HE establishments. Teachers appear to have put in far more work than they originally anticipated, and senior staff in particular have had to divert their attention to this part of the school's activity, possibly at the expense of the already demanding task of monitoring teaching and learning more closely under the eye of OFSTED.

For HEIs validating SCITT courses, the work of assessing standards and tracking a novice teacher's experience is much greater for being dispersed into a number of schools. That in itself has a cost factor which may cause validating bodies to withdraw. In early 1995, it seems too early to assess the long-term life expectancy of SCITT. It may well survive in isolated areas as a way of bringing more schools into the teacher-education process, but unless it can be clearly seen to be providing a quality training experience for the majority of participants, it seems unlikely to become the general pattern.

For my own part, I do not foresee schools wishing to make a takeover bid for the HE aspect of the training of teachers. Leaving aside the lure of the money, because it is surely an illusion to think that schools could make a significant real income out of taking on novice teachers in quantity, the responsibility and the expectations are too great. However dedicated and well-motivated practising teachers are, they simply do not have the time to read widely in the methodology of their own subject, let alone keep up-to-date on all the wider trends in curriculum development and educational management theory. It is in these fields that HE colleagues bring the experience, expertise and time essential to making the novice teacher's year stimulating and personally enriching. Functional effectiveness is not enough; there needs to be time for reflection and for the wider perspective and this is where the HE contribution is paramount.

What is needed, therefore, is a partnership in which the strengths and limitations of the partners are recognised and used. It is, for example, more cost-effective for an HEI to deal with all the administrative aspects of the PGCE year than for each individual school to get embroiled in the detail of grants, police checks, Department for Education (DFE) certification and all the attendant bureaucracy. The school's focus should be on effective performance in the classroom in relation to the specific classes to be taught. The HE tutor can provide the theoretical framework and suggest a range of methods; the school co-tutor, knowing the pupils in that school, guides the novice teacher towards the selection of styles and activities appropriate to the particular group being taught.

In relation to the specialist subjects, the school co-tutor has to ensure that students plan lessons appropriate to the classes they teach, with continuity and progression (not just produce brilliant lessons in isolation). They must make the tasks differentiated according to pupils' needs, learning to recognise the ability and attainment levels of pupils and matching activities to those levels. Within the classroom, they must learn to deliver instructions and information with clarity of language, audibility and with language variation appropriate to the various situations in which they find themselves and, at the same time, pay particular attention to pupils' language skills and seek ways of developing them. Based on a detailed knowledge of the National Curriculum, they must learn to prepare and organise resources and know how to select from resources already available.

On the other hand, the HE subject-specialist tutor's role will be primarily to introduce students to the wider methodological debate, to an analysis of practice in a wide range of schools, developing an awareness of the place of the subject within the whole curriculum and an understanding of the concepts and skills which underpin their specialist subject. In looking at how pupils learn, the HE tutor will be best placed to teach student teachers about the major current theories on how children learn and about the influence on learning of social class and cultural dimensions. The school co-tutor will observe how well the novice teacher applies that theory to the individuals he or she meets and will, in particular, provide opportunities for the student teacher to consider provision for pupils with special needs, be they learning difficulties or giftedness, and to discuss with pupils directly the learning strategies they find most helpful. This broad division of responsibilities, useful as a basic checklist, inevitably oversimplifies the issues and suggests that subject specialism can be compartmentalised from a wide range of cross-curricular issues, including gender and equity, to which both school-based and HE-based staff will make their contribution.

A similar kind of division of responsibilities can be applied to class management and assessment. Where a HE tutor has led a debate on different class-management styles, the school co-tutor will help a student teacher choose an appropriate management style for the particular class. The HE tutor will have a greater knowledge of the psychological underpinning of achievement and must transmit that to the trainee teacher; the school co-tutor will show how sanctions and rewards work in practice and will help the trainee teacher to assess the effectiveness of the techniques chosen in relation to a particular class or child.

Although the focus of the PGCE year is predominantly on the development of professional expertise and day-to-day class-management skills, the student teacher *must* become aware of wider issues. This is where the partnership is at its strongest provided that senior staff within school, under the leadership of the school ITT coordinator, play their part to the full. Heads and deputies have a wealth of experience from particular schools to bring to the issues which the HE tutor will have put in the historical and theoretical context and to which they will have contributed their experience from working in a wide range of schools. School ethos, this indefinable quality which appears to make all the difference between relative success and failure for pupils, can be discussed in sociopolitical terms and the HE tutor will have had the time and opportunity to read the background texts. Heads, deputies and other senior teachers with whole-school roles can scrutinise, with the help of student teachers, sometimes in the form of an enquiry-based approach, what it is in their particular school that creates its distinctive ethos.

The preceding list of competencies and skills, by no means exhaustive, serve to illustrate the kind of partnership which will best prepare would-be teachers for the increasingly demanding role they will undertake. The essence of the relationship between school, HEI and novice teacher is the honest recognition of what each can best bring to the process. Although the boundaries can never be rigidly drawn, each partner needs to know what she or he can rely on from each other. This exploration is time-consuming and develops its full effectiveness over a period of time. It requires sensitivity on the part of all participants to the pressures under which we all work.

A Longer-term Vision

I have referred (in the context of funding and competition) to the harmful effect on the education service of the fragmentation taking place over the last few years; this fragmentation is also likely to reduce the helpful cross-fertilisation which ought to take place between professionals working in different branches of the service. It is becoming increasingly difficult for people to move from teaching to administration, from teacher education into inspection, from research back into school. We are increasingly in danger of working within our own narrow confines; partnership, collaboration and flexibility have suffered. That is why we need to be applying our minds to a longer-term vision which will unite rather than divide the educational world and secure, among other things, the benefits to the profession of a training system that brings schools and HE into partnership.

In spite of the best intentions and individual professional integrity of those working in government-appointed agencies, I would prefer to see the professional standards, training and development of teachers within the structure of an autonomous council or college which would liaise with government but not be subject to it. New entrants to the profession would have a year of preparation along the lines of the best examples of the current internship model, followed by two years' probationary experience, in which they would have continued support from outside the school as well as agreed levels of teaching remission and support from within the employing school. Given the fluctuating employment patterns across the country and the impossibility of ensuring that teachers take up first posts within the geographical area in which they first trained, I think that the probationary or entry-level scheme would need to have national coordination and funding by means of a voucher paid to the school taking on newly qualified teachers.

Given the rapid change in educational practice, teachers need to be retrained regularly and this council, which we could call a General Teaching Council (GTC) for short, could provide a recertification structure every five or seven years. Similarly, those wishing to proceed to senior posts, whether in middle management, deputy headship or headship, would need to have accredited training before being eligible for consideration for promotion.

The GTC, while having national standards, criteria and validity, would need a regional substructure which could be conveniently designed to match a new regional structure for the governance of schools when the present LEA structure is replaced. Within a region, education and training would be under the strategic control of the Education and Training Board (ETB), which would constitute one-third nomination from the regional government, one-third directly elected and one-third coopted for their specialist interests (industry, commerce, teacher training, inspection, for example). The ETB would have 'light-touch control' of education and training within its area because individual establishments would have maximum management autonomy within a nationally agreed funding formula that would reduce the current disparities and be based on a needs-led model, of which good examples already exist.

Within such a framework and within a climate emphasising cooperation rather than competition, it will be possible for senior practitioners to move across the boundaries currently isolating sections of the education service. For example, some heads and senior teachers would train to be part of the inspection process which, while less onerous than the present four-year OFSTED model, would nevertheless be demanding and public in its accountability. Teacher trainers would also be enabled to contribute to inspection and to in-service training under the GTC model and be leaders in developing educational research in which the schools within the ETB area would be involved.

Many different models for this brave new world could be devised and clearly depend upon wider political decisions for their implementation. To some it will seem an impossible task to move from where we are now to the situation I outline. It ought to be an encouragement to us to know that progress along these lines is actually taking place elsewhere in the world, namely in the Ontario province of Canada where the recently published (1995) *Report of the Royal Commission on Learning* makes recommendations along similar lines to those suggested above. The exciting feature of the Ontario proposals is that they have all-party political support, thus allowing the educationalists to concentrate on their successful implementation without the uncertainty of periodic electoral upheaval preceded by planning blight.

The crucial element in this longer-term vision is that we must be working towards a more professionally responsible and cooperative structure, in which specialists would continue to deliver what they do best but still have sufficient breadth of knowledge and expertise to contribute to the work of others. The fundamental change needed, in my view, is a reconsideration of the balance between competition and cooperation. After a decade or so in which market forces were used to drive up standards, to make establishments more cost-conscious and to increase public accountability, it is now time to heal divisions and to reduce the waste of inter-sectional strife and tension.

The process of the initial training of teachers is integral to the process I have been outlining because it stands at so many institutional boundaries. Teacher educators have a crucial role in pushing forward this debate, and perhaps this book will contribute perspectives to assist in the wide-ranging discussion which is needed now.

CHAPTER 7

ENGLISH, HIGHER EDUCATION AND ETHICS

Carole Cox

In this chapter, I write as a practising English teacher, not as a teacher educator; as a subject specialist whose specialism is English and as a practitioner with 14 years experience. However, I also write as someone who has had close links with higher education (HE) and worked with student teachers in schools. Most importantly, I believe that English teachers need, even more than any other sort of teacher, to have the benefit of the contribution HE can make because of the profoundly ethical nature of the subject as well as of the practice of teaching.

Before outlining the reasons why English teaching in particular needs the underpinning of higher education, I wish to sketch in my understanding of the reasons behind the current government's desire to place teacher-training within the school and to marginalise the role of HE. I found two major strands to the 'rationale'. The first is found in the increasingly prevalent belief that teachers are born and not made: thus if you know your subject you can just go in there and have a charismatic effect. If you lack charisma, presumably you can be sacked on that basis.

The second strand is a faith in the ultimately reductive view that 'knowing how' takes precedence over 'knowing that' in teaching. There is the view that only 'hands on' experience, to use an interestingly technological metaphor, will enable someone to understand a subject. This view has underpinned arguments to the effect that pupils need to do *X* if they are to grasp the principles of *X*. Although mere experience of some things teach us what they are – for example, the percepts of colour and pain – experience of complexities does not automatically lead to understanding. It is also true that, you do not need to have a full grasp of the principles of motor engineering to drive a car proficiently, or an easy familiarity with computer programming to operate a word-processor. However, these kinds of activity in which 'know how' is undeniably significant are not central to pupils' education. Nevertheless, this sort of emphasis on direct experience is now central to teacher education, where prospective teachers are envisaged as teaching in a classroom to understand the principles of the profession. This emphasis certainly seems to be reflected in the expectations of student teachers themselves, on occasions – that they will be inducted into the mysteries of teaching by experienced mentors who will know exactly how to deal with 5G on Friday afternoons without any damage being incurred.

Of course, I am unconvinced, even though I still do want to know how to deal with 5G on Fridays without experiencing severe stress! I am unconvinced because I believe that it is important to reflect upon practice and to stand back in some way from it so that you can perceive the ends you wish to achieve. Purely school-based practice makes this hard for the student teacher and, also important, the on-going practice of teachers is less likely to be reflective without the opportunities provided by HE for the learner initially. The habits of mind engendered by the opportunities to reflect and to philosophise in advance of, during and after actual experience in schools enables the prospective teacher to consider practice in the light of the ends she or he and the other students wish to pursue.

When I use the term *philosophise* I mean the 'activity whereby I think as clearly and coherently as I can about what I want to achieve and why I want to achieve it'. Such thinking is practical in the sense that it encompasses my thoughts about the relationship between the teacher and the taught, and about what my subject is and how I can convey it in as clear and interesting a manner as possible. As such, philosophising is absolutely fundamental to my profession, my work, as I think about aims, objectives, means and ends as a teacher. It is not some kind of abstract exercise 'bolted on' to the actuality of teaching, but an essential component of my practice.

For example, as an English teacher I choose to teach *Edward II* by Christopher Marlowe. In thinking about my approach to this text, I consider the difficulties posed for modern youth by the language, the number of characters, the concept of 'the divine right of kings' and, of course, the great interest of the homosexual theme. In so doing I must philosophise in the sense that I must become clear in my own mind about some of the ethical dilemmas the play raises, such as the conflict between the right to a significant personal life and the political responsibilities of kingship, before I even begin to introduce the play to my students. This is because inevitably such dilemmas will be raised and if I want, as I do, to encourage my students to think clearly about such issues I must have at least tried to be coherent, if not absolutely decided, myself at the outset.

All teaching involves the ethical, in considerations of the personal relationship between teacher and taught, of what is appropriate conduct, the issues of responsibility, setting an example, and so on. However, English teaching by its very nature involves the ethical. Here, I take ethical to mean considerations not only of conduct but of the pursuit of the good life, of flourishing, as discussed by neo-Aristotelian philosophers, such as Martha Nussbaum (1986, and 1990 in particular). Inevitably, in teaching literature, in discussing the words on the page, the characters and their interaction, pupils are considering what it is to lead a good or a flawed life.

For example, in any discussion of Jacobean plays such as *The Changeling* or *The Duchess of Malfi*, students are made to consider the implications of the desire for revenge. Such a desire often finds expression in the pages of the tabloid press. When a small child is killed by other children or by an adult, for example, the relatives concerned are reported as wanting retribution of some kind, usually what is felt to be an appropriately terrible kind, upon the killer. The very difficult ethical issues here, of the difference between justice and revenge, understandable grief and unacceptable viciousness, can be talked about and thought about in a special way when discussed in the perspective of Jacobean tragedy. The students remain detached, because it is seventeenth-century literature they are discussing, and yet are engaged because these plays involve their audience by virtue of the characterisation, dramatic interplay and language. When I get my students to set up a trial of Bosola, the hired assassin of the Duchess who becomes her avenging angel in *The Duchess of Malfi*, they consider his sins but also his desire to make reparation for his sins. They also have to think about the society which made him a criminal, for the corruption of the Italian court is such that only flatterers and conspirators can 'get on'. The compassion that is finally awakened by the terrible events he is organiser of and party to also needs a great deal of attention. In just this one 'exercise', based on a knowledge and understanding of the play built up over some considerable time, students of English are involved in a discussion about the good life and that which threatens it.

In encouraging the young to write personally, to engage with and to share what they read, whether it be *Hamlet* or *Burglar Bill*, the ethical, encompassing as it does thought and feeling, the purely personal and the inquisitively detached, is endemic to practice. Central to literature teaching is the notion that the young respond as individuals to what they read, that they communicate what *they* feel about the text rather than regurgitating what their teachers say. Therefore, English teachers do spend a great deal of time attempting to provide open-ended questions for students to approach.

Frequently groups of students 'come at' texts from an angle, half-touch them, feel their way in, with the assistance of the teacher. This tentativeness, the sensitive and shared approach ~~to~~ literature, seems to have enormous relevance to the exploration of the ethical issues and questions of value that literary study inevitably addresses.

There are other areas of learning in which the ethical can be addressed, for example, in the study of science or history. It might be relevant and interesting to discuss the ethical issues involved in the deployment of nuclear power in a physics lesson, but it is not integral to the study of physics to have that discussion. It is fruitful to consider the ethical implications of the reasoning behind the combatants' decision to fight the Wars of the Roses, but it is not essential to the study of history that one ponders this element. Studying literature, on the other hand, with all the concomitant considerations of what characters choose to do and not to do in novels and plays, and of how the writer presents these choices to the readers of the works, cannot but bring ethical considerations into play.

For example, when studying *Hamlet*, students find Hamlet's moral situation genuinely interesting. They wonder about such questions as 'is it right to kill your father's killer?' or 'is it acceptable to reject your lover either because you have a new role to undertake or because you no longer love her or because you want (perhaps) to protect her?' and, a question related to the previous multiple one, 'aren't you, if you see the questions purely in these aforementioned terms, a nasty piece of work anyway?'

Hamlet, among many other things, is about means and ends and the relationship between them. Hamlet's agonising exposes the essential problems of there ever being a justification for using another human being as a means to an end. Hamlet attempts to use Ophelia, the Players, and others to find out the truth about his father's fate. His end is good, in that he does not want to kill his uncle unless there is evidence that Claudius is guilty of fratricide, but Hamlet violates the Kantian principle of not using people as means to ends as assuredly as the more obvious manipulators Claudius and Polonius do. I find that students studying the play have a working understanding of what might be called ethical theory here, but some more focused discussion of the enacted situations and dilemmas of one of Shakespeare's greatest plays enables them to come to a much more nuanced grasp of the particulars of all that 'respect for persons' involves.

It is inevitable that responding to literary works, the ways in which we feel and think about the characters, the experiences and insights they offer us, will draw us into ethical judgements. This is true of much poetry as well as the novel because the emotions explored are presented to the readers in particular ways, expressing certain attitudes and feelings towards situations that invite ethical perception. I do not think that it is possible to read 'The Love Song of J Alfred Prufrock' without having certain responses regarding what might be pusillanimity or poignant self-regard; or to engage with 'Carrion Comfort' without becoming absorbed in, what might be alien to a secular reader, the full horror of a priestly vocation.

This engagement in the ethical underlies the heat of debate regarding the depiction of black people in *The Adventures of Huckleberry Finn* and the portrayal of women in *Last Exit to Brooklyn*. Because ethical understanding is particular, and thus shaped by social change and more percipient awareness of others as persons (in some respects) as well as individuals' responses, readers find that not only their perceptions of what they read are altered by circumstances but their 'readings' of real-life situations are altered by their reading.

As a result, the prospective English teacher needs careful preparation for the very sensitivity and care which will be required to teach, for example, *The Adventures of Huckleberry Finn* in a multiracial school or to approach the topic of whether to teach it at all. The ethical dimensions to which I have referred are significant whatever the educational institution in which the teacher works, but are perhaps especially pressing in a multicultural framework.

I think here of the time when I taught Joyce's *Portrait of the Artist as a Young Man*; the students were from a range of ethnic backgrounds. A major disagreement arose when the group were met with Stephen Dedalus's decision to leave Ireland and pursue his vocation as an artist, a decision which means that Stephen's mother's aspirations for her son have to be dashed and that she must accept her son living in exile from her. A female Muslim student would not accept that it can ever be right to deny your obligation to your mother. Filial duty has to come first, the only exception being an outright infringement of the Koran. Other members of the group became increasingly frustrated in the discussion of what weight should be given to personal well-being versus familial obligation, as they felt that the debate kept hitting a moral brick wall: a certainty. Considerable care on the part of the 'chair' of this discussion, the teacher, was required for some negotiation to take place. In the end there was no resolution, except an acceptance on the part of the Muslim girl that her view was not the one that Joyce was forwarding in the novel. She did see that the way in which the 'dilemma' was presented made Stephen's decision the only right one in terms of the novel and the authorial perspective. She could not see that it was right in 'life' and her very tenacity certainly ensured that the other students and the teacher had to address their own preconceptions. This is an extreme example of the kind of contention that can arise in discussing not only artistic but ethical choices in the classroom.

Literature can also cause embarrassment and discomfort in other respects. Teaching Larkin's poem 'Sunny Prestatyn' recently I was touched by one blushing 18-year-old boy's anxious comment that 'you don't use words like that in poetry. It's not nice and I don't think I like the poem' (Larkin refers to a 'tuberous cock and balls'). [Incidentally this student was male, white and working-class.] This comment of his, I think a brave one in that he said it unsolicited in front of others, in itself raised a whole range of fascinating debates about writers' choices of words, what is and what is not acceptable or appropriate in certain genres, and how or why we try to judge such matters in the way that we do.

In preparing prospective English teachers for these and related scenarios, higher education has a very important role in focusing on questions regarding how *X* or *Y* can or should or might be taught. Furthermore, in asking such questions one is philosophising about the practice of teaching. In pursuing the best possible approach to it and wondering just what the 'best' might be, or what it might entail, you are engaged in philosophical activity. As an English teacher I find that my own experience, and that of many of my colleagues, is that the literature I have the richest and most profound understanding of and engagement with is that which I have taught. This suggests that the philosophical process of wondering how particular texts might be taught and preparing to meet all kinds of ethical possibilities raised by texts enriches not only the *preparation* for the teaching process but the experience of teaching itself.

At this juncture, it might be argued that there is more to English teaching than literature teaching. This is true, although most English teachers see books as pretty central to what they do! The teaching of writing, of the language, often involves or is enmeshed with what is read, so the ethical still suffuses the subject. Furthermore if, as Charles Taylor says, our expression of language 'is an activity which constitutes a specific way of being in the world' (1985, p.236) then writing and speaking are as ethically significant as reading.

Our styles reflect our attitudes. If I tend to speak and write in terms of 'clients' or 'end-of-line users' rather than of 'pupils' or 'students', I am expressing an ethical view of my relationship as a teacher to those I teach. 'Client' has connotations of a consumer buying a product or service, reflected in the use of the term by prostitutes with reference to those for whom they provide a service. 'End-of-line use' has all the hallmarks of the factory process, irresistibly reminding me at least of the 'hands' of Dickens's *Hard Times*. Taylor's point then is that I am a different kind of person if I feel at ease with one set of terms rather than another; 'to be' in the world requires a certain kind of perception of my relationships with it and that perception is embodied and enacted in the language I inherited and use or modify for my own purposes.

The foregoing needs considerable attention when you teach about and in the language. Encouraging pupils to write and commenting on what they write needs more than sensitivity (although it does need that): it requires an awareness of the ethical choices involved not only in responding to the words on the page but in your choice of words to use. Martha Nussbaum (1990, p.5) argues that

> *the telling itself – the selection of genre, formal structures, sentences, vocabulary, of the whole manner of addressing the reader's sense of life – all of this expresses a sense of life and of value, a sense of what matters and what does not, of what learning and communicating are, of life's relations and connections.*

Now, this is not only true of the literary artist: it has to be so too in our ordinary decisions when writing to *X* about *Y*. It may be that we cannot discuss or analyse in a deeply thoughtful way all the ramifications of our decisions to write in particular ways with the putative 5G to whom I referred earlier, but this does not mean that the written style, the choice of one word as apart from another, is not an ethical one. To take a fairly crude example,

I spend a good deal of my time as a teacher getting my students to see that 'crap' is too loose and undiscriminating to cover the various forms of opprobrium they really want it to have. Often, this all-inclusive bag of a word, perhaps apt in some contexts, is found to be insufficient to communicate the deeper dissatisfactions students wish to voice: deeper concerns about lived experience.

In focusing on what style to write in, talk in, live in, as you inevitably do in any English lesson, the ethical is endemic. There are some extreme and obvious examples here, for instance, that racist expressions are not acceptable. Being able to argue why these are not acceptable is likely to be more crucial for a practising teacher than an undergraduate student of English. Ways in which to reflect upon our approaches to stereotypical terminology, reflecting prejudices based on gender or race, which are readily made in the classroom by pupils, and to respond to pupils' choices of language, need to be considered carefully.

These sorts of issue are raised and debated in the preparation higher education offers to prospective teachers, in a way that they are not when you are studying for an English degree. The assumptions of the largely middle-class students who enjoy literature are not necessarily those of the pupils of the inner-city, multiethnic school or the predominantly white population of the rural school. Having to face challenges to your ideas of acceptable terminology, without preparation, but 'on the spot' so to speak, seems at best a clumsy and at worst a deeply distressing experience for the prospective and the practising teacher.

While practising the craft or art of teaching and 'learning by doing', I find the constraints of the needs of the syllabus, the desire to keep control and impose my authority, for example, preclude much reflection on practice. Higher education's role then is to provide the forum for debate, questioning and analysis, for philosophising in the practical Aristotelian sense so emphasised by Martha Nussbaum. This is not a matter of simply learning abstract educational theory, and it is vital for all prospective teachers. Ronald Barnett (1990, p.76) writes:

> *It is increasingly recognized that a profession will be the stronger if its practitioners are used to plan, to execute, to accept responsibility for, and to evaluate critically, their own actions. 'The reflective practitioner' is not, or should not be, a woolly piece of rhetoric. It signifies an idea of real value to both the world of thought and the world of action.*

Practice is felt to be important mainly because of the concern with teaching methodology, which is essential; and in devising apt pedagogical approaches practice does help. However, in spending time considering why certain methods 'work' better than others and, even more important, what the actual purposes of employing particular methods *are*, the student teacher is doing something of great value. In teaching, you have to make some difficult ethical choices, fundamentally concerning what to teach and why, in a culturally diverse society.

Higher education has always made valuable contributions to debates about methodology as well as about the deeper questions to which I referred. To make a general point, the very quality that can lead to disparagement of the world of HE – a certain academic detachment perhaps – can assist the student teacher or practitioner in standing back from what she or he does and considering why she or he does *X* or *Y* in this way.

In the past, university teachers of English such as F R Leavis, in his *Sketch for an English School* (1943), addressed methodology as well as rationale in analysing English teaching. Although his ideas – about collaboration between departments, moving away from examinations and towards the seminar paper and the tutorial, discussion and readings shared between teacher and taught – were put forward with reference to the university in general, many of them percolated into practice because Downing College undergraduates went into teaching and/or teacher training (see Mulhern, 1979; Walsh, 1980). There have been many other influential figures in HE, for example, Peter Abbs, whose work has been central to the development of English teaching as the fostering of discrimination (see Abbs, 1976).

Higher education enables all student teachers to reflect critically upon their practice and that of others, to consider broader issues regarding not only their own teaching but other matters, such as the ethos of one school as compared to another or the nature of the curriculum, in a way that immersion in one or even two particular schools cannot.

At this point, I could argue that student teachers already have plenty of HE experience and background by virtue of their subject degree. The prospective English teacher will have studied his or her subject for a minimum of three years within an HEI and will have had ample opportunity to consider the ethical issues raised by literature and should be, by virtue of this, capable of addressing the challenges that English teaching offers.

At present, however, English at university level is a subject dominated by literary theory. Literary critics and university teachers, if not by definition then certainly in reality, seem more interested in their own highly specialised and difficult, not to say jargon-infested, discourse, than in concerning themselves with ethical matters. In its concern for discourse, literary theory turns to various forms of continental cultural theory as a means to investigate underpinning ideologies within criticism (eg, see Day, 1993, pp.1–7) and seems intent on understanding the various levels of discourse within which literary criticism operates. The problem here is that the whole exercise risks being 'socially marginal, even redundant' (p.5), especially within teaching, where exposing the workings of an apparently parasitical and ideologically driven practice – criticism – leads to a sense of futility on the part of the pupils as well as the student teacher when addressing the question 'Why study literature?'

Contemporary literary theorists, beset by the apparently irreducibly subjective nature of literature and human responses to it, have been driven to an inappropriate 'objective' model which has little to offer English teachers in schools. Ethical criticism, to use Nussbaum's expression (1990), in which corroborative readings are 'checked' by discussion with students and other teachers, resting upon implicit standards, and following some kind of intersubjectivity, is a far better model because it is centred upon the literature itself and the questions that the texts in some sense 'ask'. In debating the how and the why of English teaching and reflecting upon practice, the prospective teacher is drawn to this approach.

Literary theorists and university teachers of English seek objectivity to give their discipline some degree of legitimacy. In an age in which the measurable and the quantifiable is the yardstick of knowledge and understanding, a sensitive preoccupation with values, a concern for what it is to lead a good life, does not appear to have any external credence. I suspect a similar concern for something being *seen* to be done underlies the enormous emphasis upon trainee teachers 'doing the job' rather than thinking about it and debating questions of ethical value. Nevertheless, thought and debate need to inform the 'doing'.

The account of practice that seems to me to be far richer and more rewarding than that underlying the 'hands-on' approach of learning by doing is that offered by MacIntyre in *After Virtue* (1981, p.177). He writes:

> *A practice involves standards of excellence and obedience to rules as well as the achievement of goods. To enter into a practice is to accept the authority of those standards and the inadequacy of my own performance as judged by them . . . the standards are not themselves immune from criticism, but none the less we cannot be initiated into a practice without accepting the authority of the best standards realised so far.*

An inculcation into the practice of English teaching itself, with its inherent standards, values and concern for the ethical, all deriving from the nature of the subject, the language and its expression by us all and by the most perceptive of us – that is literary artists – is vital to any education offered to prospective English teachers. That inculcation can only be offered by HE and then enriched by the experience that teaching English involves. Of course, this experience itself nourishes the practitioner's understanding of his or her practice and of the discipline in which she or he is working. Such an interaction of education and HE can only benefit the prospective teacher, the teacher of many years and, most important, the pupil.

References

Abbs, P (1976) *Root and Blossom: Essays on the Philosophy, Practice and Politics of English Teaching.* London: Heinemann.

Barnett, R (1990) *The Idea of Higher Education.* Buckingham: SRHE/Open University Press.

Day, G (ed) (1993) *The British Critical Tradition: A Re-evaluation.* Basingstoke: Macmillan.

Leavis, FR (1943) *Education and the University: a sketch for an English school.* Cambridge: Cambridge University Press.

MacIntyre, A (1981) *After Virtue*. London: Duckworth.

Mulhern, F (1979) *The Moment of Scrutiny.* London: NLB.

Nussbaum, M (1986) *The Fragility of Goodness.* Cambridge: Cambridge University Press.

Nussbaum, M (1990) *Love's Knowledge*. Oxford: Oxford University Press.

Taylor, C (1985) *Philosophical Papers 1.* Cambridge: Cambridge University Press.

Walsh, W (1980) *F. R. Leavis.* London: Chatto.

CHAPTER 8

THE LIMITS OF MENTORING: THE CONTRIBUTION OF THE HIGHER EDUCATION TUTOR TO PRIMARY STUDENT TEACHERS' SCHOOL-BASED LEARNING

Trisha Maynard

> *Over the last few decades the progress of primary pupils has been hampered by the influence of highly questionable dogmas which have led to excessively complex classroom practice and devalued the place of subjects in the curriculum.* (Alexander, Rose and Woodhead, 1992, para. 3.2)

> *Whereas the individual subjects which teachers will teach require academic study, the skills of teaching are essentially practical ones. They can be acquired only through experience, trial and error and careful, individual supervision.* (Lawlor, 1990, p.8)

In the last decade the appropriateness and effectiveness of the child-centred ideology, seen as an important aspect of the culture of the post-Plowden primary school, have increasingly been brought into question. Those belonging to the New Right (eg, O'Hear, 1988; Lawlor, 1990), and others considered to be close to the government (eg, Alexander, 1984, 1992; Alexander, Rose and Woodhead, 1992) have been most vociferous in their criticism of this ideology and in their advocacy of a more subject-centred approach to primary teaching.

For the New Right, the primary task for teachers is to induct the next generation of children into proven and worthwhile forms of knowledge. What is needed above all in a good teacher, they maintain, is 'sound knowledge and love of the subject one is teaching' (O'Hear, 1988, p.16). They suggest that one of the chief weaknesses of the present form of initial teacher training is the focus of higher education institutions (HEIs) on pedagogy and 'trendy' theories at the expense of subject studies. Even on teaching practice, it is argued, students are not left naturally to develop their own practical teaching skills with an open mind, but are required by education departments to apply to their practice the generalised educational (and presumably child-centred) theories that they have been taught (Lawlor, 1990).

For others close to the government, the National Curriculum appears to offer a justification for the need for primary teachers to become more 'subject-centred'. Alexander, Rose and Woodhead (1992), for example, claim that since the 'arrival' of the National Curriculum the task of the primary teacher has changed dramatically. They maintain, 'The resistance to subjects at the primary stage is no longer tenable. The subject is a necessary feature of the modern primary curriculum' (1992, para. 3.2). For these writers, the principles and values underlying the establishment of the National Curriculum are no longer open to debate. What is important now is that teachers are enabled to gain the appropriate knowledge and skills to meet its requirements.

Putting 'subjects' (rather than the child) at the heart of primary teaching has, according to these writers, significant implications not only for the content of teachers' activities but for some of those practices seen as most fundamental to the child-centred ideology. Alexander, Rose and Woodhead (1992) argue, for example, that it is unreasonable and unrealistic to expect teachers, particularly teachers of Key Stage 2 (KS2) pupils, to have the extent of subject knowledge needed to teach the National Curriculum. Teachers are therefore urged 'dispassionately' and with an 'open mind' to consider the strengths and weaknesses of 'that most sacred of primary "sacred cows"' (OFSTED, 1993, para. 42) – the class-teacher system. Moreover, they suggest that teachers also need critically to evaluate the appropriateness, efficiency and effectiveness of other important tenets of the child-centred approach: for example, of topic work as opposed to single-subject teaching, of individual or group work as opposed to whole-class teaching and of the teacher as 'facilitator of children's learning' as opposed to the teacher as 'teller'. For these writers, as for those of the New Right, the 'dogmas' of the child-centred approach unnecessarily complicate primary teaching and obstruct and impede a focus on subject knowledge.

One way of attempting to bring about a more subject-centred approach to primary teaching appears to be, unsurprisingly, through government reforms of initial teacher training (ITT). Circular 14/93 (DFE, 1993) sets out 'strict new criteria which all training courses must meet' and advocates not only that there should be a variety of routes to qualified teacher status but that schools should play a much larger and more influential role in course design and delivery. In this Circular, the content of teacher training is presented as essentially consisting of two elements: subject knowledge (learned largely, though now not exclusively, in HEIs) and practical teaching skills (learned in schools). There is little reference to those issues of pedagogy, child development and the broader social and cultural dimensions of learning that traditionally have been part of the curriculum of HE. Moreover, it notes that time in schools is 'particularly valuable for the acquisition of practical teaching skills, and allows students to apply their subject knowledge in the classroom' (DFE, 1993, para. 19). Teaching and learning to teach have thus been pared down to what is seen as their essential core – subject knowledge and practical teaching skills – stripped of those unnecessary child-centred constraints and demands that have, in the past, cluttered teachers' thinking and their practice.

From this perspective, the contribution of the HE tutor to primary students' school-based learning may appear superfluous and irrelevant. If school experience is essentially concerned with the personal development of 'practical skills' and the opportunity to 'apply' subject knowledge gained in college-based studies, what possible justification can there be for the involvement of the HE tutor?

Here, I maintain that student teachers' school-based learning is far more complex than the acquisition of simple teaching 'skills'. Furthermore, the relationship between students' subject knowledge and their classroom practice is also complex and problematic. If student teachers are to become professional educators then I maintain that there is a fundamental need to 'challenge' them critically to evaluate their thinking and their practice. In particular, there is a need to challenge students to articulate and evaluate their thinking about the content of the activities they teach their pupils. Moreover, I argue that it is the HE tutor and not the class teacher who is most able to fulfil this role. I maintain that it is the 'detachment' of the HE tutor from the day-to-day pressures, demands and 'culture' of the classroom that makes their contribution to primary students' school-based learning both unique and fundamental.

Research

In developing this thesis, I draw on findings from two research projects carried out at the University of Wales, Swansea, which aimed to explore the role of the mentor in initial teacher education.

The first project, funded by the Paul Hamlyn Foundation, incorporates three interrelated research studies. The first study documents the different stages of student teachers' learning as they develop practical teaching competence. Fieldwork was carried out with seven student teachers (PGCE and BEd) working in five schools: two secondary schools, one junior school and two primary schools. The second and third studies look more closely at the content of teachers' practical professional knowledge and at students' difficulties in developing this knowledge. Two areas were selected for particular study: classroom management and control and teachers' 'good ideas' – the content of their activities. The second and third studies involve 11 primary PGCE students working with 16 different teachers during their two block-teaching practices. The second project, funded by the Esmée Fairbairn Charitable Trust, extends this work by focusing on the process of mentoring subject knowledge in the primary school. Along with five primary teachers I became part of an action-research team which explored the possibilities and limitations of mentoring subject knowledge to 11 primary PGCE student teachers while on their school experience.

The Nature of Student Teachers' School-based Learning

To characterise the distinctive role of the HE tutor it is first necessary to examine the nature of student teachers' school-based learning. Among researchers there appears to be a general consensus that learning to teach is a complex and painful experience. Students appear to pass through a number of 'stages' or 'phases', each with their associated ways of thinking and concerns, as they develop competence, confidence and independence in the classroom (see Fuller and Bown, 1975; Calderhead, 1987; Guillaume and Rudney, 1993; Maynard and Furlong, 1993; Furlong and Maynard, 1995). Furlong and I (1995) characterise these stages as 'early idealism' (preteaching), 'personal survival', 'dealing with difficulties', 'hitting a plateau' and 'moving on'.

It is with the development of practical 'knowledge' that students' school-based learning is associated. One difficulty of discussing teachers' practical 'knowledge' is establishing exactly what is being talked about. As Johnston (1992) notes, there are many different definitions of this 'knowledge' and each term arises from a different set of assumptions and interests. Are we, for example, referring to the 'knowing' that is actually embedded in teachers' actions – what Schön refers to as 'knowing-in-action' (1983, p.25)? Alternatively, are we referring to teachers' descriptions of knowledge that is useful to their everyday practice? In characterising the distinctive role of the HE tutor it is essential to differentiate between these two aspects of teachers' practical 'knowledge'.

First, 'knowing-in-action' is embedded not only in teachers' actions but also in the particular contexts in which they are working: what teachers 'do' will depend on their priorities and aims at any given moment when working with *these* children, with *this* content and in *this* situation. Moreover, these priorities and aims, according to the teachers in our studies, are constantly and rapidly shifting. Given the urgent, immediate nature of classroom practice, teachers maintained they were not always consciously aware of the purposes of their actions at the time they were carried out; teachers often referred to their actions and responses as being 'instinctive' and 'intuitive'.

As Schön makes clear, it is possible to make descriptions of the tacit 'knowing' that is implicit in our actions. He explains, 'We may refer to the sequences of operations and procedures we execute; the clues we observe and the rules we follow; or the values, strategies, and assumptions that make up our "theories" of action' (1983, p.25). However, these descriptions are always constructions and can never represent that knowing-in-action in its entirety. For, as Schön points out, knowing-in-action is dynamic – it is a continuous activity in which awareness, appreciation and adjustment all play their parts (1983, p.25). Schön further maintains that when we attempt to articulate our knowing-in-action, our descriptions have to be tested out against observations of our actions. Through our attempts at description, this 'knowing' is converted from a dynamic to a static form – from dynamic 'knowing' to static 'knowledge'. I stress here that 'knowing-in-action' may develop without conscious deliberation and may precede teachers' understanding of and personal theories about their practice (their practical knowledge). Further, while teachers' practical knowledge may guide their actions, it is always a partial understanding of what they actually do in the classroom.

Students' practical 'knowing' and their practical 'knowledge' are not developed in a vacuum; rather they incorporate, and are shaped by, a great deal of personal and cultural learning. For example, students need to find out who they are as a teacher and this involves working with and within the constraints of who they are as a person. Moreover, if they are to teach effectively, and to survive as a teacher, students need to learn how to control themselves; that is, their desire to establish a close, personal relationship with pupils as well as the anger and frustration they may feel when pupils fail to understand, or are disruptive, or when they do not allow students to fulfil their self-image of the 'ideal' teacher. Student teachers must also learn how to protect themselves – not to take pupils' resistance to and rejection of their activities and requests personally – and they must learn how to satisfy their needs – a matter of how and when they are able to let their 'personal' selves show through (Furlong and Maynard, 1995).

Students need to find out not only who they are but who they can be as a teacher. To do this they must identify what counts as acceptable and effective practice within the culture of primary schools. If they are to succeed, students need at least to appear to 'fit in' with cultural norms. 'Fitting in' may incorporate the relatively trivial, for example, washing up their own coffee mug after morning break and not parking their car in the headteacher's parking space. It may also incorporate more profound understandings about, for example, the role of the teacher and what counts as appropriate and effective teaching and learning in the primary school. Student teachers' school-based learning, therefore, is more than the development of practical teaching 'skills'; it is concerned with the complex acquisition of practical 'knowing' and practical 'knowledge'.

Subject Knowledge

What of student teachers' subject knowledge? Following the work of Schwab (1978), there appears to be general agreement among researchers that subject knowledge can be understood as incorporating two different dimensions: substantive and syntactic knowledge. *Substantive knowledge* is knowledge 'of' the subject and will include the facts, concepts, procedures, and so on, of the subject area and also the way in which the body of knowledge is structured and organised. *Syntactic knowledge* is knowledge 'about' the subject area and incorporates an understanding of the way in which the particular body of knowledge is generated and validated. It is suggested that if they are to be effective in their teaching, teachers need to have a 'flexible, thoughtful and conceptual' understanding of subject areas (McDiarmid, Ball and Anderson, 1989). Moreover, it is maintained that teachers need to hold understandings about the nature of subject areas. Sanders (1994), for example, argues that teachers' beliefs about the nature of mathematics will profoundly influence the way in which they teach, but having a personal subject knowledge, however flexible and 'sound', is not enough. Teachers need to find ways of transforming this knowledge to make it accessible to the pupils in their class. Shulman (1986) calls this knowledge – teachers' 'subject knowledge for teaching' – 'pedagogical content knowledge'. He describes this knowledge as 'the most powerful analogies, illustrations, explanations and demonstrations – in a word, the ways of representing and formulating the subject that make it comprehensible to others' (1986, p.9).

Pedagogical content knowledge is of particular interest here in that it would appear 'overtly' to draw both on teachers' personal 'theoretical' subject knowledge developed in college-based studies and their 'practical' understandings about teaching and pupil learning developed on school experience. According to McDiarmid and colleagues (1989), for example, appropriate teaching activities derive from teachers' 'bifocal consideration of subject matter and pupils' (1989, p.194). Wilson, Shulman and Richert (1987) suggest that teachers transform their personal subject knowledge and find ways of representing that knowledge to make it accessible to their pupils through a process of pedagogical reasoning – through planning, teaching, adapting instruction and reflecting on classroom experiences.

Like Calderhead and Miller (1986) however, we found that students (even those students who appeared to have a 'sound' subject knowledge) did *not* tend to consider or draw on their personal subject knowledge when planning activities for their pupils. Rather, students preferred to copy and adapt 'good ideas' suggested by their class-teacher or tutor, found in resource books or even remembered from their own experience of being a pupil. While in part this may reflect student teachers' lack of knowledge of pupils and pupil learning and also their desire to fit in with and gain approval from the class teacher or tutor, there did seem to be a general difficulty with relating theoretical knowledge, including personal subject knowledge, and classroom action (see Russell, 1988; Calderhead, 1987). Student teachers' 'theoretical' (as opposed to 'practical') college-based studies often appeared to be in danger of becoming a 'thing apart' from their school-based practice: irrelevant in the face of the demands of 'real' teaching. For our students, then, when considering the subject-knowledge content of their activities, it appeared that 'imitation' featured more commonly than 'transformation'.

Even though students relied on ready-made 'good ideas' for activities, the way in which they interpreted these 'good ideas' often reflected what were considered by teachers and tutors to be naive and simplistic views about the nature of teaching and learning. Having gained basic competence and confidence in the classroom, our students (as those in the studies of Calderhead, 1987 and Fuller and Bown, 1975) appeared to 'hit a plateau'. Students appeared to have difficulty in 'moving on' to engage with the complexities and demands of pupil learning and the evaluations they made of their activities tended to remain – or even increasingly become – superficial. For example, students maintained that an activity 'worked' so long as the pupils enjoyed it and remained interested (Furlong and Maynard, 1995). While a few of our students did appear gradually and naturally to develop a feel for what were considered to be appropriate activities, their understandings in this respect appeared to be implicit and intuitive: they were unavailable to students' conscious thought. Here again, imitation may have been a significant factor in student teachers' learning. Moreover, *what* students came to see as being 'good' activities appeared to be more reliant on the appropriateness of these activities in child-centred beliefs about how pupils best learn than on their effectiveness in developing pupils' subject understandings. Three points need emphasis here.

1. The relationship between students' personal subject knowledge and what they actually teach may be far more complex than the government (and those close to the government) would suppose! Student teachers' practical 'knowing' appears to predominate not only the development of so-called practical teaching skills but the content of the activities students devise for their pupils.
2. It seems that students do not by themselves easily 'move on' to engage with the complexities of pupil learning. Those students whose activities appear to reflect more 'appropriate' understandings in this respect may simply be relying on imitation and intuition.
3. Without intervention, subject knowledge may not be seen by students as of particular relevance or importance either for themselves as teachers or in pupils' learning.

If student teachers are to become professional educators, then they need to be moved on from practising what Buchmann (1987) calls the 'folkways of teaching', that is, understandings gained and accepted uncritically and often intuitively through experience and imitation. What makes this move particularly fundamental is that teachers' practice is a moral occupation, it is value-laden. What teachers teach their pupils (and the way in which they teach) will represent and subsume a value position and have important educational and moral implications and consequences. Leaving the development of students' understandings about the content of the activities they teach to mere chance is untenable. While they are on their school experience, therefore, students need to be 'challenged' critically to evaluate those assumptions that are implicit and embedded in the activities that they teach.

It may be unrealistic to expect student teachers to devise activities from a broad consideration of subject knowledge and pupil learning. But students should be challenged to evaluate the content of their activities (wherever these originate), not only in pupil learning but also in their own subject understanding and in the light of underlying subject 'principles'. These principles may incorporate an understanding of how the activity relates to or reflects what the subject area is essentially about – its nature, key ideas, associated processes, and the like. It may also include an understanding of the importance of the subject area in pupils' development – why this subject area is included in the curriculum and how pupils develop their understanding of knowledge in this subject area. *These* understandings may also be evaluated in the light of what students find to be 'practical' in the classroom context.

Who Challenges?

So who is best placed to make these challenges? At first sight it may be thought that the simple and unequivocal answer is 'teachers'. Their influence and importance in students' school-based learning is beyond dispute – certainly with student teachers (Boydell, 1986; Calderhead, 1988; Duquette, 1994). However, there are difficulties with this. First, many teachers in our studies appeared reluctant to challenge students. Teachers maintained that they did not want to assert themselves and take on a role of professional authority – particularly when working with adult learners. As one teacher commented, 'I don't like being authoritarian – it's because it's another adult. That's the conflict. They're intelligent people and I wouldn't feel comfortable with that.' Another teacher commented, 'I think it's got to do with you as a person. Like the students when they go in a classroom, you want the students to like you – you don't want to go in with a big stick. To get the best out of anybody you have to be approachable and let them know you're on their side. And I think there's a bit of a conflict there from being supportive and friendly in that way to having to go in and criticise their practice. That's not a role I feel happy with at the moment.'

Moreover, teachers found it difficult to 'formulate' these challenges. Not only were they unable to articulate their practical knowledge but this knowledge was also tied to the specific. They were, for example, able to talk about *their* children and *their* school but not to generalise this knowledge to broader understandings about how children learn and the influences of different contexts on that learning. In their pedagogical content knowledge, teachers could cite examples of what they considered to be 'good' activities but were not able to articulate what made the activity good.

Furthermore, teachers acknowledged that they had difficulties with aspects of their substantive subject knowledge, particularly in mathematics and, at KS2, in science. Teachers' difficulties, however, extended beyond their understanding of the substantive content. Teachers were unable to articulate how the activities they commonly taught related to fundamental understandings within and about subject areas. For example, one teacher was unable to say how printmaking, an activity she regularly taught to the pupils in her class, related to key ideas about art and art education. This teacher commented, 'What's struck me the more I've talked to people about this is how hidden inside teachers are the reasons why we teach anything. I wasn't alone in not really being able to say . . . clearly . . . what I did printing for. . . . Is the information there and it's so underneath that we just don't recognise it or don't people know?' Another teacher maintained, 'I don't know why I do half the things I do. I do them because they seem like a good idea at the time. . . . If someone asks me why you do it, I just wouldn't be able to give them an answer. My answer would be, it says I've got to do it in the National Curriculum or I've done it before and it worked really well and the children got a lot out of it. But I wouldn't know intellectual reasons why I did certain things. And I don't think most teachers do.'

It would be easy to condemn these teachers for this apparent lack of understanding or maintain that it could easily be remedied by providing teachers with more in-service training. In fact, this may be far from the case: the reasons for teachers' difficulties and the influences on their practice were complex. Moreover, as I have indicated, what teachers know and can articulate 'off the top of their heads' (their practical knowledge) may be different from what they do in 'lived' teaching (their 'knowing-in-action').

Influences on Teachers' Thinking and Their Practice

As I have stated, the reasons why teachers failed to gain or retain an understanding of the principles underlying the subject content of their activities were complex. However, several significant (and interrelated) factors which appear to contribute to teachers' difficulties could be identified: the nature of teachers' practical 'knowing'; the culture of the primary school; teachers' attitudes towards and difficulties with subject knowledge; and the effects of time and experience on teachers' thinking and practice. Moreover, I note that each factor in some way also contributed to teachers' reluctance and inability critically to evaluate the subject content of the activities they taught.

As we have seen, the dynamic and tacit nature of 'knowing-in-action' made it very difficult for teachers to describe and articulate their practical knowledge. Moreover, these difficulties appear to be compounded by the 'culture' of the primary school. Teachers typically work in isolation; for many of the teachers in our study working 'behind closed doors' was a recognised part of primary school culture – it was considered not only acceptable but an important part of their professional autonomy. Teachers commented that it was, therefore, unusual for them to discuss their practice with colleagues, other than, perhaps, which aspects of the National Curriculum they were going to 'cover' in their particular classes. As one teacher commented, 'After qualification, no one ever questions your practice again. You are just left to get on with it.' Unsurprisingly, then, it not only was demanding but appeared emotionally risky for teachers to share with colleagues what were seen to be their personal and private solutions to problems with their practice. One teacher, for example, maintained that she did not discuss her practice with colleagues as she was worried that, 'If I say I do *that*, then someone might say, that's wrong, you shouldn't be doing that . . .'.

Teachers' attitudes towards subject knowledge were also significant when considering their difficulties with understanding and articulating the broader subject principles underlying their activities. In our second project, when teachers were asked to mentor an aspect of subject knowledge to the students in their schools, they initially voiced grave reservations about the appropriateness and relevance of this focus. Subject knowledge, it appeared, was not seen as of particular importance for themselves, for student teachers or for their pupils (see Maynard, 1996).

Teachers' opposition to subject knowledge appeared to be based, in part, on the standpoint of a child-centred ideology – an important aspect of the culture of primary schools which all of our teachers supported to different degrees. Teachers maintained that they did not think about their teaching in terms of subject areas and that pupils' intellectual development was not their only, or arguably at certain ages and stages, their main concern. Rather, teachers sought to educate the 'whole' child and this included the child's social, moral and emotional development. They further raised concerns that, 'The end result of having a greater subject knowledge might be that we go into subject specialism' – clearly something that none wanted.

However, teachers' attitudes towards subject knowledge were also supported by (or possibly masked) a need to protect their own interests and self-esteem. They acknowledged their lack of subject knowledge in certain areas of the curriculum, and were realistic about the impossibility of becoming subject specialists in all ten National Curriculum areas (including Welsh) as well as Religious Education. This strengthened their 'anti' subject and 'pro' child-centred position. As one teacher commented, 'I think in the end what I'm going *against* rather than going *for* is that we can't be subject specialists in all eleven subjects . . . it's impossible. So instead of trying to say, "Yes we must strive towards this", we have to say, "We don't need to strive towards this."'

Teachers' lack of subject understanding, particularly their difficulties with articulating the subject principles underlying their activities, appeared to be significant in teachers' ability critically to evaluate the content of their activities. Teachers maintained that not being able to articulate these understandings, not being able linguistically to represent this knowledge even to themselves, meant that they had no criteria against which they could evaluate the appropriateness and accuracy of the subject content of activities. Another teacher commented, 'I feel I can't really evaluate what I'm doing because I don't really know why I'm doing it. I can just say I did that today and it worked, I did that today and it was a complete disaster. It's such a superficial evaluation', and went on, 'I feel I have to refer back to something. I'm doing this activity but why am I doing it? What are the children going to get out of it? If I want to truly evaluate what I do then I need to base that on some bedrock of educational research or theory. And I feel very inadequate in that respect.'

It also became clear that experience can contribute to teachers' difficulties in locating and articulating the principles underlying the subject content of activities. With experience, teachers will form concepts or schemas and this helps them control, organise and order this complexity (see Copeland, 1981; Berliner, 1987; Carter and Doyle, 1987). They will, for example, develop personal concepts of what is acceptable in pupil movement and noise, concepts of 'types' of pupils, typical and likely behaviour and so on. Each comes to know *what* information will be of significance to her or him 'as a teacher' (Berliner, 1987).

Linked to the formation of concepts is the idea of routines and routinisation. Furlong and I (1995) describe three forms: routine thinking, behaviour and activities. Teachers form and use routines, possibly without conscious awareness, to structure their own and their pupils' thinking and work (Leinhardt and Greeno, 1986). They also suggest that the use of routines may free teachers from concern with the mundane to focus more effectively on the 'important and/or dynamic features' of the lesson (p.94). However, this may be an optimistic or partial view.

The formation of concepts and routinisation appeared, for the teachers in our study, also to lead to a lessening of questioning and critical evaluation of certain aspects of their practice. Experience, as Berliner (1987) warns, should never be seen as a synonym for expertise. Moreover, the nature of *expertise*, as it is used by researchers, should not be misunderstood. Expertise, as Leinhardt (1988) explains, does not refer to doing things in the right or preferred way. Rather, it is a technical term referring to 'working with speed, fluidity, flexibility, situationally encoded information schemas, and mental models that permit larger chunks of information to be accessed and handled' (p.147). While teachers may become more adept and skilful in their presentation and the orchestration of their practical 'knowing', this does not, as I intimated earlier, confer a judgement of quality on the way the content is represented (pedagogical content knowledge) or on the actual knowledge itself (personal subject knowledge). We must discriminate between teachers' skilful performance, that is, their ability to think and act on different levels, process information, convey their expectations and the like and the accuracy and appropriateness of the subject content of their activities.

The Swansea studies indicate that experience (and teachers' attitudes towards subject knowledge) may have a negative effect on teachers' willingness critically to evaluate the subject content of their activities, because 'what' they taught, as opposed to 'how' they taught, appeared to become a matter of routine and of habit. For example, one teacher maintained that she 'measured out her year by festivals – Christmas, St David's day, Mother's day and Easter'. Similarly, another teacher, when asked why she taught various activities, commented, 'I do it because. . . at this time of year I always do that.' This teacher further maintained, 'When you've been teaching a number of years you do get to think this works, and you lose the reason why you teach it. As the years go by. . . you just know it works.' Another teacher added, 'If you've had a lot of experience, built up a lot of experience working with a lot of children in different ways, then something sticks there and it becomes. . . dangerously instinctive sometimes.'

Implications

The nature of teachers' practical knowing, the culture of the primary school, teachers' attitudes towards and difficulties with subject knowledge and the effects of time and experience all seemed to influence teachers' thinking and the way they worked with students. Teachers, it appeared, focused (increasingly focused) on those issues that were the most urgent, essential and practically useful to the day-to-day business of teaching, that were most 'visible' to them and that were most supportive of the child-centred culture of the primary school. Subject knowledge and the principles underlying the subject content of their activities were not seen by teachers as particularly relevant or significant in this respect. One teacher commented, 'I think something like control is always at the front because you deal with it all the time. Whereas subject knowledge you only draw on every so often – it's not something of immediate pressing importance.' Another teacher maintained, 'I suspect I totally ignored subject knowledge. Classroom control at the beginning of every year or at some stage you're constantly tinkering with.

But subject knowledge I never have done . . . I just didn't have it there in my head.'

I do not suggest that teachers did not think about the subject content of their activities, but that they did not easily consider how, for example, the particular concept or procedure to be taught related to other concepts and procedures, or to key ideas, processes and principles associated with the subject area. Rather, teachers appeared to view this concept or procedure through the 'lens' of their sophisticated and child-centred understandings about how to teach and how pupils best learn (Furlong and Maynard, 1995), and in terms of their store of 'good ideas' for teaching activities.

Teachers' activities *were not* necessarily inaccurate of the specific concept being taught or inappropriate in the principles underlying the subject area. The relationship between thought and action is, as we have seen, very complex. McNamara (1990) comments that we need to be careful about making judgements about the quality of teachers' actions – their practical 'knowing' – on the basis of the quality of their thinking or their practical 'knowledge'. The reverse must also hold true. One teacher said that when she revisited the activities she planned for her pupils in the light of her refound knowledge of these subject principles, she discovered, in her words, 'that it was all there'. This knowledge, she maintained, had merely been assimilated into broader, underlying and tacit understandings about approaches to teaching this subject content, and commented, 'For most things *why* I'm doing it isn't in the forefront of my brain . . . that's got lost in *how* you do it.'

The important point here, however, is that the teachers in our study were not consciously aware of, and therefore not able to articulate, how the activities they taught related to fundamental understandings within and about subject areas. Whether this affected the quality of their teaching is debatable, but it certainly affected teachers' ability to mentor student teachers in this respect. When teachers *did* challenge students about the content of their activities, these challenges were essentially directed at students' understanding of how to structure activities to support pupil learning: it was from this perspective that the appropriateness of students' activities was judged. Understandably, it was *this* perspective that students gradually, if intuitively, developed and came to see as of most importance.

The Limits of Mentoring

Mentors have an important, influential and essential role to play in students' school-based experience (Glickman and Bey, 1990). Classroom teachers are able to model, support and guide students' thinking and practice in distinctive and profound ways; this is vital to students' development.

However, particularly at the stage in their development when students appear to 'hit a plateau', there is a fundamental need for someone to take on a more challenging role. To deny teachers this role could undermine their professional status having identified the difficulties mentors could, given time, 'adjust' to the new demands made of them. In part this may be true, although a major stumbling block may be teachers' lack of interest and commitment. Becoming an effective mentor is demanding and from our studies there is still a strong sense that teachers regard their main responsibility as their pupils' learning and further that they see their workload as already overwhelming. It may be tempting in these circumstances to see students as just 'another pair of hands'. While the teachers in our studies were committed to mentoring, others, as one teacher remarked, say 'Great, I've got a student, a term off.'

Improving teachers' understandings relating to subject knowledge may be more problematic. Our teachers were privileged. Through being involved in our project they had the opportunity to revisit the 'theory', and establish or re-establish the subject principles underlying the content of the activities they devised for their student teachers. Interestingly, it was precisely these principles that our teachers later came to believe were most fundamental for students to understand about the content of their activities. One teacher commented that now she viewed her student's activities in an entirely different way and realised that what she had previously put down to a lack of understanding of pupil learning she now saw as a lack of understanding of the subject area. However, these teachers were focusing on one small aspect of one subject area.

Revisiting the subject principles underlying this aspect was very demanding of their time and led to great stress and feelings of insecurity about their practice.

- How many teachers would be given or would want to take this opportunity?
- Would teachers be willing to admit to and remedy their difficulties with subject knowledge?

Certainly the teachers in this study maintained that they attended only in-service courses for those subject areas in which they already felt they had 'some confidence and real understanding'. Moreover, teachers maintained that challenging student teachers to articulate the subject principles underlying the activities they taught was simply not the best use of their expertise. One teacher said, 'I can't see the point of people who are not subject specialists doing "What is the nature of the subject?" It's not what we're good at.'

All these factors point to difficulties with teachers taking on the responsibility for challenging student teachers, and set out a clear role for the HE tutor in students' school-based learning. However, the most persuasive argument for the involvement of such tutors rests, I believe, on what is often seen as their greatest weakness – that is, they are *not* involved in the day-to-day business of teaching. I would argue that far from being a weakness this is one of their particular strengths. Tutors do not have to 'survive' the classroom, they are not in a position of having to protect their own interests and juggle priorities and needs in the face of overwhelming demands. Moreover, they are outside of the culture of primary schools *in a way that practising teachers can never be* and it is this that makes their contribution to student teachers' school-based learning unique and fundamental. It is not, for example, that the teachers in our studies failed to embrace a more subject-centred approach, but that they were simply not able 'dispassionately' and 'with an open mind' to evaluate the appropriateness or effectiveness of this approach. If primary school culture develops, in part, to support teachers, to meet their needs and protect their interests, then it does seem unrealistic to expect teachers critically to examine the structures and substance of that culture. Interestingly, even when as part of our study teachers were challenged to reflect on and critically analyse their practice, in general there did not appear to be a culture of critical evaluation for the purpose of change – rather teachers, at this point at least, seemed to be motivated solely by a desire to 'find out why I do the things I do'.

The Role of the Tutor

Traditionally, the role of the tutor is characterised as overlapping the role of the supervisory teacher (Glickman and Bey, 1990). Tutors make a series of short assessments of students' attainment, moderate teachers' informal assessments, and support (as necessary) the student teacher. Tutors comments may merely become trivial, unfair, biased towards their subject specialism or an official duplication of those of the teacher. Moreover, tutors may feel inhibited from discussing theoretical knowledge in the classroom environment (Mansfield, 1986).

What I am arguing for is not a continuation of tutors' traditional role but the formation of a new role. The difficulty in trying to characterise this role is that every student and context will be unique and have different demands and needs which indicate different ways of working. In the early days of school experience tutors should support mentors in their work with students – discussing students' 'wants' and 'needs', what is known about student learning and strategies mentors may use to work with student teachers. Tutors should be involved in moderating and monitoring students' development and they may work with teachers in the classroom, acting as 'mirrors' so that teachers may clarify and find ways of articulating their practical 'knowing'.

Tutors should also work with student teachers and, as I have indicated, this is particularly important in the later stages of students' school experience. Tutors should challenge students to examine and evaluate the content of the activities they teach, not only in embedded assumptions about pupil learning and underlying subject principles but in their own subject understandings. As I stated earlier, students should also be challenged critically to evaluate these more 'theoretical' understandings in the light of what they find to be practical in the classroom context.

However, not just students will benefit from the tutor continuing to work in this way within schools. Tutors need teachers, not only for their research but to keep them in touch with the demands and pressures of teaching. Without close links with the classroom *their* 'teaching' becomes meaningless. Teachers will benefit too. Having help to understand their practice can affirm their belief in themselves as good teachers and lead to greater control of their practice. If an appreciation of the importance of subject knowledge is acknowledged by teachers, then tutors would also provide a valuable resource for schools. Closer links with colleges could also rekindle and keep alive within schools debate about broader educational issues. Given the findings of this research, tutors would also have a vital role to play in teachers' further professional development.

Conclusion

If the government intends to change the way a new generation of teachers think and teach through a series of initiatives and interventions, then it may have misunderstood the strength and lifeblood of the child-centred ideology. A more subject-centred approach cannot be 'imposed' on teachers. Nor, it seems, will a more subject-centred approach emerge 'naturally' if students are left to develop practical teaching 'skills' through trial and error under the supervision of the classroom teacher. Personal experience and imitation appear to be key features of student teachers' school-based learning. Students are likely simply to accept what seems to 'work' not only for them but for their class teachers.

If we believe that student teachers *should* consider not only 'how' they teach but 'what' they teach and 'why' they are teaching it, then there is a fundamental need for them to be challenged in this respect and it is the HE tutor who appears best-placed to take on this role. Ironically, the role of the HE tutor in students' school-based learning becomes particularly crucial if we really are to move to a more subject-centred approach!

If HE loses its involvement in students' school-based learning, student teachers' practice may not become 'practical' in the way the government may suppose, but merely 'partial'. If teaching is to survive as a profession then schools and HE need to recognise each others' strengths and limitations. The role of the tutor then becomes neither superfluous nor irrelevant, but a fundamental part of student teachers' practical professional development.

References

Alexander, R (1984) *Primary Teaching*. Eastbourne: Holt, Rinehart & Winston.

Alexander, R (1992) *Policy and Practice in Primary Education*. London: Routledge.

Alexander, R, Rose, J and Woodhead, C (1992) *Curriculum Organisation and Classroom Practice in Primary Schools*. London: HMSO.

Berliner, DC (1987) 'Ways of Thinking about Students and Classrooms by More and Less Experienced Teachers', in J Calderhead (ed) *Exploring Teachers' Thinking*. London: Cassell.

Boydell, D (1986) 'Issues in Teaching Practice Supervision Research: A Review of the Literature', *Teaching and Teacher Education*, **2**(2):115–25.

Buchmann, M (1987) 'Teaching Knowledge: The Lights That Teachers Live By', *Oxford Review of Education* (13): 151–64.

Calderhead, J (1987) 'The Quality of Reflection in Student Teachers' Professional Learning', *European Journal of Teacher Education*, **10**(3): 269–78.

Calderhead, J (1988) 'The Development of Knowledge Structures in Learning to Teach', in J Calderhead (ed) *Teacher's Professional Learning*. Lewes: Falmer Press.

Calderhead, J and Miller, E (1986) *The Integration of Student Teachers' Classroom Practice* (Research Monograph). School of Education, University of Lancaster.

Carter, K and Doyle, W (1987) 'Teachers' Knowledge Structures and Comprehension Processes', in J Calderhead (ed) *Exploring Teachers' Thinking*. London: Cassell.

Copeland, WD (1981) 'Clinical Experiences in the Education of Teachers', *Journal of Education for Teaching*, **7**(1): 3–16.

DFE (1993) *The Initial Training of Primary School Teachers: New Criteria for Course Approval (Circular 14/93)*. London: Department for Education.

Duquette, C (1994) 'The Role of the Cooperating Teacher in a School-Based Teacher Education Programme: Benefits and Concerns', *Teaching and Teacher Education*, **10**(3): 345–53.

Fuller, FF and Bown, OH (1975) 'Becoming a Teacher', in K Ryan (ed) *Teacher Education: The Seventy-fourth Yearbook of the National Society for the Study of Education*. Chicago, IL: University of Chicago Press.

Furlong, J and Maynard, T (1995) *Mentoring Student Teachers: The Growth of Professional Knowledge*. London: Routledge.

Glickman, CD and Bey, TM (1990) 'Supervision', in WR Houston (ed) *Handbook of Research on Teacher Education*. New York: Macmillan.

Guillaume, A and Rudney, G (1993) 'Student Teachers' Growth towards Independence: An Analysis of their Changing Concerns', *Teaching and Teacher Education*, **9**(1): 65–80.

Johnston, S (1992) 'Images: A Way of Understanding the Practical Knowledge of Student Teachers', *Teaching and Teacher Education*, **8**(2):123–36.

Lawlor, S (1990) *Teachers Mistaught*. London: Centre for Policy Studies.

Leinhardt, G (1988) 'Situated Knowledge and Expertise in Teaching', in J Calderhead (ed) *Teachers' Professional Learning*. Lewes: Falmer Press.

Leinhardt, G and Greeno, J (1986) 'The Cognitive Skill of Teaching', *Journal of Educational Psychology*, **78**(2): 75–95.

McDiarmid, GW, Ball, DL and Anderson, C (1989) 'Why Staying One Chapter Ahead Doesn't Really Work: Subject-specific Pedagogy', in M Reynolds (ed) *Knowledge Base for the Beginning Teacher*. The American Association of Colleges for Teacher Education. New York: Pergamon.

McNamara, D (1990) 'Research on Teachers' Thinking: Its Contribution to Educating Student Teachers To Think Critically', *Journal of Education for Teaching*, **16**(2): 147–60.

Mansfield, PA (1986) 'Patchwork Pedagogy: A Case Study of Supervisors' Emphasis on Pedagogy in Post-lesson Conferences', *Journal of Education for Teaching*, **12**(3): 259–71.

Maynard, T and Furlong, J (1993) 'Learning To Teach and Models of Mentoring', in D McIntyre, H Hagger and M Wilkin (eds) *Mentoring: Perspectives on School-Based Teacher Education*. London: Kogan Page.

Maynard, T (1996) 'Mentoring Subject-Knowledge in the Primary School', in D McIntyre and H Hagger (eds) *Mentors in Schools: Developing the Profession of Teaching*. London: David Fulton (in press).

Office for Standards in Education (OFSTED) (1993) *Curriculum Organisation and Classroom Practice in Primary Schools: A Follow-up Report*. London: DFE.

O'Hear, A (1988) *Who Teaches the Teachers?* London: Social Affairs Unit.

Russell, T (1988) 'From Pre-service Teacher Education to First Year of Teaching: A Study of Theory and Practice', in J Calderhead (ed) *Teachers' Professional Learning*. Lewes: Falmer Press.

Sanders, S (1994) 'Mathematics and Mentoring', in B Jaworski and A Watson (eds) *Mentoring in Mathematics Teaching*. Lewes: The Mathematical Association and Falmer Press.

Schön, D (1983) *The Reflective Practitioner.* New York: Basic Books.

Schwab, J (1978) 'Education and the Structure of the Disciplines', in I Westbury and NJ Wilkof (eds) *Science, Curriculum and Liberal Education*. Chicago, IL: University of Chicago Press.

Shulman, L (1986) 'Those Who Understand: Knowledge Growth in Teaching', *Educational Researcher*, **15**(2): 4–14.

Wilson, S, Shulman, L and Richert, A (1987) '150 Different Ways of Knowing: Representations of Knowledge in Teaching', in J Calderhead (ed) *Exploring Teachers' Thinking*. London: Cassell.

CHAPTER 9

THE SUBJECT-METHOD SEMINAR AND THE ROLE OF THE TEACHER EDUCATOR

Peter D. John

Do teacher educators have distinctive expertise that sets them apart from schoolteachers and other educational consultants? This question not only is of vital significance in itself but is central to the growing debate about the future form, location and curriculum of teacher education. However, providing an answer is problematic because research still lacks a tradition of studying the beliefs, practices and pedagogical thinking of teacher educators. Furthermore, the threat to formal teacher preparation posed by recent government reforms means, as Judge (1993, p.ix) puts it, that 'We need to understand a great deal more of the lives of teacher educators, if only to avoid the pain of having to read about their collective death.'

In this chapter, I have two broad aims: first, to document the expertise of teacher educators by focusing on the subject-method seminar as one of the crucial arenas where student teachers' learning is filtered and facilitated; second, to define more clearly the role of teacher educators in initial training by offering an analytical account of their distinctive contribution.

The Literature

Teacher educators, it seems, are the missing persons on the literature on teacher education. Less than 2 per cent of the entries on the ERIC database deal directly with them, and, paradoxically people who apparently spend so much of their time studying others are themselves so seldom the subjects of study (Weber, 1988). There have been some notable exceptions: in North America numerous investigators carried out fruitful inquiries into the lives and work of teacher educators, while in the United Kingdom, Furlong and colleagues (1988) and the Modes of Teacher Education Project (Barret *et al.*, 1992) are likewise attempting to repair the imbalance.

Nevertheless, too few researchers heeded Zeichner's (1988) call to extend the arena of enquiry to include the training establishments and those who work within them. He comments thus (p.21):

> *We know very little about what actually happens inside these courses beyond what students or faculty tell us. . . . There is no tradition in our field of studying the inner workings of teacher education courses comparable to the enormous amount of work that has been devoted to studying classrooms in the lower schools.*

One reason for this apparent lack of interest may well be that teacher educators are difficult to pin down both institutionally and conceptually. Ducharme (1986) outlines five issues that make definition and study a problem: low institutional status; lack of academic legitimacy; vague *raison d'être*; an absence of a central organising body; and tentative scholarship and research.

In the early 1980s both Hultgren (1983) and Roderick (1984) addressed some of these issues by describing and critically examining the professional perspectives of teacher educators. Their findings provide interesting accounts of the lived experience of those working on methods courses and they not only highlight the creative, aesthetic and pedagogical aspects of courses but outline subject commitment, personal investment and continued advocacy as being the essential characteristics of a successful teacher educator.

A decade later a number of studies began to emerge that deal specifically with the pedagogy of the teacher education curriculum (Feiman-Nemser and Featherstone, 1993; Wilson, 1992; Clandinin *et al.*, 1992). One of the most influential is Grossman's (1990) qualitative study of the role of a teacher education method course in developing the pedagogical content knowledge of student English teachers. In it she not only describes in detail the students' emerging understandings and skills but tries to identify the sources of their professional knowledge by tracking their experiences back into their method course. In her conclusion, she outlines five general features that appear to contribute to the success of this particular curriculum and instruction course:

1. A coherent vision of teaching and learning organised around the specific subject matter to be taught.
2. A collaborative relationship among professor, supervisors and students, in which the prospective teachers helped construct their own evolving professional knowledge.
3. A shared sense of ownership.
4. The existence of necessary support or scaffolding for the student

teachers as they acquire the skills and pedagogical perspectives for teaching.

5. A reflective stance toward practice which includes a developmental perspective on learning to teach.

In two books on teacher educators themselves (Wisniewski and Ducharme, 1989; Ducharme, 1993) the tensions and incongruities among the university's mission of research, scholarship and knowledge production and the teacher educator's emphasis on teaching, service and the improvement of practice are examined. What emerges is that despite recurring pressures, teacher educators maintain a sense of dignity and a strong belief in the value and impact of their work. In conjunction with this, much of their research agenda tends to be directed at collaborative work with teachers and despite the 'publish or perish' mentality of many institutions teacher educators continue to feel close to their constituency. All the studies mentioned raise a number of important questions that frame this study:

- How is teaching and learning organised in method sessions?
- What are teacher educators trying to achieve?
- What role do they play in the seminars?
- What pedagogical strategies are adopted?
- What sorts of beliefs and understandings underpin these strategies?
- What topics, themes and issues are explored?
- What information, ideas and beliefs are exchanged?
- What type of interpersonal dynamics exist?

Data Collection and Analysis

My chapter is based on case studies of six subject-teacher educators (two mathematicians; one geographer; one modern linguist; one English and one science tutor). All are or were tutors on the Post Graduate Certificate in Education (PGCE) course at the University of Bristol. The programme has been established since the turn of the century and has developed powerful subject bases in which the tutors always exercise a high degree of autonomy within a structured framework. The course at the time of study was not underpinned by any particular paradigm of teacher education but was eclectic both in structure and philosophy.

The new 'partnership' (DFE, 1992) arrangements were in their first year of operation when the data for the study were collected. In essence the course had three definable phases: the first induction phase (Autumn term) was characterised by observation, acculturation and preparation; the second assimilation phase (Spring term) was characterised by practice, research, development and consolidation; the third and final extension phase (Summer term) was characterised by extended professional and curriculum development. The subject method seminars were usually twice-weekly encounters (every Monday and Friday) and were fitted around the school-based serial visits and extended school experiences.

The observational data were collected at various points during the PGCE year. Timetable and other restrictions meant that observations of method sessions varied. Overall, for English, nearly 40 hours of observation took place; for maths 30 hours; science 25 hours, and modern languages and geography nearly 20 hours each. Many observations were followed by exploratory and explanatory interviews which tended to be either semi-structured or open-ended. This naturalistic data were supported by an analysis of syllabuses, handbooks, teaching resources and official reports.

The analysis was undertaken at a number of different levels. The first involved creating individual case studies for each tutor and subject; this provided an in-depth portrait of each. The second stage harnessed a detailed cross-case analysis to generate patterns and themes across the data. The third level involved a more detailed comparative analysis whereby confirming and disconfirming evidence was sorted and sifted. This iterative approach was accentuated by the use of the 'conceptual memo' which according to Miles and Hubermann (1984, p.69), does not 'just report data but ties different pieces together in a cluster' and shows how a particular piece of datum can become an 'instance of a general concept'.

The Functions of the Seminar and the Role of the Subject-Teacher Educator

From the analysis of the data it appears that the subject-method seminar served five crucial functions. It had a liberalising role, a collaborating role, an enquiring role, a reconceptualising role and a modelling role. Each is discussed in turn.

A Liberalising Role

The liberalising role of the seminar was analysed at a number of levels. Initially, the tutors were concerned with developing autonomy and independent thought. Their ideal was the creation of a liberal, flexible environment where experiential learning could flourish. At the core of their beliefs was the notion that learning by doing was essentially superior to learning by other methods. To achieve this, the tutors continually stressed the importance of informality and meetings were constructed with a view to developing a 'permissive' (Abercrombie, 1953) atmosphere. Here values, feelings, viewpoints, ideas and practices were explored and discussed in an open, relaxed and constructive manner. In this sense the seminars reflected Dewey's (1902) contention that there can be no 'intellectual growth without some reconstruction, some reworking'. Progressive shifts in personal theories were regarded by the tutors as necessary for a growing appreciation of the classroom.

In most sessions, the tutors withdrew from the traditional lecturer position to challenge many of the presumptions held by the students. This shift from being the didactic transmitter of knowledge to being a facilitator of learning was seen, in part, as an antidote to the students' undergraduate education. One commented, 'many of them have been through three or more years at university where they've just been subjected to lecture-listening mode. I'm trying to wean them off the dependency culture and make them think for themselves', while another claimed that he was trying to get them to 'share their assumptions with the rest of the group in an open, liberal atmosphere'.

For the English tutor, this meant creating an alternative classroom where his students could face the challenges in a supportive environment. The seminar room was their room and in the opening weeks of term particular strategies were followed that led to the classroom being 'claimed by the students'. He commented,

> *I offer the students a widening of context; I challenge them and their latent beliefs about their subject, about learners, about literature and language. I set up situations deliberately so that they will have the opportunity to learn from their experiences and through their experiences. Teacher education is about making connections for them and with them; it's about opening up their emerging practice for debate and discussion, it's about introducing them to new propositions, it's about examining and re-examining old ones; it's about starting a journey and developing new attitudes that will stay with them for years.*

For the geography tutor, his beliefs and practices sprang from the culture of the subject. He commented,

> *If students are going to teach humanities then they have to be able to develop themselves as human beings. The whole nature of the subject means adopting a quasi-liberal disposition. We have to create that and nurture it because without it where else in the curriculum in schools will children get it from? These days teaching and learning are so instrumental, it is the humanities subjects and creative arts, I suppose, that provide the liberal underpinning. So my sessions are very much based on developing a humanistic perspective.*

To achieve such goals, rooms were quiet and comfortable and the seating arrangements reflected a variety of approaches conducive to close interaction and reasoned debate. This liberalising role continued throughout the year but was particularly noticeable during the initial few weeks of the Autumn term. Here the ambience of the seminar rooms was closely linked to a series of specific strategies aimed at inculcating more open-minded attitudes towards teaching and learning, such as the sharing of biographies, the analysis of lessons, reflections on observations and wide-ranging discussions on diverse topics such as mixed-ability teaching, assessment and the curriculum.

In addition, the seminars were also theatres where the tutors were able to express their own viewpoints and positions. Space does not permit a detailed discussion of their subject and pedagogical ideologies; however, their beliefs tended to cluster around the progressive end of the traditional-progressive continuum outlined by Bennet (1976) and Darling (1990). Here the tutors claimed to value thinking as much as the doing and the knowing, and were concerned with educating 'the whole student' and 'the whole child' both through and across subjects.

Central to these beliefs was the 'negotiation of knowledge' whereby sets of understandings and practices were explored in the hope that a personal style would emerge that would be flexible enough to be applied in a number of contexts. 'Becoming the teacher you want to be' was a frequent refrain in many seminars. This was to some extent based on the idea that the educational system serves a pluralistic society in which the values attached to what is learned as well as how it is learned vary. Throughout, the uniqueness of children's learning styles, their developmental levels and situational backgrounds were introduced as variables which can influence teaching. The mathematics tutor claimed that:

> *In some courses they go in for cloning, they have a strict view about the teaching and learning of maths; they aim to make the students pliable and they give them definite images and practices to follow. We don't follow that here. We don't have one image of good maths teaching. I recognise that each school has a different ethos and set of values and so each teacher will have to find his or her own way. I will support them in their quest, in becoming the teachers they want to be. A real first step is to get them to articulate those desires and then to get them to think about maths and the way it can be taught.*

This emphasis on getting the students to develop and formulate their own personal teaching style within a broad framework of what might be called 'progressive' or 'child-centred pedagogy' reflects the phenomenological or personalistic tradition of teacher preparation (Zeichner, 1983; Diamond, 1991). As a result, discovery methods and active-learning approaches predominated and the stress on individualism was evident in the teaching and learning styles observed.

To summarise, then, there was a strong tendency within subject groupings to create a liberal atmosphere in which the individual could flourish and explore teaching and learning. The stress on the expressive rather than the instrumental, on the being as much as the becoming, marked out the liberalising function very clearly. The epistemological basis for this position was supported by a general belief that professional knowledge is created from a fusion of many types of knowledge of which the personal and experiential is a central component.

A Collaborating Role

The quality of education is enhanced when teachers work more closely together. A growing body of literature on school improvement and teacher effectiveness reports the beneficial effects of this collaboration (Fullan, 1991, 1993; Hargreaves and Hopkins, 1991; Nias, 1989). During the 1980s, a key element in this process was the shift away from seeing individual autonomy as the basis for professionalism to the viewing of teaching as a collaborative undertaking.

The pathway to the emergence of a collaborative professional culture is strewn with difficulties, and, as Little (1990) suggests, collaboration can range along a continuum from independence to interdependence. All the subject tutors in the study, however, expressed a deep and abiding faith in the importance of collaboration as both a professional learning tool and an appropriate and correct teaching and learning strategy for use in schools.

The collaborating role of the seminars was visible at a number of levels and in a number of forms. At the purely pedagogical level, collaborative ways of working were inculcated from the outset. Working in groups and pairs, by the early weeks of the course, became commonplace and the students were soon routinised into the necessary structures. In languages, for instance, it formed the core of their working principles; rarely was a session observed where the students did not get into pairs or groups. In a typical session, students were encouraged to work together developing dialogues using a set vocabulary; at other times collaboration moved from pair work using simple everyday artefacts to the evaluation of GCSE worksheets. In mathematics, students worked collaboratively on the production of resources related to National Curriculum Attainment Targets, while in English, groups were asked to research and create a language database consisting of key theoretical articles and materials for use in school. In geography, a field trip to Dorset was planned and executed collaboratively.

At another level, collaborative working was seen as an essential element in the development of the students' professionalism. They would, they were continually told, have to work in a collaborative atmosphere in subject faculties where planning and resource production were collectively decided. Many tutors expressed the ideal that their students would, through group and pair work, develop a long-lasting commitment to seeing their learning as dependent on others, thereby carrying on the notion of collegiality.

At a third and perhaps more problematic level was the belief that in getting the students to work collaboratively the seminars were indirectly encouraging the participants to use such strategies to develop autonomous learning in their pupils. Thus by working in groups and taking responsibility for their own learning the students, it was believed, would develop positive habits of thinking and reflection which in turn would not only help them professionally but might encourage them to see the benefits of using such approaches with children.

The modern languages tutor was a main proponent of this position and commented:

> *I aim to get the students to be autonomous learners and to get them to encourage autonomous learning in their classes, so they have to work collaboratively in smaller teams and pairs. In so doing I hope that their own emancipation as teachers will follow alongside the emancipation of their pupils.*

The geography tutor's beliefs sprang from his own political views:

> *Being a socialist, just about, I still feel, even though I'm a bit long in the tooth, that people feel better and by and large do things better when they work collaboratively. But perhaps this is going out of fashion with all this rugged individualism.*

Such a finding is not new. Furlong and colleagues (1988) found collaborative working to be widespread in a number of courses. Similarly, Grossman (1991) and Wilson (1992) saw the collaborative process as an essential element in the success of method coursework. Nevertheless, a number of issues remain. Furlong and colleagues (1988) felt that although collaboration was central to courses the control of the agenda for group-work still often lay with the tutors. This meant that the flow of knowledge to the groups and the parameters within which they worked were still tightly controlled. Evidence from this study confirms this, with few instances of a negotiated agenda being offered. In addition, the relationship between voluntary and enforced collaboration and the effects this may have on the traditional workplace autonomy and independence of the teacher are important questions that need to be explored in the context of teacher preparation (Hoyle and John, 1995).

An Enquiring Role

The enquiring function played a crucial unifying role within the seminars and linked both the liberalising and collaborating roles outlined earlier to the more tangible aspects of classroom life. In the seminars, the students were encouraged to enquire into the nature of their own and their colleagues' teaching, to understand the contextual constraints that influence practice as well as to explore the personal dimensions of being a teacher. In practice this meant helping the students to clarify their emerging beliefs and values while providing a neutral theatre where they could explore their own and observed teaching styles.

Of central importance here was the concept of reflection. Despite being omnipresent in virtually all coursework documentation, very little time was spent exploring how reflection is activated and encouraged in method courses. Furthermore, the data appear to show that the tutors' conceptions of reflection were not only rooted in their personal and career histories but were bound with a web of understandings and beliefs associated with the culture and pedagogy of their subjects. For instance, the English tutor, who espoused a social reconstructionist or critical perspective, was a highly politicised individual whose politics, educational values and subject perspectives were inextricably interwoven. The others saw reflection in more utilitarian ways and tended to have a less intense personal and political commitment. They saw reflection as a purely professional process aimed at securing more effective practice through lesson evaluation and design.

In examining the role of the seminar in developing reflection, the three levels of reflection (the technical, the personal and the critical) outlined by Van Manen (1977), Carr and Kemmis (1986) and Zeichner and Liston (1987) have a useful heuristic value.

At the *technical* level a number of strategies were offered to the students that enabled them to enquire into particular aspects of classroom practice. In one instance, students were specifically trained to observe and understand an aspect of practice to be viewed in school using observational pro formas. In another, a group of students were encouraged to 'go back stage' and examine the 'in-flight' decision-making of teachers. Here the tutor showed a video of an experienced practitioner at work and then, through a carefully directed discussion, guided the students in the creation of a non-judgemental question agenda which could be used later to explore their mentor's teaching. These two examples were typical of the range observed and were aimed at developing the students' capacity to rationalise and deliberate on the technical aspects of their teaching.

Strategies aimed at eliciting the *personal* level of reflection were fewer in number. Every Friday during the Autumn term, for instance, the mathematics sessions were based on a 'burning issue' theme whereby the students' experiences were explored using a 'critical incidents' framework. Here the novices were encouraged, through observation and reflection on their own and their mentor's practice, to come up with an important personal issue. They were then asked to explain the context of the theme, give a detailed narrative of it and then comment on it. Each theme was usually related to an aspect of practice either observed or encountered during serial visits. In examples such as this, the teacher educator played a crucial role in defining the reality of schools as well as offering students tools to understand and evaluate their school-based learning.

The third, *critical* level of reflection, is recognised by both theorists and practitioners as the most difficult level to operationalise during the preservice year. Very few examples were observed or encountered during interviews and observations and those that did occur tended to happen in the English seminar. In most sessions the students had regularly to feed back and outline the wider racial, social and gender implications of each activity under examination. In one session, for instance, in an attempt to help his students overcome their preconceptions about formal grammatical structures as well as getting them to rethink their views of learners, the tutor asked the group to write a pastiche of an extract from Russell Hoban's postnuclear novel *Ridley Walker*. The purpose was to force the students to come to terms with writing, using a new lexicon and grammar. The follow-up session explored the changing nature of grammar and punctuation using various pieces of writing generated by a wide variety of school children of different classes and races together with key articles and writings from the field.

Scholars such as Ball (1992) saw the coming of the National Curriculum as a major opportunity for critical enquiry. Here the data revealed a level of reflection again differentiated by subject. In geography and English, for instance, the sessions were underpinned by a clear historical and political critique. In languages and mathematics, on the other hand, a consensus position was adopted with a narrative outline being presented through a variety of resources and material. Throughout, the emphasis was on convergence, thus leaving the students with the impression that the National Curriculum was a synthesis of 'good practice.' In this sense, as the modern languages tutor claimed, the documents were there to 'unite teachers around an acceptable notion of effective practice'.

To summarise, the findings suggest that developing reflection in method seminars is a complex business and, as Lucas (1993) points out, the perceptions of individual tutors both influence and determine their behaviour in seminars. The heavy stress on the technical aspects of teaching was mirrored in much of the reflective work undertaken in seminars, with a great deal of it being related to the utilitarian concerns of the students – hence the emphasis on observation, protected practice, lesson-planning and evaluation (John, 1991). As a result, there were very few illustrations of the third level of critical reflection. Furthermore, as a controversial issue, the National Curriculum revealed differences among the tutors; some saw it as an opportunity for critical analysis, while others viewed it as unproblematic and given. These factors raise questions about the power and latent force of subject culture to influence each teacher educator's conceptions of reflection.

A Reconceptualising Role

When teachers enter courses of professional training, they bring with them a variety of implicit understandings and beliefs about teaching, learning, their subjects and learning to teach. As Lortie (1975) suggests, this 'apprenticeship of observation' has been partly developed through the thousands of hours spent in classrooms as pupils. According to research, this 'familiarity pitfall' (Fieman-Nemser and Buchmann, 1985) is closely linked to the students' conceptions of their subject and their own personal epistemologies. These implicit theories then shape their expectations of their pupils and often guide them into believing that their own experiences, interests and abilities are generalisable across the school population. In some cases their relatively straightforward understandings of their subject also channel them into seeing learning as simply knowledge-extension, which in turn leads them to ignore what their pupils bring to the learning process (John, 1995).

Addressing these understandings and beliefs was seen as a vital part of the preservice teacher education curriculum. In the seminars observed, many strategies used were aimed at challenging the students' understandings and beliefs about their subjects and how that content was best taught and learned. This was operationalised in two ways.

First, in all the seminars the focus was on helping students rethink their subject for teaching. In all the subject areas studied a number of sessions focused on the 'What is . . .?' question. Here the purpose was to begin to make inroads into the students' initial conceptions as a precondition for them to come to understand and harness the subject so that it could be taught in new ways. In the 'What is mathematics?' seminar, for example, the tutor explored the nature of the subject by introducing various definitions from a variety of contemporary and historical sources. These were then compared to the students' own beliefs and understandings.

In science, 18 physicists, biologists and chemists were involved in a workshop on electrical currents. The groups were given a *Punch* article which included numerous misconceptions about circuits. They were then asked to take a key concept like voltage, ammeter, current, resistance and to write down and discuss what they understood by it. Named individuals then had to teach a mixed group of scientists about that particular concept. This was followed by a large group discussion in which their latent understandings were shared. Throughout, the tutor facilitated the discussion and explained and challenged where appropriate.

Overtly, this session was designed to help the students 'explore the key concepts that underpin electrical currents'; however, the underlying aim, the tutor claimed, was 'to address their conceptions of science so that they could begin to rethink their subjects for teaching purposes.' This was a common justification for the approaches used with all the tutors commenting on the limited and simplistic subject conceptions held by the students.

Second, many tutors wanted their students to see the sorts of common-sense knowledge and preconceptions pupils brought with them into lessons. The science tutor commented thus,

> *I want them to come to terms with their misconceptions and be explicit about them. There are two levels I suppose: the first sessions try to get at their subject misconceptions and I find it's the physicists who are worse when they are dealing with physics because they are operating on such a high level of abstraction they can't always see the wood for the trees. The second tries to then get them to explain their ideas so that a group of younger children can understand. They have to learn that children don't come to classes* tabula rasa, *they are full of basic scientific ideas – the problem is that teachers confuse them instead of building on their understandings, mainly because they have not come to terms with the subject themselves.*

At the core of this reconceptualising function was a constructivist perspective on learning. The tutors therefore gave a high priority to helping their students make sense of their experiences by challenging and building on the knowledge, beliefs, schemas and attitudes derived from previous encounters with their subjects. The activities also aimed at the creation of pedagogical content knowledge, defined by Shulman (1987) as the teacher's ability to make the content of a subject penetrable for pupils. The creation of such knowledge has become even more urgent of late with the introduction of a subject-centred National Curriculum. Here the tutors all echoed Bennet and Carre's (1991) view that teachers need good subject understanding so that they can 'adequately transform programmes of study and attainment targets into worthwhile and appropriate tasks, they need it to frame accurate and high quality explanations and they need it to diagnose accurately children's misunderstandings and misconceptions.'

A Modelling Role

Although the modelling role of teacher education is well-documented, very little time is spent trying to understand the process and the subtle variations within it. Oakeshott (1967, p.169) draws attention to the importance of modelling in achieving an understanding of what such an activity as teaching really means:

> *In every ability there is an ingredient of knowledge which cannot be resolved into information, and in some skills this may be the greater part of the knowledge required for their practice. Moreover, abilities do not exist in the abstract but in individual examples; the norms by which they are recognised are after-thoughts, not categorical imperatives, and each individual example has what may be called a style or idiom of its own which cannot be specified in propositions. Not to detect a man's style is to have missed three quarters of the meaning of his actions and utterances; and not to have acquired a style is to have shut oneself off from the ability to convey any but the crudest meanings.*

This definition provided a useful conceptual lens for the exploration of the types of modelling found in the method seminars. Repeatedly students were asked to role-play particular classes and were required to participate in the model lessons from the children's point of view. In this sense they were taken through lessons and the learning process step-by-step and were encouraged to empathise with the pupils. In a typical maths session on probability, for example, the students had to improvise their roles using the performance of the tutor as their guide. At the end, the group returned to student mode and carried out a detailed debriefing of the pedagogical strategies and tasks they had encountered.

In geography, three demonstration lessons were delivered, each with a different focus. Again the students were encouraged to be the learners and to work through the tasks and activities. These then formed the basis for micro-teaching sessions whereby the students in pairs were responsible for planning and executing lessons that were part of their teaching programme in schools. The model lessons also served as an entry point for a wider exploration of lesson-planning.

A central element in this modelling process was the attempt by the tutors to get the students to see the point of the lesson from the point of view of the learners while offering the students 'suggestions for practice' (McIntyre, 1992).

This *direct* modelling of actual teaching and learning processes was complemented in the seminars by what might be termed *stylistic* modelling. All the tutors talked at length about the need for both the form and substance of sessions to be understood in equal measure. This led them to model the various styles of teaching they espoused in their own practice: a process that was felt to be central to the learning of their students. The science tutor claimed that he was a 'definite role model' and that he had to 'do things professionally'. He went on to say 'I prepare well and take a lot of time over my seminars. I am also very open and share with the students my preparation and reflections.' Another tutor introduced the concept of teacher education as learning by 'vicarious experience'; here his teaching style was deliberately constructed so that the students could see the preparation and organisation that went into it, thus actively engaging them in the process of learning .

Throughout the seminars the subject-teacher educators were engaged in helping their students learn practices that could be used in particular classrooms while trying to develop the ability in them to adjust to variable conditions. The first emphasises a fund or store of techniques whose function is anticipatory; the second emphasises resourceful practice in the face of uncertainty and the unanticipated. Such viewpoints reflect similar themes in other studies. Fieman-Nemser and Featherstone (1993) outline the need for teacher educators to model a particular sort of teaching which 'can help students examine their preconceptions and work out some reasonable and defensible ideas about teaching for themselves'. From an action research perspective Adler (1993) comments on the need for teacher educators to be explicit about their own reflections if they are successfully to model the practices they wish to inspire in their students.

The Distinctive Contribution of Subject-Teacher Educators

Judge (1989, p.vii) argues that 'If universities can only do (better or worse) that which other professional agencies can also do (more or less expensively) then there is little reason for them to remain in serious business.'

The remainder of this chapter addresses Judge's point by offering an analytical account of the role of HE tutors in relation to the institutional locales within which they operate. By drawing on the more descriptive data outlined earlier, I provisionally sketch the distinctive contribution that subject-teacher educators make to ITT.

Recent attacks on the institutions of teacher formation raise in a new form old and persistent questions related to the knowledge and skills required of teachers as professionals, the sites in which these are best acquired and the role of teachers and HE tutors in that process. The challenge posed by these attacks has had some beneficial effects. It means closer collaboration between schools and HE and the setting up of a wide variety of partnership arrangements across Britain. The teachers' role is more clearly defined and their expertise honoured and partly rewarded; the challenge also means a radical rethink for those whose prime responsibility is to work with student teachers – the subject-teacher educators. However, problems remain, many of which hinge on the crucial relationship between institutional context and the teacher-education curriculum (Alexander, 1984).

Clearly, higher education and schools have different institutional and cultural histories, they embrace different value structures and address different challenges, all of which require different mindsets on the part of those who work within them. Yet both are crucial to the functioning of high-quality teacher-education courses. Freidson (1970), in his seminal study of the medical profession, documents the existence of these two cultural milieus and suggests that the settings create differentiated orientations, what he calls the clinical mentality and scientific mentality. Although somewhat oppositional, the framework is a useful one for evaluating the descriptive data outlined previously and apart from some terminological alterations the basic concepts and ideas remain true to Freidson's original categories.

Reflection and Action

Whatever may be claimed, the first priority for the practitioner is action. Numerous studies of teachers and teaching note that teachers have little time to think, deliberate and reflect. Much of their preparation may be more deliberative but a great deal of their teaching is still intuitive. Furthermore, the coming of the National Curriculum and the plethora of structural and managerial initiatives intensify this process. The pressure to produce and act is immediate; classroom action is *hot* action; however, where the action is cool, the consideration of ideas, beliefs, principles becomes more feasible, there is more space for trial and experimentation and personal style is less pervasive (Eraut, 1988). So if experimentation, adjustment and reflection are to be developed, student teachers need time and space.

Since HE tutors' prime responsibility is to their student teachers (unlike teachers, whose prime responsibility is to their pupils) they are ideally placed to help students resist the dive into action. As shown in the first part of this chapter, reflection and deliberation were considered central features of the enquiring and reconceptualising role of the subject sessions. Throughout the seminars, the tutors strove to get their students to deal constructively and creatively with their emerging understandings and skills. The tutors helped their students review alternatives, explore their own and others' indicators and counterindicators for action and impressed on them the need to consult carefully before acting.

Scepticism and Direct Intervention

Because of their action-oriented environment, teachers must exhibit a certain confidence in the efficacy of their interventions. Given this commitment to practical solutions, often in the face of ambiguity, practitioners manifest a certain will to believe in the value of their practices rather than exhibit a sceptical detachment. HE tutors, on the other hand, because they work in a neutral environment which treasures autonomy and independent thought, are ideally placed to help their students evaluate and when necessary throw doubt on the efficacy of what they observe and practice. At the same time, alternative approaches are offered directly through the modelling of reasoned practice or indirectly either through the discussion of the discrepancies observed and experienced at school and by collectively sharing practice in a decontextualised environment.

Theory and Pragmatism

According to Freidson the clinician often judges the success of an intervention purely on pragmatic grounds, often the immediate, observable effect being enough to justify its efficacy. 'It worked' is a common term used by both experienced and novice teachers alike. HE tutors, as has been shown, are often suspicious of such pragmatism. Having a base in HE allows them to gain access to a wide variety of research and professional literature which can call into question the atheoretical nature of many practical actions. The way this shelf-knowledge is integrated into the emerging understandings of student teachers is a unique feature of teacher education.

Furthermore, knowledge that helps prospective teachers develop a sense of the overarching purposes for teaching their subject and that which challenges the powerful effect of personal and firsthand experiences may be more influential in the long run than is currently supposed. In addition, an understanding of the theoretical principles underpinning a particular choice of teaching style or strategy can also help new teachers justify and defend their choices if their practice is seen to run counter to standard approaches used in a particular institution.

Scholarly and Personal Justifications

By allowing student teachers to explore the connections between theoretical knowledge and classroom practices, HE tutors can help their novices make the connections between theory and practice and vice versa. Being scholarly is an essential prerequisite of working in academia. For tutors this usually means not only examining the literature in the field but engaging actively in research and scholarship. Sifting this knowledge and filtering it down to prospective teachers combine as one of their essential roles. Similarly, sharing the findings of their own research not only is regarded as good practice in HE but can provide the link between generalisable knowledge and personal knowledge.

Teachers, on the other hand, are prone to trust their accumulated personal knowledge and craft wisdom. This is founded on concrete practical action and its efficacy is based on a distillate of contemplated experience (Freidson, 1970). It is also highly personalised and has a unique relationship with the knower, while its plausibility is based on its similarity to the experiences of others.

Universal and Particularistic Experience

Here the uniqueness of a particular context is counterposed by the more universal environment of the HE establishment. Often student teachers are so bound up with the specifics of their particular experience that they are unable to see beyond the monolocational environment they inhabit. As can be seen from the descriptive data, HE tutors can and do use their unique 'peripatetic' knowledge gained from hundreds of hours watching, evaluating, examining and discussing practice with experienced and novice teachers. This allows them not only to play a vital moderating role in assessment but, in method seminars, to make generalisations about particular practices and their effectiveness. Finally, since they are experienced practitioners themselves, this broad multilocational view creates a vast database not only of ideas and approaches but of local knowledge about subject faculties and departments.

Conclusions

Clearly, from the evidence presented in this chapter, subject-teacher educators perceive themselves to be playing a fundamental role in the education of new teachers. In their seminars they act as role models, supporting and challenging at every opportunity; they question, clarify, comment and criticise; they help student teachers define the realities encountered in schools as well as helping them account for the discrepancies and inconsistencies that occur. Finally, they communicate and filter a wide variety of theoretical and conceptual ideas and encourage reflection, deliberation and experimentation.

The seminars serve a series of vital functions from the more generic liberalising role to the modelling of reasoned practice. The beliefs and practices underpinning the tutor's role create a fusion of the craft wisdom gained from years spent in the classroom combined with the more universal experience of being a teacher educator within the culture of HE. The latter is vital in creating a unique mindset characterised by reflection, a sceptical detachment, theoretical understanding, a scholarly approach and a breadth of vision.

Ultimately, subject-teacher educators are concerned to pass on the multiple live traditions in which their practice is embodied. Teaching and learning to teach, from this perspective, is clearly not, as some commentators would have it, simply a matter of the teacher or mentor shaping the student's behaviour. It is more a matter of passing on the traditions of principled thought and action which define the life of teacher and taught. In the words of R S Peters (1963, p.18),

> *The teacher (educator) is not a detached operator who is bringing about some kind of result in another person who is external to him. His task is to get others on the inside of the public form of life that he shares and considers to be worthwhile.*

References

Abercrombie, MLJ (1953) 'Emotional Security as a Condition for Change', *Health Education Journal,* **11**(3): 112–117.

Adler, S (1993) 'Teacher Education Research and Reflective Practice', *Teaching and Teacher Education* **9**(2): 159–169.

Alexander, R (1984) 'Innovation and Continuity in the Inital Teacher Education Curriculum', in R Alexander, M Craft and J Lynch (eds) *Change in Teacher Education: Context and Provision since Robbins.* London: Holt, Rinehart & Winston.

Ball, S (1992) *Markets, Morality and Equality in Education.* London: Tufnell Press.

Barrett, E, Barton, L, Furlong, J, Galvin, C, Miles, S and Whitty, G (1992) 'Initial Teacher Training in England and Wales: A Survey of Current Practices and Concerns', *Cambridge Journal of Education,* **22**(3): 293–307.

Bennet, N (1976) *Teaching Styles and Pupil Progress.* London: Opie Books.

Bennet, N and Carre, C (1991) 'No Substitutes for a Base of Knowledge', *Times Educational Supplement,* 8 November.

Carr, W and Kemmis, S (1986) *Becoming Critical: Education, Knowledge and Action Research.* Lewes: Falmer Press.

Carter, H (1984) 'Teachers of Teachers' in J Raths and L Katz (eds) *Advances in Teacher Education,* vol. 1. pp.125–143. Norwood, NJ: Ablex.

Clandinin, DJ, Davies, A, Hogan, P and Kannard, B (1992) *Learning to Teach, Teaching to Learn.* New York: Teachers College Press.

Darling, J (1990) 'Progressivism and Individual Needs', in N Entwhistle (ed) *Handbook of Educational Ideas and Practices.* London: Routledge.

Dewey, J (1902/1964) 'The Child and the Curriculum in', JA Boyden (ed) *John Dewey: The Middle Works, 1899–1924,* vol. 2. Carbondale: South Illinois University Press.

Department for Education (1992) *Circular 9/92.* London: DFE.

Diamond, CT (1991) *Teacher Education as Transformation.* Milton Keynes: Open University Press.

Ducharme, E (1986) 'Teacher Educators: Description and Analysis', in J Raths and L Katz (eds) *Advances in Teacher Education*, vol. 2, pp.39–60. Albany, NY: SUNY Press.

Ducharme, E (1993) *The Lives of Teacher Educators.* New York: Teachers College Press.

Eraut, M (1988) 'Knowledge, Creation and Knowledge Use in Professional Contexts', *Studies in Higher Education*, **10**(2): 117-132.

Feinman-Nemser, S (1983) 'Learning To Teach', in LS Shulman and G Sykes (eds) *Handbook of Teaching and Policy*. New York: Longman.

Feinman-Nemser, S and Buchmann, M (1985) 'Pitfalls of Experience in Teacher Preparation', *Teachers College Record,* **87**(1): 53–65.

Feinman-Nemser, S and Featherstone, H (1993) *Exploring Teaching: Re-inventing an Introductory Course*. New York: Teachers College Press.

Freidson, E (1970) *The Profession of Medicine*. New York: Dodd, Mead.

Fullan, M (1991) *The New Meaning of Eduational Change*. London: Cassell.

Fullan, M (1993) *Changing Forces: Probing the Depths of Educational Reform.* London: Falmer.

Furlong, J, Hirst, VJ, Pocklington, PH and Miles, S (1988) *Initial Teacher Training and the Role of the School.* Milton Keynes: Open University Press.

Goodman, J (1983) 'The Seminar's Role in the Education of Teachers: A Case Study', *Journal of Teacher Education,* **24**: 44–50.

Grossman, P (1990) *The Making of a Teacher: Teacher Knowledge and Teacher Education*. New York: Teachers College Press.

Grossman, P (1991) 'Overcoming the Apprenticeship of Observation in Teacher Education Coursework', *Teaching and Teacher Education,* 7(4): 342–359.

Hartley, D (1991) 'Democracy, Capitalism and the Reform of Teacher Education, *Journal of Education for Teaching,* **17**(1): 81–97.

Hargreaves, D (1989) 'PGCE Assessment Fails the Test', *Times Educational Supplement,* 6 October.

Hargreaves, D and Hopkins, D (1991) *The Empowered School.* London: Cassell.

Hultgren, F (1983) *Reflecting on the Meaning of the Curriculum Through Hermeneutic Interpretation of Student Teaching Experiences.* Paper presented at the annual meeting of the American Educational Research Association, Montreal.

Hoyle, E and John, PD (1995) *Professional Knowledge and Professional Practice.* London: Cassell.

John, PD (1991) 'Course, Curricular and Classroom Influences on the Development of Student Teachers' Lesson Planning Perspectives', *Teaching and Teacher Education*, 7(4): 359–373.

John, PD (1995) 'Understanding the Apprenticeship of Observation in Initial Teacher Education: Exploring Student Teachers' Implicit Theories of Teaching and Learning', in G Claxton, M Osborne and T Atkinson (eds) *Liberating the Learner: Lessons for Professional Development*. London: Routledge.

Judge, H (1989) Introduction, in R Wisniewski and E Ducharme (eds) *The Professors of Teaching: An Inquiry*. Albany, NY: SUNY Press.

Judge, H (1993) Foreword, in E Ducharme (ed) *The Lives of Teacher Educators*. New York: Teachers College Press.

Lanier, J and Little, J (1986) 'Research on Teacher Education', in M Wittrock (ed) *Handbook of Research on Teaching*, 3rd Ed. New York: Macmillan.

Lortie, D (1975) *Schoolteacher: A Sociological Study*. Chicago, IL: University of Chicago Press.

Little, JW (1990) 'The Persistence of Privacy, Autonomy and Initiative in Teachers' Professional Relations', *Teachers College Record*, **91**(4): 509–536.

Lucas, P (1993) 'Light Half-believers in Our Casual Creeds: Tutors' Interpretations of Reflective Practice', *Higher Education Review*, **25**(2): 50–61.

Lawlor, S (1992) *Teachers Mistaught*. London: Centre for Policy Studies.

McIntyre, D (1992) 'Theory, Theorising and Reflection in Teacher Education', in J Calderhead and P Gates (eds) *Conceptualising Reflection in Teacher Development*. Lewes: Falmer Press.

Miles, M and Hubermann, MA (1984) *Qualitative Data Analysis: A Sourcebook of New Methods*. Beverly Hills, CA: Sage.

Nias, J (1989) *Primary Teachers Talking: A Study of Teaching as Work*. London: Routledge.

O'Hear, A (1988) *Who Teaches the Teachers?* London: Social Affairs Unit.

Oakeshott, M (1967) 'Learning and Teaching', in RS Peters (ed) *The Concept of Education*. London: Routledge.

Popkewtiz, T, Tabachnik, R and Zeichner, K (1979) 'Dulling the Senses: Research in Teacher Education', *Journal of Teacher Education*, **30**: 58–72.

Peters, RS (1963) *Education as Initiation*. London: Evans Brothers.

Raths, J, Katz, L and McAninch, A (1989) 'The Plight of Teacher Educators: Clinical Mentalities in a Scientific Culture', in R Wisniewski and E Ducharme (1989) *The Professors of Teaching: An Inquiry*. Albany, NY: SUNY Press.

Roderick, J (1984) *Perspectives on the Self as a Teacher: Cracks in the Technocratic*. Occasional Paper no. 28, University of Alberta.

Shulman, LS (1987) 'Knowledge and Teaching: Foundations of the New Reform', *Harvard Educational Review*, **57**: 1–22.

Van Manen, M (1977) 'Linking Ways of Knowing with Ways of Being Practical', *Curriculum Inquiry*, **6**: 205–228.

Weber, S (1988) 'The Teacher Educator's Experience: Cultural Generativity and Duality of Commitment', *Curriculum Inquiry*, **20**: 141–159.

Weber, S (1993) 'The Narrative Anecdote in Teacher Education', *Journal of Education for Teaching*, **19**(1): 71–82.

Wilson, S (1992) 'The Secret Garden of Teacher Education', *Phi Delta Kappan*, November, pp. 204–9.

Wisniewski, R and Ducharme, E (eds) (1989) *The Professors of Teaching: An Inquiry*. Albany, NY: SUNY Press.

Zeichner, KM (1983) 'Alternative Paradigms of Teacher Education', *Journal of Teacher Education*, **34**: 3–10.

Zeichner, KM (1988) *Understanding the Character and Quality of the Academic and Professional Components of Teacher Education*. Paper presented at the annual

meeting of the American Educational Research Association, New Orleans, LA.
Zeichner, KM (1993) *Reflections of a Teacher Educator Working for Social Change.* Paper presented at the annual meeting of the American Educational Research Association, Atlanta, GA.
Zeichner, KM and Liston, DP (1987) 'Teaching student teachers to reflect', *Journal of Teacher Education*, **34**(3): 23–48.

PART 3

Principles Guiding the Future of Higher Education in Initial Teacher Training

CHAPTER 10

REASSERTING PROFESSIONALISM: A POLEMIC

Margaret Wilkin

> *Let me see if I have got this right. At primary level children should learn less by 'doing' and more by being told, while their future teachers being trained in college should spend less time being told and more time learning by 'doing' on the job in schools. It's a funny old world, isn't it?* (Letter to the *Times Educational Supplement (TES)*, February 1995)

At first glance the above letter appears to be a rather neat response to the criticism of Her Majesty's Chief Inspector of Schools, Christopher Woodhead, that primary education remains dominated by the ethos of 'doing' and learning by discovery and that a more didactic or 'telling' approach might have beneficial results in pupil learning (*TES*, 27 January 1995). The letter, however, is more memorable for what it reveals about the state of teacher education in the UK today. First, its tone is political. Through the clever use of words the writer gains satisfaction from scoring a point against the government. He does not mention the government by name; he does not need to. Readers will know the target of his barbed comments about school-based training. Second, the letter discloses a reluctance to confront the changes that have taken place in initial training over the last few years. They have not been assimilated into the writer's thinking. He fails to recognise that students are still 'told' but that the 'telling' is now done by the mentor, or it should be. There is difficulty in acknowledging that power has been transferred to teachers in schools and that they are now worthy and skilled practitioners in training in their own right.

My chapter is a plea to members of the teacher-training profession in the higher education institutions (HEIs) to free themselves, ourselves, from the political sniping and the Nelson syndrome exemplified in the opening letter. Both these tendencies deflect us from what should be our central and serious concern: the improvement of the quality of initial training through the constant review, monitoring and critical evaluation of our practices as teacher educators. We are always stressing to our students the need to be reflective about their classroom activity. The assumption is that if they are reflective they will strive with an open mind to appraise the advantages and disadvantages of their current action within a defined situation. In the main, the criteria for judging action will reflect a concern for pupil learning. In what way and to what extent does this or that course of action either impede or enhance the ability of pupils to learn? Sometimes, however, the immediate concern of the student will be personal survival in the classroom. Then feelings of anger and fear will displace questions such as these which are at the heart of learning to be a good teacher.

Are there parallels here with the situation in which we currently find ourselves? Government initiatives in initial training over the past decade distracted the profession from its true purpose, that of seeking and practising the best form of training for student teachers. A series of circulars and other measures have criticised the established form of training and have reduced the power of the institutions both financially and *vis-à-vis* the schools. Powerful objections were levelled against a tradition of training which was well embedded in consciousness and habits; jobs were threatened and the contribution of the lecturer to student learning diminished and demeaned. This is highly uncomfortable and it is to be expected that anguish would express itself in fierce reaction (Gilroy, 1992).

In our responses to government measures, education and politics have become confounded as in the opening letter. Yet engagement in political stone-throwing is time-wasting. It reduces the time available for educational activity, and if continued over many months may attribute more credibility to political arguments than they deserve (Berrill, 1994). Energy and interests have become directed outwards in a battle which cannot be won by a return to the status quo even if this were perceived as desirable, for changes in the structure of courses and in the involvement of schools in training have gone too far for easy reversal.

It is time to take the broader view, to forsake grieving and to concentrate on a reappraisal of government initiatives and their value for training. There are those who will argue that the profession has already done this and concluded that there is little merit in the changes imposed. Some might interpret such a move as capitulation or weakness or a loss of integrity. Surely the reverse is the case? It would be a demonstration of the strength and maturity of the profession and a restatement of our commitment to rightful concerns, were we to exercise reflective judgement purged of anger about the contribution of the government and ourselves to the current situation. Pring (1994, p.175) says that we should not just dismiss the charges against us as though there is no element of truth in them. For example, how was it that for so long, with the exception of one or two schemes such as the Sussex Partnership Scheme and the Oxford Internship Scheme, we granted teachers only nominal power as 'partners' in training? Should we not also accept that the form that training takes may change over time, perhaps through political intervention but perhaps for other social or historical reasons, and that the task of those engaged in training the next generation of teachers is to take responsibility for rationally assessing these changes for their benefits as well as their disadvantages, their truths as well as their falsehoods?

Critical Reflection as the Internal Dynamic of Initial Teacher Training

Reviewing the history of teacher education since the Robbins Report of 1963, I find it possible to discern the strong critical trend that is the dynamic of its progress. The continuous appraisal and analysis of current practice by those in the institutions, particularly the philosophers of education, is motivated by an active concern that students should receive the best preparation for a career in the classroom that current thinking can devise. Most changes that have come about over the years as a consequence are evolutionary developments in the balance between theory and practice, developments which are supported and justified by reference to the inadequacies of existing training methods (Wilkin, 1996).

Well before the Robbins Committee recommended that the college course be elevated to degree status with the extension of the academic dimension of the curriculum that this implied, there were those advocating exactly this on the grounds that 'real scholarship in the teacher is a prerequisite' and that 'the undue emphasis in some training colleges on teaching practice to the neglect of problems of theory . . . (is) symptomatic of those traditional views' that 'stand in the path of educational change and accentuate social lag' (Holmes, 1954, p.5). From the perspective of today, this emphasis on theory and the concomitant dismissal of the importance of practice ('Of minor importance in teaching practice is the learning of teaching techniques'[*sic!*] [p.13]) seems strangely outmoded. Yet this development represented an amazing step forward, a very real advancement on the low intellectual demands which characterised the college training courses of the day.

Having been introduced into the training curriculum of the colleges through a government initiative, the disciplines of education then became the object of critical review, and, as a result, their role in training in turn was transformed. From being the determinants of practice they became the means of clarifying that practice (Hirst, 1979). Much later, 'educational theorising' and its irrelevance for the tasks facing student teachers in school is listed as a 'Problem To Be Overcome' in the setting up of the Oxford Internship Scheme (McIntyre, 1990, p.20). Once again the restructuring of training, and particularly the reconceptualisation of the relationship between theory and practice was being justified on the grounds that this is an improved way of preparing students to teach. Hargreaves (1990), with his proposals that initial training should be school-based and that teachers should be the principal partners in training, is part of this continuous quest for a more effective way of training the ideal teacher, as also is Berrill (1994), a teacher who robustly criticised the teacher-training establishment for elitism and who defended the ability of schools to take responsibility for training. In turn his arguments were challenged by Furlong (1994) who defends theory and the contribution of the HEIs and notes that 'evidence that consistently high quality teacher education can be achieved if schools "go it alone" is not strong' (p.119). And so it continues. Arguments go back and forth and the balance and role of theory and practice in training gradually shift once more as improvements to the current form of training are sought.

It can be concluded then that within teacher training there is a well-established tradition of debate in which the values and priorities of current practice are constantly subject to critical review by those who are themselves engaged in that practice. That the debate is honest and open is indicated by the participation in it of both supporters and opponents of the issue of the day. An early example was a lecturer in a college who, at a time when the opposition to the dominance of the disciplines was growing, proposed that the student's main subject should be replaced by courses in those same disciplines! (Price, 1966). It is unlikely that he slowed the decline in the importance of theory, but nevertheless his rather extreme views may well have caused others to reassess theirs and they will have contributed to the liveliness of the exchange. The value of this debate lies in the diversity of views expressed as well as the quality of their presentation. Mainstream ideas are challenged and these challenges may redirect events, perhaps force a reconsideration of routinised thinking or sink without trace.

Within teacher education today this necessary and lively critical tradition continues. Lecturers are joined by teachers, who are now themselves trainers (Berrill, 1994). When we look beyond the confines of HE and confront the initiatives of the government, the reluctance to exercise this same responsibility as academics, to consider both sides of the question before making up our minds, remains strong. Even now, we are still in such a state of shock at what is perceived as the temerity of the government in intervening so forcefully in the training curriculum and at the subsequent speed of reforms to initial training, that we have difficulty in meeting that fundamental obligation that we share as members of the HE community – the need to be sceptical, critically evaluative and, so far as we can, unbiased at all times. There are now early signs that the new forms of training which have been introduced by the government are being reassessed. In their study of two school-administered and two HE-administered ITT programmes, Evans and colleagues (1995) do not dismiss the former but are attuned to the problems they confront, and they suggest a number of ways in which this form of training might be improved. The competencies, originally greeted with such caustic criticism when first introduced, are now 'worthy of more exploration than teacher educators sometimes assume' (Whitty, 1993, p.270); it is also acknowledged that they are 'neither narrowly technicist nor exclusive. In theory, institutions can still do other things' (Barton *et al.*, 1994).

The purpose of these comments is to promote the teacher-training policies neither of the government, nor of any other external body for that matter; it is to put a case for renewing our commitment to the student in training and to keeping his or her needs at the forefront of our collective mind. To evaluate political initiatives fairly in these terms, and then to act upon our conclusions (see below), is to reaffirm our expertise and to strengthen our position as professionals. We need to step aside and pause and make a less frenzied (because angry and anxious) assessment of each item or aspect or consequence of policy, asking ourselves the age-old questions:

- Does this significantly advantage the student?
- Will it help him or her become a sound teacher?

Although we may not have had much purchase on policy-making in the recent past, we can influence policy-implementation. The last major political intervention which had an effect across the teacher-training curriculum was at the time of the Robbins Report. In subsequent years, the profession appraised what the report introduced and decided that they liked the idea of graduate status for teachers (which was retained), but that they did not like the overvaluation of theory (which in time was rejected)[1] for the reason that it ill-equipped the student for the task of classroom teaching which lay ahead. It is this principle of independent judgement that is being advocated. These judgements are made on the basis of professional expertise and understanding and are unclouded by political antagonisms. We should not allow 'political arguments [to] dominate more strictly educational discourse' but with 'sober consideration' 'separate some of the underlying arguments and consider them in their own terms' (Bridges, 1993, p.52). This is not easy to do.

The political and the educational are closely intertwined, and we have all felt that our response to government policy has been determined by real and well-placed concern for the quality of training. While, on the one hand, it is impossible to disregard the political origins of the many initiatives in training; on the other hand, this is exactly what has to be done. We must focus on them *ab initio* to assess their value for professional preparation, and this should be so whether the politics are of the right or the left. We lose stature and we undermine our credibility by subordinating our educational priorities to lengthy political diatribe, for it then appears that we are unable to confront these new ideas and deal with them. Surely, it will help the profession to retain a sense of self-worth if we exercise our expertise by asking of *any* change from whatever source:

- Are there, or could there be, any benefits for training in this situation, and if so, how can we incorporate them into the current curriculum?
- Which aspects of these changes should we disregard since we can see no professional merit in them although we have viewed them from every angle?

Practical Action

All of this is of course easy to state! What would it mean in practice? First, we need to operate with an open mind not only within our own academic community but with regard to our relationships with external agents. In a neat, punchy and convincing paper, Hare and McLaughlin (1994) represent open-mindedness as an attractive and desirable quality. Being open-minded does not mean being either indecisive or neutral, for 'ongoing open-mindedness is plausibly associated with having taken a position' (p.240). What it does mean is being willing 'to form or revise beliefs in the light of evidence and argument' (p.239). They quote from a text by Montefiore (1975). Retaining an open-minded attitude means being 'always ready to take into fresh consideration any new facts and any new interpretations of old facts which might seem to have any relevance'. These writers are not talking of being easily swayed in one's opinions: they are advocating reasoned debate and attention to evidence.

Second, we have to agree – and surely there is no difficulty here – that teachers should be more than token participants in training. With one or two exceptions, it has taken institutions far too long to acknowledge that the many and complex skills and judgements required to manage pupil learning and behaviour, which are the particular province of classroom teachers, are best made available to students by *them*. Teachers have this knowledge of their craft and they should be invested with the power and authority to take responsibility for conveying it to the novice student. That this is still not universally acknowledged is indicated by the letter that opens this chapter. Only when time spent in school is structured, developmental and accountable will it be possible to say that schools 'will have a leading responsibility for training students to teach their specialist subjects' (DFE, 1992, para.14). For the time spent by the student in school to become training rather than mere experience, it will be necessary to introduce a clearly defined curriculum of training in each subject area, as there is in the institutions. Some partnerships have already gone a long way down this road, schools and institutions working together to devise a total curriculum in which the contribution of each party is clearly defined and integrated. In addition, literature which offers schools some suggestions on how they might introduce and implement training is becoming more commonplace. In the best examples teachers and lecturers work together on these projects (Hagger *et al.*, 1993).

Third, as already implied, we must honestly review political initiatives for their potential professional benefits and then act confidently upon our evaluations. One example of this is the way in which many institutions, in conjunction with their partnership schools, have taken the bare bones of the competencies (any one of which it would be difficult to disagree with as a fundamental aim of training), and exercising professional choice and discretion, prioritised, shaped and developed them to provide a curricular framework that reflects particular interests and concerns. Another (unlikely) example comes from the Licensed Teacher Scheme, which when first mooted, was strongly criticised for the way in which it transferred teacher training from the professional to the occupational sphere (Hoyle and John, 1995). However, it was also a scheme which was minimally prescribed and therefore provided opportunities for alternative interpretations and for the creative use of interstices. The MOTE Report (1993) describes one scheme where there was strong collaboration between the LEA and HEI, and where the HEI had a significant input into the training programme. Here both parties, the LEA and the HEI, were convinced that licensees needed time out of school to reflect on their in-school experiences and to learn, yes, some theory which would enhance their understanding of pupil learning, say, when they returned to their classes. The HEI input to the course was well-received by the licensees, one even commenting: 'Now looking back on it it was brilliant. It provided everything you needed' (p.67). Political strategy is not the reason for adapting government policy in this way. The motive is professional. Examples such as these of grassroots modification of political initiatives represent an attempt by those in the HEIs with their school partners to continue to provide what they jointly believe to be the best form of training for their students, and there is nothing wrong in this. It is an appropriate response to innovation. One great benefit of recent government initiatives is that they oblige us to look again at our own assumptions. We may decide that we would wish to retain some aspects of our (recent) forms of training and work towards doing this as the two preceding examples indicate. On reflection, we may decide that we would prefer to discard other aspects, these changed preferences emerging from a rational appraisal of current principles and practice.

Fourth, and most crucially because those engaged in training, whether in schools or HEIs, are convinced that both theory and practice are necessary elements in students' professional preparation, we need to safeguard this relationship. There is no need to insist that the two elements should always be juxtaposed in the same way. The marginalisation of theory in initial training provides an excellent example of a politically generated change which demands independent apolitical assessment and invites creative thinking. Maybe, once schools become fully 'tooled up' for training and mentors are confident in their ability to convey the knowledge and skills of teaching to the student, trainee teachers could profitably spend an early period as apprentices in school. Working through a defined curriculum under skilled mentors, they would acquire the basic skills of classroom management and an initial understanding of how schools operate. Only when this is followed up by some theoretical and reflective school-related study or studies, either in or with the support of an HEI, would the trainee be granted qualified status. There is some limited evidence that such a consecutive approach to their training makes sense to students (Tann, 1994). I must stress that although it would be in two stages, this form of training would *not* be hierarchically elitist.

The order of practice (for training in the 'what' and 'how') followed by theory (for education in the 'why') is a matter of logic. The first priority of students is coping: coping with classroom management and control and with the demands of lesson preparation and marking. In Griffiths and Tann's (1992) five levels of reflection, they are now at the state of 'reaction'. The 'retheorising and reformulating' stage of reflection on personal practice with reference to what these authors term 'public theory' lies ahead. Maynard and Furlong (1993) would agree. They suggest that before students are ready to engage in reflective practice, they must achieve sufficient mastery of essential teaching skills to enable them to forget their concern with self and instead to feel confident enough to look outwards and focus on pupil learning and how it can be facilitated. This model of training, in which the student is placed in school under the guidance and direction of the mentor, and then later works under the guidance and direction of the lecturer, might appear to distance educational theory from practice in school once more.

Have we not been here before? seems a relevant question at this point. The answer is No. The situation is not the same as it was in the 1960s or 1970s when criticism of the place of the disciplines in training was rife. First, today's student has a much broader base of practical experience, and in time more reflective 'Why?' questions may be generated by this experience than arose out of discussion on classroom practice in the past. Once students acquire a certain level of competence and confidence in their ability to start and conclude lessons, to ask and respond to questions or to give directions clearly and so on and they begin to observe pupils as learners, the desire for theoretical explanation about the learning process could become persistent and demanding. Whether this were so would depend upon the mentor's ability to stand aside from the prevailing occupational culture (Elliott, 1991) and encourage the student to do likewise. So there are implications here for the selection of mentors.

Here we come to the second difference: such a form of training would place a considerable obligation on the lecturer to ensure that his or her theoretical knowledge and concerns remain relevant, of interest and above all of *use* to the student. To qualify the trainee student would have to undertake some theoretical study directly related to his or her practice, and as that trainee's resource and facilitator the lecturer would have to be able to provide the necessary support and guidance. Because schools and their staffs are changing rapidly in response to political, social and economic factors they could do this only if they were to move forwards themselves within their respective disciplinary area through the processes of research and reading. In other words, the HEI would need to become a lively community of scholars. Theory, whether subject or educational, is not separated from practice at all, but rather the point in training when their relationship is investigated by the student trainee comes later. Such a scheme, which echoes the James Report, would enhance the professionalism of all concerned. Teachers in school would have real and acknowledged responsibility for training the next generation of teachers; training itself would become more akin to master's degree work for the lecturer would be teaching students who had sustained experience behind them and for whom the disciplines become 'sources of ideas which can be eclectically utilised in situational problem-solving' (Elliott, 1991, p.316); and lecturers would be expected to contribute to the body of knowledge which underpins practice and which is the hallmark of a profession.

Would it be possible to introduce such a scheme of training in the UK? It is not impossible. It would bring our professional qualification nearer to those of our continental colleagues and in the future there might be pressure for this. Although somewhat lengthier than the current PGCE, it need not necessarily be vastly more expensive. It would mean rethinking our relationship with the schools once more. Partnership here would mean going our separate ways because each side at last had confidence that the other would do a sound professional job. For the institutions this might not be easy. It would mean 'letting go' of students and trusting the schools to maintain standards of training. In the past, there has been a marked reluctance to do this (Patrick *et al.*, 1982). It would also mean recognising that the form that training shifts over time, but that the direction of these shifts is at least partly within our power to determine. Seen from this perspective, the current form of collaborative partnership is a *necessary* step to the greater professional autonomy of each side in the future, and for this reason should be protected.

Conclusion

Underlying these comments is the more fundamental issue of how we as individuals and intellectuals relate to the State. This is an issue which is far too vast to consider here and which I am unqualified to address, but which has been the concern of sociologists and philosophers from Mannheim and Gramsci to the present day (Maclean *et al.*, 1990). In the UK we have been more fortunate than other countries which have experienced oppressive regimes that dominate through diktat and terror. Relatively speaking we have a history of moderate government. Perhaps this is one reason why the teacher-training profession has been so stunned by the degree of penetration and the relentlessness of recent legislation. Our initial reaction was to shout 'foul, foul' from the rooftops yet to submit – what has been called the 'toadying factor' (Price in Gilroy *et al.*, 1994). More recently there have been signs that the profession, or its representatives, the subcommittees of the Universities Council for the Education of Teachers (UCET), are reassessing the situation. The Teacher Training Agency (TTA) is admittedly anxious to consult and the institutions have a responsibility to respond (UCET Minutes of Management Forum, 15 February 1995). Perhaps more significantly, it was suggested at a recent meeting of the Funding Council (UCET, 12 January 1995), that UCET should offer to work with the TTA and undertake a series of case studies representing the different models of training. The benefit of this exercise would be that it 'might help to give UDEs a better idea of expenses and so how to manage their own budgets, and also show schools and the TTA what costs actually are' (p.2). This is surely the way ahead even though the underlying motivation for such an exercise might be the hope that the outcome would favour the institutions. There is recognition that change may be necessary, that collaboration is possible, that the institutions may have lessons to learn from their own evaluations, that there are initiatives to be taken, and that those in the HEIs have skills and expertise which they can make available to the teacher-training world at large as a contribution to the resolution of current dilemmas.

We should take time to assess policy initiatives for their value for student learning and training, and where they seem to offer benefits be sufficiently open-minded to admit this. Where they do not, *collectively* we 'just say no, in a very proper protest' (Griffith, 1994). Saying No does not mean that we then ignore our responsibility to scrutinise rigorously our own attitudes, practices and priorities. In a commentary headed 'Time To Stop Being Grumpy', Russell and Triesman (1994) make a plea for government and academics to work together. I would like to conclude with an extensive quotation from this piece.

We must discover a new road to influence and with it a new sense of ownership. . . . Yet our influence is plainly not all it could be. For fifteen years, governments, as a matter of ideology, have barely spoken to unions or professional bodies. Other problems are arguably of our own making. All professions have sometimes found it more comfortable to be grumpy from the sidelines than to be insistent players, and academics' professionalism is broadly defined by commitment to their students and disciplines. Universities must be centres of intellectual integrity, and therefore critical centres in society. That role is protected by defending academic freedom – it implies the class of ideas and universities must be guarantors of debate. . . . Rigorous debate reaches the parts which other approaches do not at present reach, questions what universities should do, how their independence can be protected . . . and how best to accomplish individual professional objectives and development.

Notes

1. There is an interesting parallel here. At the time of the report, 90 per cent of students were trained in the colleges. However, there was no college representation on the Robbins Committee or at the Hull Conference where it was decided how the report's recommendations should be implemented. This meant that the majority of those who were engaged in teacher training had far-reaching changes in the curriculum imposed upon them, as today.

References

Barton, L, Barrett, L, Whitty, G, Miles, S and Furlong, J (1994) 'Teacher Education and Teacher Professionalism in England: Some Emerging Issues', *British Journal of Sociology of Education*, **15**(4).

Berrill, M (1994) ITE: Crossroads or By-pass?, *Journal of Education for Teaching*, **24**(1).

Bridges, D (1993) 'School-based Teacher Education', in D Bridges and T Kerry (eds) *Developing Teachers Professionally*. London: Routledge.

Department for Education (1992) *Circular No: 9/92 Initial Teacher Training (Secondary Phase)*. London: DFE.

Elliott, J (1991) 'A Model of Professionalism and Its Implications for Teacher Education', *British Educational Research Journal*, **17**(4).

Evans, L, Abbott, I, Goodyear, R and Pritchard, A (1995) *Hammer and Tongue: The Training of Technology Teachers*. Association of Teachers and Lecturers.

Furlong, J (1994) 'Another View from the Crossroads', *Journal of Education for Teaching*, **24**(1).

Gilroy, P (1992) 'The Political Rape of Initial Teacher Education in England and Wales: A JET Rebuttal', *Journal of Education for Teaching*, **18**(1).

Gilroy, P and Smith, M (eds) *International Analyses of Teacher Education*, JET Papers 1. Abingdon: Carfax.

Gilroy, P, Price, C, Stones, E and Thornton, M (1994) 'Teacher Education in

Britain: A Symposium with Politicians', *Journal of Education for Teaching*, **10**(3).
Griffith, J (1994) 'Just say No, in a Very Proper Protest', *Times Higher Education Supplement*, 25 November.
Griffiths, M and Tann, S (1992) 'Using Reflective Practice to Link Personal and Public Theories', *Journal of Education for Teaching*, **18**(1).
Hagger, H, Burn, K and McIntyre, D (1993) *The School Mentor Handbook*. London: Kogan Page.
Hare, W and McLaughlin, T (1994) 'Open-mindedness, Commitment and Peter Gardner', *Journal of Philosophy of Education*, **28**(2).
Hargreaves, D (1990) 'Another Radical Approach to the Reform of Initial Teacher Training', *Westminster Studies in Education*, **13**.
Hirst, P (1979) 'Professional Studies in Initial Teacher Education: Some Conceptual Issues', in R Alexander and E Wormald (eds) *Professional Studies for Teaching*. Guildford: SRHE.
Holmes, B (1954) 'The Teacher of Teachers', *Education for Teaching*. Paper no.34, Association of Teachers in Colleges and Departments of Education (ATCDE).
Hoyle, E and John, P (1995) *Professional Knowledge and Professional Practice*. London: Cassell.
McIntyre, D (1990) 'Ideas and Principles Guiding the Internship Scheme', in P Benton (ed) *The Oxford Internship Scheme*. London: Gulbenkian.
Maclean, I, Montefiore, A, and Winch, P (eds) (1990) *The Political Responsibility of Intellectuals*. Cambridge: Cambridge University Press.
Maynard, T and Furlong, J (1993) 'Learning To Teach and Models of Mentoring', in D McIntyre, H Hagger and M Wilkin (eds) *Mentoring: Perspectives on School-Based Teacher Education*. London: Kogan Page.
Montefiore, A (1975) *Neutrality and Impartiality: The University and Political Commitment*. Cambridge: Cambridge University Press.
MOTE (Modes of Teacher Education) Survey: Barrett, L, Galvin, C, Barton, L, Furlong, J, Miles, S and Whitty, G (1993) *The Licensed Teacher Scheme*. Obtainable from the Health and Education Research Unit, Department of Policy Studies, Institute of Education, 55–59 Gordon Square, London WC1H 0NT.
Patrick, H, Bernbaum, G and Reid, K (1982) *The Structure and Process of Initial Teacher Education within Universities in England and Wales*. University of Leicester.
Price, G (1966) 'Education as a main course', *Education for Teaching*. Paper no.70. ATCDE.
Pring, R (1994) 'The Year 2000', in M Wilkin and D Sankey (eds) *Collaboration and Transition in Initial Teacher Training*. London: Kogan Page.
Russell, C and Triesman, D (1994) 'Time to Stop Being Grumpy', *Times Higher Education Supplement*, 20 May 1994.
Tann, S (1994) 'Supporting the Student Teacher in the Classroom', in M Wilkin and D Sankey (eds) *Collaboration and Transition in Initial Teacher Training*. London: Kogan Page.
Whitty, G (1993) 'Education Reform and Teacher Education in England in the 1990s', in P Gilroy and M Smith (eds) *International Analyses of Teacher Education*, JET Papers 2. Abingdon: Carfax.
Wilkin, M (1996) *Initial Teacher Training: the Dialogue of Ideology and Culture*. Lewes: Falmer Press.

CHAPTER 11

DO STUDENT TEACHERS NEED HIGHER EDUCATION?

John Furlong

The passing of the 1994 Education Act was a vitally important milestone in the history of initial teacher education in Britain in that it marked the formal separation of the initial teacher education system from the rest of higher education (HE). In the future, funding for all forms of initial teacher education in England (though not in Wales) will be the responsibility of the Teacher Training Agency (TTA) rather than the Higher Education Funding Council for England (HEFCE) which funds all other higher education.

Even more significant, however, was the Act's confirmation that in the future, consortia of schools can develop their own SCITT (School Centred Initial Teacher Training) teacher-training schemes (DFE, 1993a) without reference to HE at all. This innovation poses the most fundamental challenge to those professionally involved in initial teacher education; it raises in stark and unavoidable terms the question whether trainee teachers really do need HE at all. If even a small number of graduates from SCITT schemes can achieve qualified teacher status without ever setting foot in a university or college department of education, we can no longer avoid questions about the value of the contribution of HE to a teacher's early professional development.

My aim in this chapter is to contribute to the debate as to what the rationale for the continued involvement of HE in initial teacher education actually is. In doing so I intend to engage with the writing of Ronald Barnett, one of the most insightful contemporary writers on the 'idea' of higher education. Before turning to my main theme, however, I ask how it is that we have come to be in this position. How is it that the contribution of HE to the professional development of teachers has come to be questioned in such a profound way? In answering this question I find it useful to consider what Barnett (1990) describes as the 'sociological' and 'epistemological' undermining of HE.

According to Barnett, HE is traditionally founded on two axioms. First, there is the realm of objective knowledge; there are recognised truths to which students are to be introduced and about which they are expected to be able to demonstrate some assurance. This Barnett calls the *epistemological axiom*. Second, there is what he calls the *sociological axiom*. This is the idea that objective knowledge is most effectively maintained and disseminated in institutions which are relatively autonomous from narrow social interests (such as the state) and in which members of the academic community can enjoy comparative freedom. Truth, it is traditionally argued, can only be pursued in institutions that are themselves freed from outside interference. However, as Barnett demonstrates, both axioms have, in recent years, come under attack or been put in doubt throughout HE.

Higher Education's Role

The 'Sociological' Undermining

On the 'sociological' front, Barnett argues that in recent years, HE has been 'swept up' by the state, so much so that a large amount of what goes on is now prescribed.

> *Having expanded the system very rapidly and dramatically, (the state) came to have doubts about both the economic value of higher education and, in the wake of the radical movement, its wider social value. The state turned to maximising its investment in higher education. . . . There is a new emphasis on value for money, accountability, planning, efficiency, good management, resource allocation, unit costs, performance indicators and selectivity and reduced opportunities for tenure. Subjects within the curriculum are favoured to the extent that they make a clear contribution to the economy: the sciences and technological subjects are supported . . . the humanities and social science subjects try to prove their worth by developing skills-oriented courses.* (p.26)

Certainly, this is the experience of most of those professionally involved in initial teacher education. Teacher educators' own explanations for the undermining of their role is that it comes about largely as a result of state intervention.

Direct intervention first began in 1984 with the issuing of DES Circular 3/84 (DES, 1984). It was with this circular that the Government established the Council for the Accreditation of Teacher Education (CATE) which was charged with the responsibility of overseeing initial teacher education in Wales and England. In retrospect, the substantive changes introduced by Circular 3/84 do not seem particularly radical. However, constitutionally the Circular was revolutionary (Wilkin, 1991). For the first time it established the right of the Secretary of State to have a say in the detailed content and structure of initial teacher education in the UK.

Since 1984 there has been a range of further interventions that have extended and elaborated central control and further challenged the contribution of HE. Circular 24/89 (DES, 1989) reformed the organisation and powers of CATE while introducing far more detailed specification of the content and form of initial teacher education courses. Between them Circulars 3/84 and 24/89 challenged the *autonomy* of those in HE to organise the structure and content of courses in the way they saw fit. Nevertheless, HE still had a major role to play in the process.

More recent Circulars (DFE, 1992, 1993b) went much further in that they explicitly *limit* the role of higher education. For example, the secondary circular (DFE, 1992) states:

> *The Government expects that partner schools and HEIs will exercise a joint responsibility for the planning and management of courses and the selection, training and assessment of students. The balance of responsibilities will vary. Schools will have a leading responsibility for training students to teach their specialist subjects, to assess pupils and to manage classes; and for supervising students and assessing their competence in these respects. HEIs will be responsible for ensuring that courses meet the requirements for academic validation, presenting courses for accreditation, awarding qualifications to successful students and arranging student placements in more than one school.* (para. 14)

The primary circular is equally forceful. As a result of these two circulars, teacher education in the future is intended to be narrowly focused, functional and technical with HE playing a more limited role than in the past.

The Response

To understand the full force of the present challenge to the role of higher education, it is not sufficient simply to focus on current government regulations. We must also ask how universities and colleges responded to earlier changes. Only by so doing can we appreciate the context into which current legislation entered. Here it is useful to refer to evidence provided by the Modes of Teacher Education Project (MOTE) (Furlong *et al.*, 1994). The MOTE project is monitoring changes in initial teacher education over a five year period (1992–1996). What we discovered in the first phase of our research was that by 1992, immediately prior to the introduction of the latest government circulars, most courses had responded to the government's increasing emphasis on practical training in the previous eight years by changing the HE rather than the school-based parts of their training programmes. Course leaders introduced substantial changes in the structure, content and pedagogy of their HE-based programmes to make them more 'relevant' and 'practical' for students. There had also been a substantial change in personnel, with significant numbers of new lecturers being recruited directly from schools. By contrast, the changes introduced to school-based work were, in most courses, modest. In 1992, school-based work was still predominantly planned, supported and assessed by university and college tutors; the formal role assigned to teachers in the process remained minimal. Rather than sharing power and responsibility with schools and *together* finding ways of responding to government criteria, during the 1980s, colleges and universities had, for the most part, I would suggest, taken it on themselves to deliver a practical training.

It could be argued that by 1992, those in HE still controlled the provision of teacher education but maintained that control at considerable cost. In moving to highly practically oriented courses, many started to lose sight of what their distinctive contribution actually was. As a result, they were particularly badly placed to respond to the government's demand that the responsibility for practical training be passed largely to schools. The cumulative effects of the sociological undermining of their work were profound.

The 'Epistemological' Undermining

Higher education has, according to Barnett (1990), not only experienced a 'sociological' undermining; it has also been profoundly 'epistemologically' undermined too.

> *So the idea of objective knowledge is central to higher education. But from various theoretical quarters – philosophy of science, sociology of knowledge, epistemology, critical theory and post-structuralism – the ideas of objective knowledge and truth have come under a massive assault. What if anything is to replace objective knowledge is unclear. Pragmatism, relativism, 'metacriticism' and even 'anything goes' are all proposed. The very diversity of the alternative opinions is testimony to the collapse of some of our basic epistemological tenets.* (p.11)

As I indicated, British teacher educators interpret the undermining of their role as largely resulting from government intervention. In reality such an analysis is highly partial; profound epistemological difficulties must also be admitted. Those epistemological difficulties concern the nature and worth of theory understood as 'propositional' knowledge in education.

As Hirst (in this volume) reminds us, controversy over the role of 'theory' in education has a long history; it is a highly complex and largely partisan debate showing little sign of resolution. Where there has been agreement, however, is in dissatisfaction with the teaching of propositional knowledge in the form of 'the disciplines' of education – sociology, psychology, philosophy and history. The move away from such an approach to professional education in reality commanded widespread support; it was only hastened, not fundamentally caused, by the government. There is far less consensus about what to replace disciplinary knowledge with. Uncertainty, in what Schön (1987) characterises as 'the swamps' of professional knowledge, is endemic. The only firm ground is at the extremes - those who remain committed to the essential role of formal theory in teacher education and those supporters of SCITT schemes who see induction into the 'craft of teaching' as sufficient in itself (O'Hear, 1988; Lawlor, 1990).

In 1984, Alexander pointed to the 'possibility' in British initial teacher education of moving away from a concern with theory to a concern with 'theorising'. Since then, as the MOTE project confirms (Furlong *et al.*, 1994), within the vast majority of British teacher-education programmes, notions of 'theorising', 'theory as process' and particularly 'reflection' largely displaced the teaching of theory as propositional knowledge. The popularity of the idea of theorising through reflection has not led to conceptual clarity. As Calderhead (1989) points out, 'researchers, teacher educators and other writers in the field hold a range of beliefs about teaching and teacher education into which they have incorporated their own particular notions of reflection' (p.45). In reality there are probably as many different definitions of reflection as there are supporters of the idea. Once again the very diversity of proposed alternatives to the teaching of propositional knowledge is testimony to the collapse of certainty. No wonder in the 1980s teacher educators responded to government initiatives by embracing 'the practical'; articulating any secure version of educational knowledge other than the practical was, and remains, immensely problematic.

Those involved in HEIs devoted to initial teacher education face a double crisis today for they are both epistemologically and sociologically challenged. The certainty of the value of their knowledge and the autonomy of their control over the content of their courses are undermined. Bridges (in this volume) reminds us, teacher educators should not assume that they are unique in this regard; many other fields look on us with some sympathy and a good deal of nervousness, recognising the same symptoms in their own field. A loss of certainty and a loss of autonomy is now endemic in HE. What perhaps is distinctive, however, are the lengths to which the government went in recent years in its attempts to control teacher education. This, in combination with epistemological difficulties felt widely throughout professional education (Schön, 1983, 1987) and elsewhere, makes our crisis particularly pointed.

However, it is because teacher education is not alone in its current crisis that there can be no going back. Academics who yearn for the good old days of academic freedom where they alone could determine the curriculum untroubled by the complexities of engaging with the real world of schools will be disappointed. I argue elsewhere (1991), the government – any government – will continue to want to have a strong hand in teacher education as it will in the rest of higher education; the days of complete autonomy for any of us are over. Moreover, as I will seek to demonstrate in the second half of this chapter, we do not want to go back to a world of detached 'academic' knowledge either. Higher education has a vitally important role to play in professional preparation, but if it is to be relevant to the profession of the future, it must have a very different role from that which it had in the past. This will raise important challenges for those in HE but the potential rewards could be significant.

Higher Education and Practical Professional Training

What then is the contribution of higher education to initial teacher education? First, we should recognise that those in HE do have an important role in supporting the development of students' practical professional competence – this is a responsibility that universities and colleges *share* with schools. In my view, the assumption that HEIs can and should take total responsibility for this central aspect or professional preparation could never really hold water. One strength of the government reforms of the last few years is that they have forced those in HE to recognise the importance of systematically involving practising teachers in their work. In many courses, I suggest that the quality of professional training offered is already significantly better for that involvement. Nevertheless, HE currently has a vital role to play in this aspect of training in at least four key ways.

1. Students benefit from being introduced to a great deal of the practical business of teaching *away* from the complexities of the classroom. For example, they need a chance to look at the National Curriculum in detail, they need to work on the preparation of lesson plans and to examine different strategies for assessing pupils' work. All this work is highly practical in nature, but particularly in the early stages of their professional preparation, there are clear advantages to students if they engage in this work away from the complexities of actually performing as teachers. Classrooms are highly complex places with a great many different things happening at the same time. Students must learn to cope with that complexity, but there are definite advantages if parts of their practical professional preparation take place outside of the classroom.
2. Those in HE can contribute through the vitally important process of modelling good practice. It is no coincidence that all of the tutors we spoke to in the MOTE research referred to (Furlong *et al.*, 1994), regarded their own pedagogy in their HE-based sessions as one of their key strategies in professional preparation. Pedagogy was always chosen with care. Through it, tutors were able to model a wide variety of teaching strategies for their students, and as our interviews with

students confirmed, that modelling was a rich source of ideas for them. Many tutors would also deploy the strategy of putting a group of students back into the role of learners themselves. Through this process, tutors could raise complex issues about teaching, learning, and the nature of knowledge in an extremely effective manner. These sorts of learning opportunity for students, however, demand that they are *taught* and that they work together as a group; the same ends cannot be achieved through direct practical experience in school.

3. HE can contribute to practical professional preparation by broadening the students' experience. Through their teaching, through the use of a well-stocked professional resources centre, by arranging visits and visiting speakers, HE tutors can broaden students' practical knowledge and skills. Again, this form of practical training is no substitute for direct experience in the classroom; it is nevertheless a vitally important complement to it. One great stimulus to developing a deeper understanding of the principles behind professional practice is to have a broad range of practical experience oneself – what John (in this volume) calls 'peripatetic knowledge'. Within the confines of an initial training course, the number of opportunities to teach in different contexts is strictly limited. Nevertheless, because of their knowledge of practice in a wide range of schools, those in higher education are particularly well-placed to provide students with 'indirect' practical experience of this sort.
4. The final contribution is different in that it concerns quality control – monitoring school-based work and making sure that schools are able effectively to perform their role. At the end of the day we must recognise that any one school or any one teacher has responsibility for initial teacher education only on a year by year basis. Schools, unless they are part of a SCITT scheme, have no statutory responsibilities for initial teacher education while those in higher education clearly do. It is, after all, universities and colleges that are validated and accredited. This means that however much schools are partners in the development of students' practical professional preparation, the ultimate responsibility for the quality of that training in most cases remains with HE. It is the responsibility of those in higher education to make sure that students are appropriately placed in school; that they are well-supported in school; that mentors give them the time that they should, and that their mentors have the right skills for working with them. Given that some schools will be better than others in supporting students and that mentors change – currently about 25 per cent per year nationally – there is a long-term role for HE here. To say that HE 'carries the can' and therefore has a responsibility to be involved in the detail of students' school-based work is not being arrogant (Berrill, 1994), it is to recognise that in an HE-based course those are lecturers' responsibilities.

So HE today retains a vitally important role in the development of students' practical professional preparation. University and college lecturers have built up a great deal of expertise in supporting students' practical learning in the ways I have outlined, and for the present at least, government legislation places the responsibility for quality control on them. Those in HE should not apologise for or minimise the importance of these contributions to practical professional training, for they are essential if the quality of initial teacher education is to be maintained.

However, we should also recognise that none of these functions, essential though they are, necessarily has to be undertaken by those in HE. Universities and colleges may be well-placed to take on these tasks; there may be important economies of scale in allowing them to do so; and they may have staff who have appropriate forms of expertise. The tasks I identified could, I would suggest, quite effectively be undertaken by a local education authority (LEA) or even perhaps by a consortium of schools. They are not tasks that are *in principle* something that only those in HE can do. Therefore, now I want to turn to the question of what, if anything, is distinctive about the contribution of HE to ITT.

The 'Essential' Nature of Higher Education

In developing an understanding of the distinctive contribution of HE to professional training, I must begin by asking what is distinctive about HE per se. As we have seen, traditional definitions of HE centred on certainty of knowledge and academic autonomy. In the field of teacher education, as elsewhere, these have been profoundly undermined. What then remains of the idea of HE at the end of the twentieth century? Once again, Barnett (1990) provides the most persuasive answer. Barnett argues that whatever the current challenges, the essential nature of HE is not compromised in its contemporary form if it maintains its commitment to the pursuit of truth. However, following Habermas (1970, 1974), Barnett suggests that truth is not an end point. 'Rather truth is the description we give to a particular kind of human transaction' (p.59).

This transaction, Barnett suggests, is a conversation, but not just any kind of conversation. Within such a conversation, participants can say what they want provided they are trying to get at the truth, provided that they are sincere, that they mean what they say, that their contribution is internally coherent and is intelligible to the other participants in the discussion.

Participation in this sort of intellectual debate imposes certain demands – people have to be heard, people have to listen attentively and participants need to be able to understand the discussion. Participants also need to be sincere, coherent and committed. Most fundamental of all, according to

Barnett, is the willingness to expose one's viewpoint to the critical gaze of others.

> *Intellectual debate is not cosy, or permissive; it is critical, judgemental and stern. Higher education in this view of truth, cannot simply be a matter of truths disseminated to the student; it is a much tougher and more demanding process. Through it, the student emerges able to begin to take up an informed position of his or her own, or at least to have some awareness of what that involves.* (p.60)

The commitment to the pursuit of truth in this manner is not merely something that is imposed on students within HE. Crucially it is a discipline that is also imposed on lecturers too.

> *So far as higher education is concerned, the idea of a discourse freed of unnecessary constraint works on two levels. First there is the discourse in which the student is a participant, with opportunities available to the student to form and communicate ideas either with other students or with teachers. Secondly there is the discourse of academics, a discourse which advances and sustains their own disciplinary communities.*

Higher Education and Initial Teacher Training

Whether Barnett's vision of higher education is, as he claims, appropriate for all disciplines and for all institutions, is open to debate. You could also question whether the pursuit of truth in the way that he defines it is self-evidently a 'good thing'. If the process of engaging in a critical discourse is to be raised to the pre-eminent principle of HE, it clearly needs more detailed justification than he provides. Nevertheless Barnett's analysis does throw significant light on the role of HE in ITT. Moreover, as I demonstrate below, his emphasis on the process of the pursuit of truth can be justified; it does have an important contribution to make to the vocational education of student teachers.

Following Barnett's line of argument I find it clear that an initial teacher education programme that involves a significant contribution from HE will be distinctive in two important ways. First, it will involve a commitment to engaging students in 'conversations' about educational practice – their own and other people's. These will be conversations where students are encouraged to pursue 'truth'; to offer their own views; to take an open and critical stance in their evaluation of practice; to form their own judgements, and to strike out on their own. In pursuing these objectives students will need to be sincere, coherent and committed and willing to expose their own practice and ideas to scrutiny.

Second, lecturers who support their professional development will themselves have something distinctive to offer. While the topics of professional knowledge they cover may well overlap with those offered by teachers, their approach may be very different for there is a demand on lecturers themselves to be engaged in the open and critical scrutiny of their professional knowledge. They too must actively engage in 'conversations' with other colleagues in their academic community through writing, research and scholarship; they too must be actively involved in the pursuit of 'truth'.

The potential contribution of HE to ITT is therefore very different from that of the school. For while individual teachers in schools may foster an open-minded commitment to the pursuit of truth, there is, as Maynard (Furlong and Maynard, 1995) demonstrates, no guarantee of this happening. This is because the essential purposes of schools and HEIs are fundamentally different. The school is not a seminar – far from it. For the practising teacher responsible for teaching *this* curriculum, to *these* children, *now*, the imperative is to act. If teachers stopped to question every action they simply could not teach. As a result, the essential contribution of teachers to professional development is fundamentally different from that of HE; it stems first and foremost from the skills, knowledge and understandings that derive from that need to act.

To recognise that higher education has a distinctive contribution to professional education does not necessarily provide a rationale for why that contribution is necessary. Having in a society some institutions dedicated to the pursuit of 'truth' in education may be of value to the profession at large in reasserting its own sense of professionalism, but why should students in the first stages of professional development need to engage with such complexities themselves? Given that the central purpose of initial teacher education is to provide a form of practical preparation that is directly vocational, I find that the value of insisting that students engage in this form of critical discourse is not self-evident.

In the final part of this chapter, I address this question and suggest that there are two fundamental reasons why such an approach is necessary for effective initial teacher education. The first derives from the fact that teaching is a highly complex activity; the second from the fact that teaching is a profoundly 'moral' activity.

The Fundamental Reasons

Controlling Complexity

In clarifying the value of higher education's contribution to teacher education I consider the limitations of the alternative 'technicist' approaches to professional training (Furlong, 1991). Can teaching, one must ask, be learned and carried out entirely as a 'technical' process? This is the argument put forward by a number of those who support SCITT schemes. For example, Hargreaves and his colleagues (Beardon *et al.*, 1992) argue that basic teaching can be undertaken at an entirely technical level; basic teaching is no more than 'competence'. It is because this is the case that *initial* teacher education can take place entirely in school. For Beardon and colleagues, the more complex dimensions of teaching, which they recognise are important, do not need to be, and are best *not* addressed until later in a teacher's career. HE, they argue, is not essential for initial teacher education; universities and colleges should focus instead on further professional development and leave initial teacher education largely to schools.

Research into how students learn to teach which I and Trisha Maynard (1995) recently carried out led us to a very different conclusion. Our research made us aware that teachers' practical professional knowledge is held at many different levels of sophistication and that this observation is vitally important for understanding how students learn to teach. Thus a 'bright idea', say, for teaching about life in Elizabethan Britain to year-5 pupils, may be understood at the level of a concrete recipe or routine – a strategy which students are capable of copying and implementing without fully appreciating why it takes the form that it does. Alternatively, the same lesson plan may be understood in rich and complex ways, drawing on a sophisticated appreciation of how children learn and a flexible understanding of the substantive and syntactic structure of historical knowledge incorporated within it. Recipes for teaching include and subsume within them these more complex educational, moral and other issues in ways that novice teachers seldom recognise.

Our research on the stages of learning to teach indicated that while it is possible to 'act like a teacher' simply by following routines and recipes established by others, becoming an *effective* teacher demands a deeper understanding of the processes involved in teaching and learning. The experienced teachers with whom we worked were able, even when they were unable to articulate the process to us or their students, to 'frame' (Schön, 1983, 1987) or interpret teaching situations by drawing on richer and more complex understandings. When confronted by new or difficult situations, they had a deeper understanding than their students had of the assumptions they were making in their framing. As a result, they were able to bring that teaching more directly under their own control.

Experienced teachers, in our study, demonstrated that competent teaching involves much more than behavioural skills; in learning to be effective, teachers have to develop a deeper and richer understanding of their teaching than is captured in the notion of 'competence'. They have to develop what Elliott (1990) calls 'intelligent skill knowledge'; knowledge which is still essentially practical but which involves an implicit appreciation of the complexities on which it is based. Students, if they are to begin to control their own teaching, do need to look beneath the surface of their own and other people's practice. Effective practice, even at an introductory level, demands a deeper understanding than the idea of 'competence' normally implies; through developing these deeper understandings, students progressively learn to bring their teaching under their own control.

Higher education, with its commitment to the forms of critical conversation I have outlined, has an essential role to play in supporting students' practical training for it can promote the development of these deeper understandings. Given their breadth of practical experience and that they too are involved in critical conversations, tutors have access to a powerful range of questions that can help students confront the complexities underlying practice. Through the challenge of such questioning, through being forced to look at their assumptions, articulate them and expose them to critical scrutiny, students learn to bring their practice more effectively under their own control. What I describe as the essential purposes of HE can be seen to be vital to the development of effective forms of practical training. Once again, because of their necessary commitment to action rather than reflection, there is no guarantee that schools will take on this role.

Teaching and Values

The second reason that the distinctive contribution of HE is essential in ITT is because teaching, in all its dimensions, is a value-laden activity. Values are not abstract and remote, they affect every decision you make as a teacher: what you teach, how you teach it, your aims and purposes, your ways of relating to children and to other teachers. Values in education are ubiquitous. As a result all examples of practice to which students are exposed when they are in school are by definition ideological. They are examples of *particular* forms of practice embodying *particular* aims, assumptions and values. This, however, is a problem if we remain committed to the idea of a pluralism of values within the profession with students developing their own professional commitments.

As part of professional training, students obviously need to be rooted in the realities of ideological commitment that come from working in particular classrooms and schools. If values are so central to our profession, then it is vitally important that we take their education seriously. To leave such education to chance, to assume that somehow student teachers will develop an informed and rational approach to educational values simply by being immersed in particular schools, is inadequate.

I suggest that the only sure way to secure pluralism within the profession is to insist that teacher education programmes are at least partly rooted in a culture *committed* to open-minded critique of practice. If values are to be fostered in a rational way, an exploration of values, including their own, must be a central part of students' professional preparation. Once again it is HE, with its commitment to open-minded critique, that is best placed to contribute to this aspect of training. As I have indicated, lecturers take part in a professional discourse when their own professional knowledge and commitments are constantly subject to scrutiny and debate. It is this process that moves them on. Through their involvement in HE, students engage in the same process – with each other and with lecturers. As a result they can come to have a clearer understanding of the assumptions and values they are implicitly and explicitly supporting in their school practice. It seems to me that only by recognising and confronting these values – by discussing the aims as well as the means of education – can pluralism within the profession be ensured. Not to take this aspect of professional education seriously would, I suggest, be damaging to our profession and eventually to our democracy as well.

Conclusion

The Challenge and The Prize of Partnership

The challenges of what has happened in recent years to teacher education in England and Wales are immense. Schools are now being asked to take much greater responsibility for the professional education of young teachers than they have ever done in the past. Such a demand has considerable implications both in resources and professional commitments. Yet, as I argue elsewhere (Furlong *et al.*, 1988, 1994; Furlong and Maynard, 1995), if the quality of the professional preparation of the next generation of teachers is to be maintained, then the contribution of schools is vital. To a very considerable extent the future of the profession is now in their hands.

In this chapter, I argued that the challenges to HE, although of a different kind, have been equally significant. The contribution of HE to professional education is profoundly undermined both sociologically and epistemologically, so much so that a few universities and colleges have started to question their continued involvement. This I regard as deeply worrying: worrying for the long-term quality of the profession and worrying for the quality of the education of our children. Universities and colleges must, for the reasons I have outlined, continue to work closely with the teaching profession in their communities and teachers in those communities must insist that they do. Equally worrying is that although the vast majority of HEIs remains committed to ITT, an increasing number do not seem to have any clear rationale for what their continued participation can and should be in the changed circumstances that face them.

What I try to demonstrate in this chapter is that HE does have a continued and vitally important role to play in the professional education of teachers. However, what is clear is that that contribution is and will continue to be very different from before. There is no going back to the certainties and autonomy of the past.

If HE is to deliver its promise in relation to student teachers then it must do more than it did in the 1980s when it stood behind closed doors but became largely practically oriented. Schools can do that job equally well if not better. What HE must do, through its new found partnerships, is engage in detailed debates about professional practice – both that of students and teachers themselves. Such debates must take place both inside the classroom and in the seminar room; the notion of partnership must be carried into the detail of educational practice for the benefit of students, teachers and lecturers alike. Such an engagement is immensely challenging to those in HE for it is no longer possible for them to hide behind the certainties of propositional knowledge untroubled by the complexities of educational practice. It is, I suggest, equally challenging to bring the culture of HE into school, encouraging teachers to expose their practice to critical scrutiny. The promise of establishing a close and routine dialogue between HE and schools is immense. It is the prize of developing a more genuine discipline of education than we have had in the past – one that is at once both practical and theoretical. From my visits to teacher education courses up and down the country I see the first, faltering signs of this new flowering. Other disciplines that are feeling equally uncertain in the changed circumstances that face higher education would do well to watch how we in education respond to these challenges in the years to come.

References

Alexander, R (1984) 'Innovation and Continuity in the Initial Teacher Education Curriculum', in R Alexander, M Craft and J Lynch (eds) *Changes in Teacher Education: Context and Provision since Robbins*. New York: Holt, Rinehart & Winston.

Barnett, R (1990) *The idea of Higher Education*. Buckingham: Open University Press.

Beardon, T, Booth, M, Hargreaves, D. and Reiss, M (1992) 'School-Led Teacher Training: The Way Forward', *Cambridge Education Papers No 2*. Cambridge: University of Cambridge Department of Education.

Berrill, M (1994) Review of *Cambridge Journal of Education* special edition 22(3), 'Initial Teacher Education at the Crossroads', *Cambridge Journal of Education*, 24(1).

Calderhead, J (1989) 'Reflective Teaching and Teacher Education', *Teaching and Teacher Education*, 5(1): 43–51.

Department of Education and Science (DES) (1984) *Initial Teacher Training: Approval of Courses (Circular 3/84)*. London: DES.

DES (1989) *Initial Teacher Training: Approval of Courses (Circular 24/89)*. London: DES.

Department for Education (DFE) (1992) *Initial Teacher Training (Secondary Phase) (Circular 9/92)*. London: DFE.

DFE (1993a) *School-Centred Initial Teacher Training (SCITT). Letter of Invitation. 5.3.93*. London: DFE.

DFE (1993b) *The Initial Training of Primary School Teachers: New Criteria for Course Approval (Circular 14/93)*. London: DFE.

Elliott, J (1990) *Competency-Based Training and the Education of the Professions: Is a Happy Marriage Possible?* Norwich: University of East Anglia, Centre for Applied Research in Education (unpublished paper).

Furlong, VJ (1991) 'Reconstructing Professionalism: Ideological Struggle in Initial Teacher Education', in M Arnot and L Barton (eds) *Voicing Concerns: Sociological Perspectives on Contemporary Educational Reforms.* Wallingford: Triangle.

Furlong, VJ, Hirst, PH, Pocklington, K and Miles, S (1988) *Initial Teacher Training and the Role of the School.* Milton Keynes: Open University Press.

Furlong, VJ and Maynard, T (1995) *Mentoring Student Teachers: The Growth of Professional Knowledge.* London: Routledge.

Furlong, VJ, Whitty, G, Barrett, E, Barton, L and Miles, S (1994) 'Integration and Partnership in Initial Teacher Education – Dilemmas and Possibilities', *Research Papers in Education,* **9**(3).

Habermas, J (1970) 'Towards a Theory of Communicative Competence', *Inquiry,* **13**.

Habermas, J (1974) *Theory and Practice.* London: Heinemann.

Hargreaves, D (1994) 'A New Professionalism: The Synthesis of Professional and Institutional Development', *Teaching and Teacher Education,* **10**(4): 423–438.

James, Lord (1972) *Teacher Education and Training (The James Report).* London: HMSO.

Lawlor, S (1990) *Teachers Mistaught.* London: Centre for Policy Studies.

O'Hear, A (1988) *Who Teaches the Teachers?* London: Social Affairs Unit.

Patrick, H, Bernbaum, G and Reid, K (1982) *The Structure and Process of Initial Teacher Education within Universities in England and Wales.* Leicester: University of Leicester, School of Education.

Schön, D (1983) *The Reflective Practitioner.* New York: Basic Books.

Schön, D (1987) *Educating the Reflective Practitioner.* San Francisco, CA: Jossey-Bass.

Wilkin, M. (1991) 'The Development of Partnership in the United Kingdom', in M Booth, VJ Furlong and M Wilkin (eds) *Partnership in Initial Teacher Training.* London: Cassell.

CHAPTER 12

THE DEMANDS OF A PROFESSIONAL PRACTICE AND PREPARATION FOR TEACHING

Paul H Hirst

Many distinguishing features have been suggested for demarcating professions from other occupational groups. Of these, two I suggest are central to what are seen as the great caring professions such as medicine, law and education. First, these professions are concerned with achieving for individuals some end which is held to be a fundamental, universal good like health or justice. Second, the achievement of that good for individuals necessitates specialised knowledge, understanding and skills which individuals cannot themselves, in general, be expected to possess or readily acquire. In medicine or law, achieving the desired good in a given case requires both careful discernment of what would constitute health or justice in this instance and the successful pursuit of that particular goal. In our contemporary context, the general concepts of both health and justice are in major respects disputable. Even where there is agreement at this general level, their significance in particular cases is often difficult to determine. What is more, the achievement of these goals is frequently a complex and highly specialised business. It is little wonder then that sophisticated university education and training is considered an essential part of basic professional preparation if practice in these areas is to be handled intelligently and effectively.

Where education is concerned, the problems of determining clearly the general good it serves, the specific goals for particular clients or pupils and the best way to achieve these are at least as complex and difficult. What is more, only in relatively recent times have these become the subjects of sustained, systematic study which sought to explore thoroughly the nature of the enterprise. Not surprisingly, the achievements of this work have to date been limited. The response of some to this situation has not been for more informed and detailed study by all aspiring professionals, rather they have seen the demands on professionals as way beyond what contemporary knowledge and expertise can provide, advocating a simplistic and reductionist account of educational goals and procedures with minimal practical training to match. Such an approach, however, is merely an evasion of the demands that contemporary professionals constantly face whether they like it or not. To fail to equip them from the start with as informed a grasp as possible of the nature and significance of the activities in which they are engaged is surely irresponsible. To fail to equip young entrants to the profession with as clear and critical a grasp of at least the most defensible goals and practices of education leaves them and their pupils at the mercy of prejudice and ill-considered ideology. It is also to render almost impossible the systematic development of education in any truly coherent and rational way.

This essentially distorting and damaging reconstitution of both education and the professional preparation of teachers has been pushed hard for political reasons against almost universal opposition from those who have closely examined the issues involved. What has, however, weakened the force of that opposition is a growing recognition among both academic educational theorists and self-critical professionals that the foundations of their own approach to educational theory and practice may well have been widely misconceived. Throughout the postwar period, a particular paradigm of what rational practice demands in all areas of human activity dominated attempts to establish educational goals and procedures. With that paradigm now undergoing major criticism, it is not surprising if educational practices, like those of many other professional areas, are increasingly seen as, at present, insecurely grounded. In this chapter I wish to argue that a new paradigm for rational practices must be formulated and that this is now taking shape. I maintain that this indicates forcefully how the professional practices of education must be reconceived and what kind of preparation professionals must henceforth receive. It is only within this new conception that I think we can now begin to formulate clearly what the proper role of higher education (HE) must be in initial professional education.

In the 1960s, the emerging postwar consensus about the general good that education pursues was most clearly set out. Under the spell of the rationalist climate of the time, the aim of education was seen as providing the foundations of a good life for everyone by promoting their development as rationally autonomous individuals. To that end it was seen as necessary to initiate them into the achievements of reason in knowledge and understanding and to promote the application of such knowledge in all areas of experience and action. The good life was seen as the rational life, the product of each individual applying in her or his own context the ever-increasing knowledge and understanding provided by the physical sciences, the social sciences, the humanities, the arts, religion and so on. Such studies could provide a grasp of the ends and means for the good life, and the disciplined assertion of the will could bring it all about. In these terms the professional's role in education was seen as judging rationally what knowledge, understanding and skills should be pursued by each individual at each stage, judging how best that pursuit might be conducted and then setting about this enterprise to maximum effect. To fulfil this role, obviously professionals must themselves have mastered the knowledge, understanding and skills they were promoting but, in addition, must have mastered the knowledge, understanding and skills necessary to making rational, justifiable, educational decisions and providing justifiable educational activities.

This specific professional mastery was seen as to be found only in the disciplined philosophical, psychological and sociological study of educational aims and processes and by the systematic application of the findings of these foundation studies in practice.

This ambitious, seemingly clear-cut enterprise to develop education as a sophisticated professional practice began to take shape in some impressive work in these so-called foundation theoretical disciplines, but before long it became apparent that these studies could not begin to provide clear answers to the immensely difficult theoretical questions they addressed. Even when there seemed to be answers, these could not begin to add up to the answering of the extremely complex practical questions they were expected to tackle. What was more, it began to emerge that the rationalist foundations of this whole enterprise might themselves be rationally untenable.

Three of its major tenets have now come under severe attack and are widely considered unsustainable:

- its doctrines of the good life
- the nature and function of reason
- the relationship of individuals to society.

Yet rationalist notions of education and its professional pursuit presuppose these very doctrines as providing the terms in which education is good and its practices can be adequately conceived. If we are to make real progress in our understanding of professionalism and preparation for it in this whole area, there seems no escaping the reconsideration of these basic doctrines and their educational significance. In the first place, the rationalistic approach very briefly outlined above takes the exercise of the cognitive capacities of human beings as fundamental to all areas of experience within the good life. Other capacities, those of say feeling and affect, will and action, are considered to operate properly only when informed by, or when subservient to, the achievements of our power to conceptualise, form propositions and principles, make judgements of truth and validity, achieve knowledge, understanding and rational belief and action. In these terms the good life is essentially a life that is ordered in all respects by the conclusions of reason, acting independently of and spectatorially on all other human attributes. The rational ends and means for a good life are considered to be cognitively, indeed theoretically, determined, our disciplined executive capacities then being exercised to realise our rational conclusions in the ordering of our lives individually and collectively.

Such a high view of the place and function of cognition in our lives is far from easy to defend. Is it the case that human good is to be found in what satisfies the independent exercise of our cognitive capacities with everything else in life made subservient to its demands? If human nature is instead conceived of as having a diversity of attributes that carry with them their own possibilities for satisfaction and fulfilment, then a very different picture of the good life begins to emerge.

Human beings can be understood as endowed with wide-ranging physical, psychological and social needs whose satisfactions constitute of themselves forms of human good. We have many diverse capacities also, not only those for cognition but those for sensation and feeling, for activity and construction, for relationships and social patternings as well. The exercise of these all carry with them their own distinctive kinds of fulfilment.

In these terms it makes sense to see the good life as a life that achieves the greatest human satisfaction across our diverse possibilities overall and in the long term. If that is so, then the place of reason is not that of the dominant capacity whose satisfaction alone is paramount, rather it is one of a range of capacities and one that can, above all, be instrumental in our achieving the overall fulfilment of our natures. Reason is then understood as concerned not with the formulation of theoretically constructed ends and means but as the instrument for the articulation of wide-ranging practical ends and the means for achieving these. This richer, more adequate view of human good has progressively made the rationalist view seem like an overintellectual myth, an ideal construct that may be hugely impressive when carefully elaborated, but one quite incapable of practical realisation because of its inadequate conception of human nature. On the richer view of the good life, the good that education seeks can no longer be mapped in the knowledge, understanding and skills that make the rationalist life possible. Instead the good for education will be seen as a matter of each of us developing our capacities across that range and in that pattern which will form a satisfying and fulfilling life overall. That will be a very different enterprise, particularly as the nature and function of reason within it can no longer be construed adequately in narrow, rationalist terms.

A second central feature of rationalism is its persistent restriction of reason to the pursuit of propositional truths and justified beliefs. On this basis, understanding, experience and action are rationally ordered only when thought and practice conform to what is objectively known in propositional terms. The good life is thus conformity in practical living to what is judged to be the case empirically, morally, aesthetically and so on, as that is expressed in abstracted, theoretical truths that can be formulated in shared symbolic systems. Yet there are the strongest grounds for judging that what it is rational to do practically is not discerned by first determining a set of justified propositions expressing a body of practical principles that are then applied. In our earliest experience our cognitive capacities come to be exercised in classifying entities and situations that do or do not satisfy our basic needs. In the interests of our practically attaining certain desired goals, we understand our world, its objects, events and our own movements within it. Far from our ends being first understood propositionally, our ends are given in the satisfactions we need and desire. Our understanding is harnessed to and determined by these ends. We articulate in practical propositions what fulfils rather than frustrates our needs, thus discovering in practice what it is rational to pursue. Having a reason for an action is thus basically the product of practical experience in which we discern where satisfaction is to be found. Progressively our practical grasp on our world not only expands but becomes increasingly differentiated with our needs becoming more specifically articulated and developed.

By experiment we discover and construct new, richer and more complex expressions of our desires and their satisfaction. Since we are social beings who have not only interlocking needs but common needs and capacities, the process of trial and error has led to the establishment of great webs of social practices developed for the best achievement of human satisfactions. In different societies, and in any one complex society, practices have emerged that serve to answer our needs and expanding interests in alternative ways: not in any simple direct sense either but in inter-related networks of varied needs and satisfying activities.

By a *practice*, I mean a coherent pattern of activity socially developed, traditionally or by deliberate institution, engaged in for achieving certain forms of satisfaction or goals which may be consciously formulated only in part. Engaging in this may involve elements of knowledge, belief, judgement, criteria of success, principles, skills, dispositions, feelings, elements encompassing any or all of our capacities and their achievements. These elements are inextricably locked together in any given practice, each taking its distinctive character in part from its relationship to other elements, the whole constituting the very nature of the practice. Such practices can range from the primarily physical to the primarily academic or theoretical, from relatively simple skills to complex professional activities. They are typically nested with simpler pursuits subsumed under more complex wholes, though a larger whole is never a mere sum of its parts. In that it is of the essence of practices that they develop in the doing, their development can involve changes in many of their interlocked constitutive elements, changes that may be of considerable personal significance for individual participants. The public features of practices, the objects, movements and events they involve, especially the shared language that articulates them, identifies them and makes them rationally developable.

In common language we created practical discourse that in its concepts, propositions, rules and principles encapsulates our practical experience of our world. That understanding in practical discourse expresses what is discovered in the pursuit of satisfaction and fulfilment. In this discourse, practical principles are the outcome of successful practice, generalisations are valid only insofar as they capture what successful practice entails. The more complex the practice and the more it is connected with differences in human attributes and differences in contexts, then the less such generalisations can possibly hope to capture what the practice entails. Yet it is in these terms that reason operates for the development and conduct of practices for the achievement of human good. In the critical examination of practices in the terms of practical discourse itself, new and more rational, that is successful, practices can be conceived and experimentally assessed. This is not merely the pursuit of more successful means for reaching existing goals but the pursuit of new specific goals and activities that more adequately embody what is our good.

In this pursuit, the activities of practical reason must be sharply distinguished from those of theoretical reason and its concerns. As distinct from the achievement of successful practices, theoretical reason is directed to the achievement of theoretical truths, of propositions expressing in detached, objective, spectatorial terms what is the case. To this end concepts and propositions are developed solely in understanding and explaining our world, in the pursuit of truth irrespective of any practical purposes. Concepts are formed identifying objects and qualities of situations and events independently of their significance for human needs or interests other than those of the desire to understand and explain. This very abstraction from other practices is of the essence of theoretical reason and means that its achievements are in themselves incapable of generating successful practices of a different character.

The pursuits and achievements of practices serving non-cognitive goals cannot begin to be captured in merely theoretical terms, but if theoretical reason cannot itself provide the basis for generating rational practices that is not to say it cannot provide crucially important knowledge and understanding of ourselves and our physical and social context. Such knowledge sets out the boundaries, the framework within which rational practices can be developed. In practices for the satisfaction and fulfilment of our physical needs and interests, the physical sciences have so generated theoretical knowledge that the generation of rational practices has thereby been transformed. Yet such developments as those of modern technology demand far more than abstract knowledge from fundamental sciences. They demand complex and sophisticated practical experiment directly concerned with attaining practical goals. Rational practices come in the exercise of practical reason that recognises the nature and limits of the given within which it must work. Where practices for the satisfaction and fulfilment of psychological and social needs are concerned, the theoretical forms of knowledge and understanding available in the disciplines of the social sciences, the humanities and the arts are crucial to rational development. The place of such theoretical insights in the generation of practices is difficult to disentangle. Yet without the illumination that theoretical knowledge can provide, the experimental development of rational practices in any area is proceeding on inadequately examined presuppositions. To that extent such development is in major respects liable to be not only blinkered but seriously misconceived. The process of developing rational forms of living has been and still is manifestly tortuous and alarmingly random in many areas of personal and social concern.

We have yet to learn effectively two linked truths: that rational practices for the achievement of our good must in all areas be practically, not theoretically, developed, but also that if our efforts are not to be constantly thwarted they must be illuminated by all the insights fundamental theoretical critique can provide. The altogether wider conception of reason that is here outlined as operating in two distinct but related modes leads inevitably to a reformulation of our notions of the good life and the good that education can legitimately pursue.

At the centre of both notions must be found not the bodies of theoretical knowledge and understanding plus the skills of application that rationalists demand, but that vast web of rational practices that are socially developed in the pursuit of satisfying and fulfilling lives. Within this web, the practices of pursuing theoretical knowledge and understanding have a vital place but in no sense is that their primary or basic role. In these terms the good life for us individually is a question of achieving satisfaction and fulfilment overall and, in the long term, through engagement in those rational practices that meet our personal character and circumstances. The good that education pursues is then for each of us a matter of initiation into those particular practices that can constitute our good life, respecting fully their nature as complex rationally developed wholes.

If we are now beginning to shift our notions of human nature and of reason so that education is seen as a matter of fulfilling practices, there is yet a third rationalist notion that has ensnared us for too long. In spite of massive evidence to the contrary, we continue to hold to an impossible individualism as if we were all in essence isolated, free, atomic beings associating with others in pursuing our individual interests only insofar as we choose. On the contrary, careful thought reveals that we are by nature dependent on physical and social relationships with others, so that from the start every aspect of our lives is socially structured.

In huge measure, our natural physical, psychological and social needs have an openness that means they take specific shape and structure under social influences. The food we eat, the physical movements we make, the relationships into which we enter are in their specific character socially organised. The concepts we employ in making sense of our world and ourselves are not individually and privately created but are socially constructed and handed on through language and socially patterned situations and activities. To develop as a person is to come to share in those socially constructed practices that have been progressively developed to satisfy human needs and interests. We are then social beings not only in our given nature but in our very character as persons. In thought, emotion and action, in wants, desires and interests we are socially formed, and it is only in relation to that externally and socially structured world that our lives can coherently be conducted.

With our very selves patterned in this way by the practices of our social context, our good, our satisfaction and fulfilment can only come by living in relation to those practices. Not that we are incapable of exploratory initiatives in exercising our capacities or that we must necessarily conform to the content of the practices we encounter, but the practices provide the terms in which our lives must be built and against which or within which we must find or form ourselves. The good life is thus fully constituted by the pursuit of living in relation to those social practices through which our socially formed natures find overall and in the long run their satisfaction and fulfilment. In no sense can we cognitively stand back from these practices and freely choose our lives.

At any stage we are the product of those practices into which we have been intentionally or unintentionally initiated, and it is in exploratory response to these and other practices which surround us that we must find our way. Even then, the terms of our exploratory initiatives and reflections are socially patterned. So the good life is a question of our discovering in practice, in the activities of living, that form of life that is most fulfilling among the rationally developed and developing practices of our society. That discovery is itself a rational practice we must progressively master as we mature if the pursuit is to be successfully conducted among the irrational and rational practices which surround us. We must thus each engage in the construction of a personal narrative in which we form a coherent and meaningful response to our context.

From this notion of the good life, the good that education seeks must be the individual's initiation into constructing just such a personal narrative in the social practices available. Some are clearly necessary for a satisfying life in our context, being practices to do with such requirements as the maintenance of physical health and safety, the basic management of possessions and money, the conduct of effective communication with others and the sustaining of personal and wider social relationships. All relate very directly to basic needs and the satisfactory exercise of given capacities. Education must surely seek to initiate everyone into these. Beyond these though are the alternative and optional practices that can constitute the substance of a richly fulfilling life according to individual endowments and given social circumstances. In these areas, education must clearly offer as wide an opportunity as possible. The complex practices that constitute the goals of education are thus of great diversity, but they cannot be composed to form an individual 'narrative' good life without initiation also into that higher order rational practice that can continuously discern and achieve one's personal good overall in the present and foreseeable future.

Such a picture of the good life and the good for education presupposes the existence of rational practices as public social deposits. It sees these as embodied in observable objects, events and actions and in practical discourse. Their rational creation and development is seen as a matter of practical experiment which involves the public exercise of shared critical reflection in both practical and theoretical terms. In this reflection the proper exercise of practical reason can be no more an individual matter than is the exercise of theoretical reason in the question of theoretical truths. The product in these two domains is radically different in character. As said earlier, practices and the satisfactions they serve are only in part linguistically expressible and the propositional truths and principles of practical discourse are loaded with affective and conative purport in addition to their cognitive meaning.

In addition, practical concepts have application that is restricted by the common features of the participants in practices and by their social and individual, as much as their physical, contexts. The justification of practical propositions and principles is quite different in character from that of theoretical propositions and principles. Yet none of this should be taken to obscure the fact that the commonalities there are among participants and contexts in any given society, both as a whole and among major subgroups, are considerable. It would be surprising if things were otherwise granted on the one hand common, naturally given needs and capacities and a largely common natural environment on the other. The existence of many domains of rational practice within any advanced society is thus unremarkable. But the systematic pursuit and development of such practices has not infrequently proved elusive. What is surely needed repeatedly is much more carefully conducted and more critically examined practical experiment engaged in publicly by significant social groups. What we tend to get instead is, on the one hand, ill-considered ideological or doctrinaire social change or, on the other, experimentation by individuals concerned primarily with the development of their own personal practices. We need well-considered experimentation in which more refined discourse is generated to embody widely applicable practices open to public examination, criticism and transmission. In numerous areas of social life, including education, there is at present little commitment to serious rational development of this kind.

What has been said about the nature and development of the rational practices which the good life and the good for education presuppose, has implications for how individuals can rationally act within those practices. This manifestly involves the mastery of the practices in their many complex interlocking features including their public discourse and the structuring of personal capacities that they demand. What that entails can only be discovered in attempting the internally coherent conduct of practices in the pursuit of the satisfactions and achievements with which they are concerned. This is necessarily a reflective process that recognises the differences in situations that are experienced and sensed as much as conceptually identified in analytically discreet terms. Practical discourse and public activity, however, are necessary instruments for creating and maintaining personal judgement and action that are adequate to particular circumstances.

What is required is the refinement of these individually through personal critical use of the discourse and development of more sensitive actions based on your own and others' practice. In most areas of life we come to much early mastery of practices in the disciplines of family and social living and in the conversations and communication of every day. These implicitly operate to a significant extent in practical reason to varying degrees of validity. For each of us, a great deal turns on the rational adequacy of the social practices of those about us and the range and depth of critically reflected insight they display. Beyond these influences our development as rational beings is, clearly, profoundly dependent on the formal education we receive and within that on the professional abilities of the teachers we encounter. If these are based on mistaken rationalist notions of the good that education should pursue for us, and of the means to that end, or on mere personal judgement, the prospects for attaining individually and collectively a satisfying and fulfilling form of life must thereby be seriously hampered. What is now needed is a new professionalism grounded in the new concept of the good that education seeks and of its practices built on the primacy of practical rather than theoretical reason.

If the good for education is reconceived as I have sought to outline it, as a matter of initiating individuals into those established social practices in which they can construct a good, a rational life, then the professionalism of teachers must be directed to their discerning and achieving that goal. They need a personal mastery of those practices they are handing on, but their professionalism rests in the mastery of the practices of initiation in which they can rationally determine and pursue their pupils' specific goals and activities. Those professional practices of initiation are, however, not to be conceived of as basically individual constructions. Individual professional practice can take place only as a rational enterprise insofar as it is the teacher's rational exercise of a practice that has been rationally developed as a public deposit. Teachers must themselves be initiated into mastery of the best available, the most rationally defensible existing professional practices. In these they must come to participate in the rational reflective process of discerning and pursuing their pupils' specific good.

Having for so long implicitly and at times explicitly embraced rationalist notions of educational good, we have professionally built up practices for initiating pupils into forms of theoretical knowledge above all. Even there the body of successful practices exists in a relatively unsophisticated form as their systematic development has itself been neglected or rationalistically misconceived. Yet the demands for successful practice will out, and at all levels. Concern, enquiry and experiment has persistently sought the furtherance of experientially successful practices in initiating pupils into major areas of educational good. With the increasing recognition of the inadequacies of the rationalist approach to professionalism, practical professionalism comes more and more to the fore. Public discussion, writing and research directly concerned with educational practice has increased considerably. Analysis of practice in the concepts it itself generates is becoming much more widespread. The idea of a reflective practitioner is even fashionable, but the demands of rationally reflective practice are as yet little understood. I argue that the difference between rationalistic reflection that seeks to apply the propositional achievements of theoretical reason and practical reflection that engages in the achieved practices and discourse of practical reason lies at the heart of the matter. Without a sharper grasp of what this distinction entails, genuine advance in professionalism, I suggest, will remain haphazard and uncertain. To conceive of professionalism as reflective practice rooted in an array of specialist knowledge – theoretical, propositional knowledge and practical knowledge – is to capitulate to the rationalist myth. Instead we must reconceive the notion of reflective practice according to the demands of the exercise of practical reason.

The conception of professionalism here outlined requires two major developments. In the first place it requires the commitment of professionals to the establishment in much more coherent, recognised, public ways of a body of practices that can for pupils demonstrably achieve mastery that contributes to their good lives. That necessitates far more open professional collaboration in critical enquiry than is currently practised. It necessitates too the leadership that can only come from ever-more sophisticated advanced study, research and experiment directly concerned with the rational development of educational practices. On the one hand, that work needs to focus directly on educational practices themselves as understood and assessed in practical discourse itself. On the other hand, it needs to engage in examination of the basic theoretical presuppositions that underpin our educational practice and its discourse. As argued earlier, it is only if experimental practice is informed by justifiable philosophical, psychological, sociological and other theoretical beliefs that it can hope to generate practices adequate to achieving personal and social goods of the kind that education seeks.

Granted professional commitment to the corporate building up of a body of rational educational practices, there must, in the second place, be alongside that the training of individuals to engage adequately in these practices. Mastery of any practice, it has been argued, can only come by engaging in that practice itself, assimilating its concepts, experiential awareness, discourse, judgements, actions, principles, dispositions and all the other content of qualities and achievements that, as a whole, constitutively make the practice what it is. To practice professionally as a teacher requires initiation into the best, the most rationally justifiable, practices established in some areas of education.

The individual exercise of the practice, however, is manifestly a complex employment of the practice's elements in constantly critically reflective activity. The best way to initiate would-be teachers into this is itself an inadequately developed practice. Yet in seeking to develop that in critical reflection on experience to date, I find that it is hard to escape the conclusion that such initiation demands teacher trainers with the most sophisticated analytical grasp available of the inter-related elements of the practices of teaching. Only with such an analytical grasp can trainers begin to understand what implicit and explicit features of the desired practices would teachers require to master. Only with this grasp can they really hope to help students engaged in training to discern in their own and others' practice the complex good they are pursuing in a given context, how activities can be directed to achieve that end and how to assess the outcome. Though the rational practice of teaching requires analytically reflective capacities of a high order, the training of such teachers demands the explicit exercise of these to a far greater degree. In the daily activities of teaching, many crucial elements of the practice must come to operate unconsciously in a manner thoroughly appropriate to rational practice in this context, practice well able to promote the maximum good for pupils. In professional training, students' many relevant capacities and qualities have to be developed or reshaped for appropriate exercise in professional practice. Successful teacher trainers need to be able consciously to discern what a student's development may require across the full range of the practice's demands. Such analytical expertise, though it presupposes high professionalism in the practices of teaching, is not in this form a necessary part of a teacher's daily professional practice. It can be expected only of those who make such analysis their specialist concern.

The analytical mastery in an area of educational practice is, however, not only vital to professional training; it is equally crucial in the critically reflective process central to the rational development of socially established practices. Therefore, it is not surprising that, out of much experience in the professional training of teachers and the study of education, universities have developed specialists in the analysis of areas of educational practice and the use of that in teacher training and in the experimental development of the practices of teaching. Clearly, such specialism can only be successfully deployed in those areas of university teaching and research if used in direct involvement with practice itself. Recent university-based developments in professional education and research, and development work on teaching, have sought to establish relationships between schools and universities that make both these areas of activity genuinely collaborative. Suitably structured, such joint work is surely set to provide just the context in which the new view of professionalism for which I argue can flourish and bear fruit. Just what pattern the professional preparation of teachers can best take is still uncertain and how best within that students can be initiated into the critically reflective practice of teaching needs detailed practical experiment and research.

Fundamental philosophical reflection on our past professional practices suggests that they have presupposed untenable rationalist beliefs. What we need to do now is to build anew our notions of the educational good that professionals must pursue, the practices they can best engage in to that end and the form of professional preparation that this requires. In all this, it is the primacy of practical over theoretical reason in all matters of education and teaching that must be our guide.

CHAPTER 13

THE UNIVERSITY, THE ACADEMIC TRADITION, AND EDUCATION

David McNamara

During the past decade educationists working within the university system have experienced two sorts of substantial change. First, as the contributions to this volume testify, government control of the teacher training has become more intrusive. The 'reforms' first introduced by Sir Keith Joseph (DES, 1984) were taken further by his successors as Secretary of State for Education. It may be a hostage to fortune to suggest that they have now reached completion with the establishment of the Teacher Training Agency (TTA) and the consequent removal of the funding for teacher education from the Higher Education Funding Council for England (HEFCE) and the transfer of a significant proportion of the teacher-education budget to the schools.

Second, the universities within which teacher educators engage in their teaching and research, have, themselves, undergone unprecedented change. Over a short-time scale the established universities and the polytechnics merged into a single system with common funding, mass higher education (HE) was introduced in the UK, and unit costs were reduced. Throughout this time, universities in general and teacher education in particular, were relatively powerless to resist various 'reforms' (which I acknowledge, have not necessarily been detrimental).

As has possibly been inevitable during this period, teacher educators attempted, as moderate people concerned with the quality of their students' professional preparation, to accommodate successive imposed modifications. They have, quite reasonably, assumed that to be seen to be cooperating with government policy in a positive and productive manner would result in a period of stability during which forced revisions could be consolidated and subsequently evaluated. This has not been the case; during a period of some 10 years the Council for the Accreditation of Teacher Education

(CATE) modified its own criteria on two further occasions (see DES, 1989a; DFE, 1992, 1993; and for incisive criticism by a member of CATE: MacIntyre, 1991) only to face its own demise when the TTA was established. It would seem that nothing that teacher educators did do or could have done has prevented them being successively 'reformed' within an HE system which itself is undergoing significant change. While educationists should be particularly concerned for their own area of professional expertise they must also appreciate that from the point of view of university managers, facing continuing financial pressures themselves, teacher education is a field in which there is a measure of concern over its future.

During this period of unprecedented uncertainty, the formal study of education must continue to be located within the university system. As I shall hope to demonstrate, this is more than a matter of professional self-interest. At a time when we may need to fight for the study of education's survival within the university sector it becomes necessary to establish what constitutes the essential core of university educationists' contribution to the study of education and teacher education, and why it is necessary for educational studies to retain its presence within the higher education system. If universities are to be convinced that it is essential for the study of education to continue to prosper within higher education then educationists must establish their unique contribution which can only be effectively undertaken within the university sector.

Teacher Education as Political Plaything

Teacher education does not have a secure place within HE. To appreciate teacher education's somewhat precarious situation within universities we must look beyond our immediate parochial experience. Until comparatively recently graduates in the UK could enter the teaching profession without any formal training (for a brief history, see Dent, 1977); it is only since 1970 (for primary) and 1974 (for secondary) that there has been a compulsory requirement that graduates must be trained before being able to teach in maintained schools. Within a wider context there is considerable variation in the extent to which nation-states invest in teacher education and the degree of involvement of the university sector in that training (Tisher and Wideen, 1990; Gilroy and Smith, 1993). International data indicate that the average age when primary teachers complete their teacher training is 19 (Garrido, 1986, p.189). Whatever the way in which teachers are trained, a common phenomenon throughout the developed world is the attempt by government to gain greater control over the teacher-training system (Gilroy and Smith, 1993).

What we have been experiencing since the mid-1980s is not unique to the UK (Popkewitz, 1993). The national case studies generated by

Popkewitz's comparative research project demonstrate that however professionally worthwhile the aspirations of contemporary governments towards teacher education, the inevitable upshot is that they seek greater control over the system. Changing teacher education in one way or another in the name of development or progress is a habit acquired by politicians in all contemporary industrial societies. Perhaps the most telling illustration of the fickleness of government policy is the example of France 'reforming' its teacher-education system by bringing teacher training into newly created university institutions at precisely the time when the British government is seeking to shift teacher education away from the universities and towards school-based training (Judge *et al.*, 1994).

The historical and comparative study of teacher education demonstrates that the university has no agreed or necessary contribution to make to the professional preparation of teachers, and that governments are prone to 'reform' teachers' training by changing the status quo, whatever this may be. History suggests that teacher education in developed countries proceeds through a reasonably well-defined pattern (Zeichner, 1983; Liston and Zeichner, 1991) with the balance between 'theory' and 'practice' changing in a cyclical manner, with consequent adjustments in the involvement of HE in teacher training. We can predict that politicians will continue to employ a policy of 'reforming' teacher education, whatever its condition, as one of the ways in which to demonstrate to their electorates that they are concerned to improve the quality of the education system (McNamara, 1993). It is a comparatively inexpensive policy to implement and teacher educators have little power to resist. Government can always find overseas examples to justify their 'reforms', such as the New Jersey model of school-based training (DES, 1989c) and play down those examples which are inconvenient for its cause, such as France (DES, 1989b).

While teacher educators should maintain that the quality of teachers' professional education is enhanced by locating it within the HE system (as they rightly do in the chapters in this volume) we have to accept that the university has no self-evident or necessary claim to take the major responsibility for teacher training. It is demonstrably the case that other parties are now taking on aspects of teacher training, which, until recently, were accepted as the preserve of HE. It would be presumptuous, at this stage, to claim that the schools are not making a success of school-based training.[1]

If teacher education is to have a central and enduring contribution to make to the study of education and professional training it is necessary, in the first instance, to eschew making the case on grounds of quality and attempt to ascertain the essential contribution of the university which cannot be undertaken by other parties.

The Essential Contribution of the University

Perhaps it is easier to identify what the essential contribution is not. As previously intimated, I suggest that it is not necessary to contribute to student teachers' practical training in the schools and to extend the theme it is not to provide practical in-service training for established teachers. To say this is not, for one moment, to insult colleagues or to denigrate the contributions which generations of dedicated university educationists made to the enhancement of high-quality teacher education. Moreover, it is not to fall into the trap of assuming that there is some naive distinction between one entity known as 'theory' and another identified as 'practice'. Classroom practice is inevitably overtly or covertly informed by 'theory'. All I wish to establish at this stage is that the training, advice and support associated with students' practical training can be, and frequently are, provided by other parties such as schoolteachers and local education authority (LEA) advisory services and, in the case of in-service training, even by privately established independent consultancies. Furthermore, there is no reason to presume that these bodies cannot undertake this work effectively.[2]

The teacher must be a reflective practitioner whose practice is informed by theory and the university's distinctive contribution is that it ensures that teachers are educated and trained in a manner which develops their capabilities as perceptive and critical specialists who think carefully about the nature and quality of the learning experiences they provide for children (for reviews of the field, see, eg, Furlong *et al.*, 1988; McNamara, 1990). It is possible to acknowledge and agree with this claim, but at the same time it must be recognised that there is no reason why reflective practice cannot be engendered by other parties. Until the introduction of school-based training, teachers, unlike other professionals, had not been directly involved with and given a measure of responsibility for the training of their new colleagues; giving serving teachers some responsibility for professional training should promote their abilities to reflect upon their own classroom practices.[3]

A further strong argument for locating teacher education within universities is that teaching is a profession and that one defining criterion of the professions is that their education and training is linked with universities. This ensures that professional preparation remains independent from political control, guarantees the requisite intellectual rigour which informs reflective practice and provides the institutional mechanisms which scrutinise the standards of education and training and maintain the quality of the professional qualification. There are, however, counterarguments. First, through the award of high-quality first degrees universities contribute to teachers' professional recognition and standing (Warnock, 1989). Second, so far as the more practical side of teacher preparation is concerned, universities are no longer able to determine the content of training courses and are not well-placed to withstand political pressure (for an extensive and detailed analysis, see Wilkin, 1994). Hence universities are no longer able to provide the independent contribution that is associated with professional preparation. Third, given that the universities, among other things, seem willing to award their honours degrees for three-year concurrent teacher-training programmes, which include the study of six subjects for comparatively short periods of time, we must question whether universities are prepared to maintain their traditional academic standards for the honours degree.

There are indications that with the advent of mass HE in Britain at the very time when universities are having to find alternative ways in which to generate their income some institutions will redefine their 'missions' so as to embrace forms of education and training which, heretofore, have not been associated with universities. Pring (1994) argues that we must question how far university departments have moved, under the new political and financial arrangements, from the distinctive university contribution to professional development.

These observations are not made to argue that the university has no contribution to make to the education and training of teachers. My purpose is to demonstrate that at a time when both the universities and teacher training are undergoing rapid change and are being subjected to various pressures we must reassess HE's contribution to teachers' professional training. In our own defence and to secure our longer-term future and involvement with the teaching profession we must ask what is it that the universities can contribute which cannot be provided by other institutions.

One may begin to illustrate the essential nature of HE's contribution by indicating, with respect to the current scene, what would be irretrievably lost if universities were not involved with the study of education and teacher education; for instance:

- As the National Curriculum has become established in primary schools there is considerable discussion about teaching methods and styles. This includes matters such as whether children should be taught individually, in groups or together as a class and whether the curriculum should be organised and communicated within the framework of conventional subject categories or according to other integrating principles such as topics or projects. The various issues and the contrasting arguments were drawn together and summarised in the 'Three Wise Men's Report' (Alexander *et al.*, 1992). This document could not have been produced without the university contribution because, in essence, it is a summary of the available empirical research and critical commentary on primary education produced by academic educationists working in universities both in Britain and abroad.[4]
- There has been considerable controversy about academic standards in

our schools, especially during the primary years. Much of the debate, which is enthusiastically pursued by politicians, is characterised by hortatory argument and harking to an idealised 'golden age' when standards were much higher than at present. It has been academic educationists who have provided firm evidence which can actually inform our judgements (eg, see Foxman *et al.*, 1993).

- Politicians have made much of the phenomenon that some schools are more effective than others at promoting educational achievements among their pupils, even when they share similar environmental circumstances. They are keen to publish 'performance indicators' which demonstrate to the public, especially parents, which schools are most effective. It has, however, been the academic educationists who have conducted the empirical studies which sought to identify the characteristics of effective schools (eg, Reynolds and Cuttance, 1992) and develop the complicated statistical models which permit the more rigorous and systematic identification of those schools which genuinely 'add value' to their pupils' achievements, when their circumstances and abilities at the time of their entry into the school are taken into account (eg, Gray, 1993; for an overview see McPherson, 1993).
- Since the time of the publication of the 'Great Educational Reform Bill' up until the 'Dearing Reforms' British education has been in a state of more or less continual upheaval; there have been successive revisions and changes heralded by deluges of documentation. Dearing's intervention was a tacit admission that politicians had attempted to impose upon schools a National Curriculum and associated assessment procedures which would not work in practice. It is salutary to reflect that without the critical commentary and documentation generated by the academic community there would be no independent record of one of the most turbulent decades in our recent educational history. It may be retorted that in addition to the academics' contributions much of the literature describing and commenting upon recent events has been generated by other parties such as the teachers' unions and journalists (notably, Haviland, 1988). This is fair comment but it reminds us of an additional essential function of the university system; namely that its libraries provide the repositories where formal knowledge is stored and made easily accessible to future generations. Without the university connection the experience and lessons of the last 10 years would not be available for tomorrow's teachers. It is not so much that the 'Thatcherite reforms' would become history; there would be *no* history.
- One may also mention an important dimension of educational discourse which should be of serious concern to the wider community as well as teacher educators and their students which is currently being expunged from professional training at both the initial and in-service levels. Namely, any discussion about the meaning and purpose of education and what we are educating young people for. With the formal

designation of the 'aims of education' in the 1988 Education Act debate about educational aspirations is going by default. In-service courses, for instance, have understandably become increasingly instrumental and tied to the specific demands of the National Curriculum.[5] At a time when society itself is changing rapidly and when we can hardly predict what knowledge, abilities and skills future generations of children will need it is worrying that the area of study which may be generally described as the philosophy of education has, with the weakening of the university contribution, been erased from many teachers' professional training.

These examples will have to suffice to illustrate the nature of what is the universities' special contribution to teacher education. This may be articulated and summarised in Popper's (1972) distinction between different forms of knowledge, which provides a useful way of formally demarcating the university contribution to teachers' professional training. Popper argues that a major task for philosophers is to develop pictures of the world which are imaginative, critical and of theoretical interest. In his Thesis of the Three Worlds he distinguishes between:

- World One – the world of physical states that includes machines and all living forms
- World Two – the world of mental states or of conscious experiences that includes our perceptions, experiences, memories, imaginings, thoughts, actions, and dispositions
- World Three – the world of ideas in an objective sense that includes possible objects of thought, theories in themselves, theorems, problems and critical arguments.

World Two is essentially the world of our subjective experiences which can interact with either World One or World Three knowledge. Popper demonstrates that World Three knowledge has an independent existence by means of two 'thought experiments'. In the first, all machines and tools are destroyed as are our subjective memories of science and technology, but libraries and our capacity to learn from them survive. Clearly, it would be possible after much effort to recreate our civilisation if World Three knowledge survived. In the second, all World One and World Three knowledge is destroyed. In this case, without the objective knowledge collected in libraries and books our civilisation would be obliterated and we would lack the capacity to recreate it.

The essential mandate for higher education, I suggest, is to contribute to the development of that World Three knowledge which has a bearing upon the formal study of education and educational practices. There can be little doubt that teaching (of a sort) can be founded upon practitioners' World Two knowledge (essentially their subjective experiences) but if teaching is to be based upon something more than each new generation of teachers 'working it out for themselves' in the light of practical experiences and if it is to remain founded upon a formal corpus which includes ideas, theories and critical reflection then the cardinal role of the universities is to develop and preserve World Three knowledge and to assist the teaching profession in the acquisition of that knowledge (this argument is worked out in detail in McNamara, 1994).

The preceding examples of World Three knowledge were deliberately chosen to illustrate that formal knowledge, of the sort generated in universities, may not have a direct and immediate bearing upon teaching practice and that students could probably become effective teachers without having encountered these issues during their training. Obviously I hope, of course, that this would not be the case. Nevertheless they are, I suggest, examples of the sorts of knowledge of which teachers, as professionals, ought to be aware and which they need to acquire if they are to remain concerned about educational issues and contribute to the enhancement of professional practice during their careers. They are certainly examples of the sorts of knowledge that must be located within academic libraries and made available to interested parties. Only an ideological despot could assert that such information should be expunged from the academic record so that it was no longer available for use in universities and accessible to the teaching profession.

In sum, the distinctive role of HE is to contribute to the acquisition, development and deployment of educational knowledge which may be accommodated within Popper's World Three. In saying this it has to be accepted that those academic educationists who are responsible for generating World Three knowledge may not have an indispensable contribution to make to student teachers' practical training. I stress that it would be regrettable if this was to be the position and, as the chapters in this volume demonstrate, universities do have an important contribution to make to school-based teacher education. At the risk of repetition, my purpose is to identify the core function of university departments of education at a time when their purpose and existence are being questioned. The most important reason why university departments of education should continue to be supported is because they are the organisations that have the accumulated knowledge, expertise, and resources to maintain the scholarship and research which make up the academic study of education. They are also located in the sorts of institution, namely universities, where the ambience and culture should support the pursuit of disinterested and critical study. It should go without saying that in the eventuality of departments of education not continuing to be directly concerned with students' practical training, they should sustain a close working relationship with schools and practising teachers.

A final gloss on this theme. It was Mrs Thatcher who, as Secretary of State for Education, received (but did not implement) the Report of the

James Committee of Enquiry into the Education and Training of Teachers (DES, 1972), set up to enquire into the education, training and probation of teachers in England and Wales and to make recommendations. The report argued that HE had a distinctive part to play in the education and training of teachers but at the same time it made a much clearer distinction between the academic study of education and practical training. Practice was to be informed by theory, notably during the first year of the second cycle of training, but essentially the academic study of education, which was regarded as necessary, was to be the preserve of HEIs while practical training was to be the responsibility of the schools. It is unlikely that a major report on teacher training produced under the chairmanship of a past High Master of Manchester Grammar School escaped the attention of Geoffrey Parker, the first Chairman of the TTA.

The School of Education in the Future

At a time when HE is becoming less directly involved with teacher training and losing resource as a consequence, university departments must assess their future prospects. Given present uncertainties this should not entail rash policies such as the unilateral withdrawal from teacher education, but it must involve departments deciding what their necessary and distinctive contribution to education is and organising their work and resources so as to give it priority. An obvious concern with a policy which places much greater stress on the 'academic' study of education is that cutbacks in the involvement with student teachers' practical training would have a dramatic effect upon the funding which departments receive from the HEFCE (and TTA, in due course). This could render many departments non-viable or lead to smaller units. This is undoubtedly the case but retrenchment is inevitable and is already occurring. The Darwinian imperative is to survive in some form and it must not be mere continuance; university education departments must have a presence which stands for something worthwhile that is recognised within the academic community of the university system. To adopt the current unfortunate idiom, we must have a distinctive mission.

I suggest that in the future the typical university education department should aspire to become more like the typical university department. It should be much more concerned with the academic study of education. The bulk of its teaching would contribute to the university undergraduate and postgraduate academic programmes. It would, obviously, make what contribution it could to initial and in-service teacher training but this would probably be limited to formal 'academic' inputs. Just as university English, politics and religious studies departments are not in the business of producing authors, politicians or priests but engaged with the academic study of those areas of human activity, so too, the education department should focus more on the study of education rather than training teachers. The consequences must be faced.

Inevitably teacher education departments will become smaller, and there will be an essential requirement that their staff have the academic background, training and expertise to enable them to engage with the academic study of education.[6] It is entirely possible that in future many people appointed to education departments will not have been school teachers. We must accept that at present there are cutbacks to education departments with the inevitable early retirements and failures to replace vacated posts as the impact of school-based teacher training affects departmental budgets. While the current financial uncertainty continues, it is unlikely that investing in education departments will be among university managers' priorities. Rather than face a scenario where many education departments could wither on the vine unsure of their future and beholden to the vagaries of politicians' education policies, it would be preferable, I propose, for education departments to assert that within the HE system they are confident that they have a distinctive role and contribution to make to the study of education: one that is credible within universities and financially realistic. I also venture to suggest that education departments which were independent from teacher training, in that they would no longer have to accede to the specific requirements of the CATE criteria or the TTA, could gain much more respect from the teaching profession and the academic community. Teacher trainers have, for instance, been rightly critical of many CATE criteria and many aspects of the National Curriculum, but their criticism and voice have been muted as they have been required to train students according to DFE requirements. Education departments beholden to the DFE for their teacher-training places are not best placed to act as independent critics of government education policy. The thrust of government teacher-training policy over the past decade may be interpreted as an attempt to emasculate the presumed baleful influence of teacher trainers (see, eg, Lawlor 1990; O'Hear, 1988).

A telling example of how the integrity of university education departments is being undermined and their academic values are being compromised arises from the manner in which the 'outputs' of teacher education programmes are being cast as a series of 'competencies' (see especially TTA, 1994). The academic study of the relevant voluminous literature reveals that the competency approach to teacher training has reappeared on a number of occasions during the past 100 years and that it is a notion which hardly bears critical scrutiny and one which may actually militate against effective teacher education (see, eg, McNamara, 1992). The essential role of university educationists should be to expose the competency movement to critical scrutiny and analysis and independently decide whether this is a viable and educationally worthwhile way in which to prepare teachers. The nature of government teacher-education policy is such that universities are being forced into a position where they must define and assess their students' teaching abilities in competencies. What is more, the universities themselves contribute to the development of the competency approach (see UCET, 1991).

The issue of how education departments are to be funded must be addressed. There are already cutbacks in many education departments. A policy which emphasises the academic study of education at the expense of practical training would accentuate this process. Education departments may need to face the prospect of becoming smaller units. Without a major involvement in teacher education, however, there would be significant savings in money, time and administrative effort (liaising with schools, organising and paying for school practices etc.), and there would be less need for dedicated teaching space. Education departments would require funding at about the same levels as the typical arts or humanities department and make comparable demands upon university teaching space and resources. Possibly the most dramatic change occasioned by disengaging from teacher education would be the freeing up of time and the capacity to use this key resource in a more flexible manner. The 'teaching year' would be reduced from 38 (in primary) and 36 (in secondary) to 30 weeks. Substantial periods of unproductive time would also be saved.[7] Those staff who did remain in post would be able to employ their time in alternative productive ways. These include undergraduate teaching, postgraduate and post-experience teaching and research.

Undergraduate Teaching

Some universities[8] have a tradition of offering educational studies as an honours-degree programme, but it is unrealistic for departments contemplating the move into undergraduate teaching to imagine that at a time when student numbers in HE are being consolidated the HEFCE would earmark new undergraduate places for academic honours-degree courses in educational studies. There are, however, emerging opportunities. Many universities are now modularising and semesterising their undergraduate programmes, and the trend looks set to continue. Alternative pedagogues are emerging in HE (Ainley, 1994) which allow students more choice and flexibility when selecting optional units within modular degree schemes.

Educational studies modules should prove very attractive for students, especially mature students and those who may be contemplating careers in teaching. They do not build upon a 'school' subject, they are concerned with policy and practice in an important area of contemporary society which bears upon their lives, they should be interesting, and if educationists practice what they preach they should be well-taught.[9] So long as education modules do not provide too large a proportion of degree programmes, students opting for education courses do not have a significant effect upon the resources allocated to the departments, which are the major providers of undergraduate teaching, but the aggregate effect of the various individual choices made by students opting for education courses could be substantial in departmental resource allocation. Many university departments in the more popular arts and humanities areas experienced dramatic increases in undergraduate numbers during the past few years; educationists may find that hard-pressed departments may welcome the introduction of new courses which take some pressure from them.

Postgraduate and Post-experience Teaching

The burden of my proposals implies that university departments of education should focus less upon providing the more practically oriented in-service courses and should concentrate upon the more academically rigorous programmes associated with, say, advanced diplomas and masters' degrees. Given that in recent years a substantial part of the funds which the DFE makes available for in-service training has been earmarked for special purposes, for example, matters associated with the practical implementation of the National Curriculum, it may be argued that it is unwise to promote forms of post-experience training where it will be more difficult to attract candidates and the fees which they bring with them. Academic arguments should carry more force than pragmatic considerations, especially given the erratic nature of in-service funding. There is a strong argument to the effect that serving teachers' continuing professional development is not necessarily best served by offering courses directly related to classroom experience and practice. The value of firsthand experience and 'doing it' has been challenged by a number of recent commentators who argue that teachers need a break from the 'reality' of their every-day classroom experiences if they are to develop insights into their professional behaviour and improve their practice. The role of the teacher educator, the argument goes, is to introduce perspectives and insights drawn, for example, from literature and the arts, so as to provide more worthwhile heuristics in which teachers may reflect upon their practice and question the 'givens' of their experience (see particularly the papers collected in Buchmann and Flodden, 1993).

Research

A necessary corollary of my proposals is that education departments must preserve and strengthen their research and scholarship. The circumstances should be created in which research and the scholarly and critical study of education flourish, and it will have to do so if funding is to be protected. We must remember that the essential resource required for much worthwhile educational scholarship is time; as intimated previously, withdrawing from practical training should make more of this precious resource available.[10] An issue that has concerned educationists in recent years is that a significant part of the grant aid available for empirical research has been directly linked to government policy and subject to political control, and academics have not always been free to publish their findings.[11]

There must also be concern that the funding for research which will be transferred to the TTA will not be available for the disinterested pursuit of educational research and that its use will be prescribed by the TTA. In the longer term, a policy which encourages educationists to become less dependent upon research grants associated with political or policy initiatives and to develop their roles as independent commentators may enhance their standing among the teaching profession and within the university community. I suggest that many of the more enduring and influential contributions that continue to inform education emanate from the work of scholars who, while being concerned with educational practices, engage in rigorous and independent scholarship.

In Conclusion

Like it or not, teacher educators in HE will continue to face an uncertain future where the only certainty is that they face a diminution in their resources and will have a less important part to play in the education of teachers. I am not proposing that education departments should unilaterally disengage from teacher training. I am suggesting that they need to articulate more clearly their distinctive contribution to education and implement policies which bring that to the forefront of their work. The role of the LEA and their advisory services has been emasculated as a consequence of government education policy, as has the independent voice of HMI. Teacher education is, among other things, beset with competencies and criteria extending to the number of hours primary students must spend learning how to teach arithmetic, many of which are part of a political rather than an educational agenda. In such an environment the study and pursuit of education needs an independent voice; it should be provided by the universities. Education is an essential and vital institution within society, and it has as strong a claim as, say, religion, politics and economics to be formally studied and researched within the higher education system.

Notes

1. For instance, the informal feedback from many students on my own institution's school-based secondary course suggests that they now regard their partnership training school as the base to which they owe their primary allegiance; they take time out from the partnership school to visit the university, no longer is it the other way about.

2. I must say that it is a moot point as to whether they can undertake the work on a cost-effective basis.
3. Incidentally, there are teacher educators who are sometimes prone to criticise teachers for not being thoughtful and reflective practitioners. I suggest that this is a dangerous argument to deploy because who selected these people for teacher training in the first place and then awarded them teaching qualifications, and what does it say about the university's contribution to teacher education?
4. One has only to glance at the bibliography appended to the document to appreciate how university educationists have set the agendas and contributed to discussion about the nature of primary practice.
5. Ongoing research by Mike Bottery at the University of Hull sponsored by the Paul Branton Foundation includes surveying primary and secondary teachers and questioning them about what their INSET priorities would be in an ideal world. They are predominantly implementational and geared to responding to external directives. They very seldomly address ethical and political issues.
6. There is the argument that the sorts of people who have the cast of mind, dispositions and personal qualities to make committed and effective teacher educators are not necessarily the sorts of people who have the expertise and qualities to become successful academic educational theorists and researchers (see, eg, Lanier and Little, 1986); this is not to imply that the pursuit of one of these activities is better than or preferable to the other.
7. In my own institution, for example, the average round trip to a secondary partner school is 50 miles and return journeys may involve two hours or more on the road.
8. Such as Lancaster, Warwick and the Scottish and Welsh universities. Note also that the James Report foresaw the academic study of education being included in HE programmes which did not lead to teacher training.
9. For instance, in my own university we introduced modular courses in 'education and psychology' and 'education and society' during the past two years and had no trouble filling them to capacity.
10. It is instructive to note the way in which some colleges of HE and ex-polytechnics who won 'R' resource for education from the HEFCE for the first time as a consequence of the last Research Assessment Exercise have clearly earmarked the money to appoint educationists with a strong academic record specifically to pursue research and scholarship.
11. The concern has even extended to the press (see Abrams, 1995).

References

Abrams, F (1995) 'No Time To Think Things Through', *Independent*, 5 January.

Ainley, P (1994) *Degrees of Difference: Higher Education in the 1990s*. London: Lawrence & Wishart.

Alexander, R, Rose, J and Woodhead, C (1992) *Curriculum Organisation and Classroom Practice in Primary Schools: A Discussion Paper*. London: DES.

Buchmann, M and Flodden, R (eds) (1993) *Detachment and Concern: Conversations in the Philosophy of Teaching and Teacher Education*. London: Cassell.

Dent, HC (1977) *The Training of Teachers in England and Wales 1800–1975*. London: Hodder & Stoughton.

Department of Education and Science (DES) (1972) *Teacher Education and Training*. London: HMSO.

DES (1984) *Initial Teacher Training: Approval of Courses*, Circular 3/84. London: DES.

DES (1989a) *Initial Teacher Training: Approval of Courses*, Circular 24/89. London: DES.

DES(1989b) *Initial Teacher Training in France: The Training of Secondary Teachers in the Académie de Toulouse*. A paper by Her Majesty's Inspectorate (HMI). London: HMSO.

DES (1989c) *The Provisional Teacher Program in New Jersey*. London: HMSO.

Department for Education (DFE) (1992) *Initial Teacher Training (Secondary Phase)* Circular 9/92. London: DFE.

DFE (1993) *The Initial Training of Primary School Teachers*, Circular 14/93. London: DFE.

Foxman, D *et al.* (1993) 'Standards of Literacy and Numeracy', in *Briefings for the Paul Hamlyn Foundation National Commission on Education*. London: Heinemann, pp. 135–50.

Furlong, VJ *et al.* (1988) *Initial Teacher Training and the Role of the School*. Milton Keynes: Open University Press.

Garrido, J (1986) *International Yearbook of Education, Volume 38 – Primary Education at the Threshold of the Twenty-First Century*. Paris: UNESCO, International Bureau of Education.

Gilroy, P and Smith, M (eds) (1993) *International Analyses of Teacher Education*. Abingdon: Carfax, pp.263–75.

Gray, J (1993) *Value-Added Approaches in School Evaluation: The Experiences of Three LEAs in England, Lessons and Challenges*. The Audit Office, HMI. Edinburgh: The Scottish Office.

Haviland, J (1988) *Take Care Mr Baker*. London: Fourth Estate.

Judge, H *et al.* (1994) *The Universities and the Teachers: France, the United States, England*. Wallingford: Triangle.

Lanier, JE and Little, JW (1986) 'Research on Teacher Education', in MC Wittrock (ed) *Handbook of Research on Teaching*, Third Edition. New York: Macmillan, pp.527–69.

Lawlor, S (1990) *Teachers Mistaught: Training in Theories or Education in Subjects?* London: Centre for Policy Studies.

Liston, D and Zeichner, K (1991) *Teacher Education and the Social Conditions of Schooling*. New York: Routledge.

MacIntyre, G (1991) *Accreditation of Teacher Education: The Story of CATE 1984–1989*. London: Falmer Press.

McNamara, D (1990) 'Research on Teachers' Thinking: Its Contribution to Educating Student Teachers To Think Critically', *Journal of Education for Teaching*, **16**(2): 147–60.

McNamara, D (1992) 'The reform of Teacher Education in England and Wales: Teacher Competence; Panacea or Rhetoric?, *Journal of Education for Teaching*, **18**(3): 273–85.

McNamara, D (1993) 'Towards Reestablishing the Professional Authority and Expertise of Teacher Educators and Teachers', in P Gilroy and M Smith (eds) *International Analyses of Teacher Education*. Oxford: Carfax, pp.277–91.

McNamara, DR (1994) *Classroom Pedagogy and Primary Practice*. London: Routledge.

McPherson, A (1993) 'Measuring Added Value in Schools', in *Briefings for the Paul Hamlyn Foundation National Commission on Education*. London: Heinemann, pp.1–15.

O' Hear, A (1988) *Who Teaches the Teachers?* London: Social Affairs Unit.

Popkewitz, TS (ed) (1993) *Changing Patterns of Power: Social Regulation and Teacher Education Reform*. Albany, NY: SUNY Press.

Popper, K (1972) *Objective Knowledge: An Evolutionary Approach*. Oxford: Clarendon Press.

Pring, R (1994) *Universities and Educational Studies*. Paper read at the Universities Council for the Education of Teachers (UCET) annual conference.

Reynolds, D and Cuttance, P (1992) *School Effectiveness Research Policy, and Practice*. London: Cassell.

Teacher Training Agency (1994) *Profiles on Teacher Competencies – Consultations on Draft Guidance*. London: TTA, Circular letter, November.

Tisher, R and Wideen, M (1990) *Research in Teacher Education: International Perspectives*. London: Falmer Press.

Universities Council for the Education of Teachers (UCET) (1991) *Annual Conference, Symposia on Competencies*. London: UCET.

Warnock, M (1989) 'The Authority of the Teacher', *Westminster Studies in Education*, **12**: 73–81.

Wilkin, M (1994) *Ideology and the Initial Teacher Training Curriculum 1960–1990*. University of Cambridge, doctoral thesis.

Zeichner, K (1983) 'Alternative Paradigms of Teacher Education', *Journal of Teacher Education*, **34**: 3–9.

CHAPTER 14

SOMETHING FOR THE GROWN-UPS

Richard Smith

Socrates sat down and said, 'It would be very nice, Agathon, if wisdom were like water, and flowed by contact out of a person who has more into one who has less, just as water can be made to pass through a thread of wool out of the fuller of two cups into the emptier. If that applies to wisdom, I value the privilege of sitting beside you very highly'. (Plato, Symposium [trans. W Hamilton], 175c)

But what can one do? Dearie, you can't do anything for the children till you've done something for the grown-ups. (WH Auden (1933) 'Private Pleasure', *Scrutiny* 1(2), p.194)

There are always some – politicians especially – who appear to believe that education is a pretty simple business. It would be very nice if teachers would just get on and deliver the curriculum. Then standards would rise astonishingly, and the shades of teachers and thinkers from Plato on who have found the whole thing rather more complicated would be ashamed to have missed the point for so long. So too with training, especially that of teachers. Despite the intense controversy that surrounds most aspects of training – competencies and outcome-based programmes, enterprise and capability, the transferability of skills – those responsible for changing the way teachers are prepared show no interest in engaging with the complexity of the issues involved, appearing to believe either that what enables teachers to do their job can be passed easily from one person to another, like the water Socrates speaks of, or that the whole messy business is best left to market forces as the new, diverse forms of 'initial training' compete with each other. (I use the term 'initial training' for brevity, but it is not a matter of indifference whether we talk of 'training' or of 'education'.)

The modes of 'initial training' with which we are familiar have been widely criticised, though many of these criticisms, particularly those emanating from the political right, have been ill-conceived and others, such as Kenneth Clarke's famous attack on 'barmy theory', puerile and headline-seeking. It is reassuring to note, as David McNamara explains elsewhere in this volume, that politicians invariably seek credit by 'reforming teacher-training', whatever form they find it in. However, I accept that the basis of the practice of the last 30 years or so is flawed by deep confusions; I argue that these are more far-reaching than is normally supposed. In this chapter I unravel some of these confusions. In the first section I argue that 'theory' has been cast in the wrong role: it should be seen as supporting, enriching and stimulating – in short, 'doing something for' – *persons* rather than primarily as informing 'practice'. In the second section, 'Technical Reason', I suggest that teaching and the preparation of teachers have wrongly been viewed as almost exclusively *technical* activities, and in the third I propose that judgement and practical wisdom are the central ideas to help us make sense of them. 'The Getting of Practical Wisdom' consists of remarks about what learning practical wisdom might involve, and the last section indicates what role institutions of higher education (HE) might play in that learning, what they might do for trainee teachers *as people*, and how they might need to change in order to do so.

Theory

Whatever else higher education does in the training of teachers it is generally supposed in some sense to 'do the theory', introducing students perhaps to the psychological, sociological or philosophical theories that underlie education. Now 'theory' in general does not have a particularly good name in our culture ('That may be all very well in theory, but . . .'), and recent critics and detractors of initial training find it convenient to play on the conventional distinction between theory and practice and to portray educational theory as remote from the 'real world' of the classroom. There is certainly anecdotal evidence that when theory took the form of the teaching of the separate disciplines (psychology, etc.) of education it was widely perceived by students as of little relevance. What I want to raise here, however, is the possibility that this was at least partly the result of two serious mistakes: first of conceiving theory as something to be 'taught to' students – transmitted, as it were, from the outside – and second of supposing that its purpose was primarily to illuminate the world of the classroom and thus 'lead to practice'.

On the first point, I argue elsewhere (Smith, 1992) that we need to start instead from a recognition of the *ineliminability* of theory, in education as in the rest of our world. To take theory seriously is to understand that phenomena come to us shot through with interpretation, such that we need to stand back and consider what other interpretations, what other perspectives on them, are possible and desirable, and I suggested that to grasp that the world is the world-as-seen, rather than as blankly and unalterably *given*, may be a source of interest and delight. To 'do theory', then, is to *theorise*: to think things through rigorously in some depth and with imagination for different possibilities, and to examine one's own presuppositions. To fail to do so (or to assume that you can rely on 'common sense') is simply to continue holding the implicit theories with which you started. In my 1992 article, I give examples of the kinds of theory students bring with them to their initial training courses: theories that children are natural learners whom teachers should be careful not to thwart, theories that, on the contrary, they will learn nothing without didactic teaching, theories about goodness and values and indoctrination, and much more. To 'do theory' with these students is among other things a matter of challenging the implicit theories that they already hold and of encouraging them to consider the adequacy of their existing frameworks and perspectives. When 'theory' is understood in this sense it is clear that the crucial question is not *whether* there should be theory in the preparation of teachers but rather what form theorising, as described, should take.

On the second point, it may seem obvious that the function of theory in the preparation of teachers should be to improve their performance in the classroom, so much so that to advance an alternative view is merely perverse. To see how this may not be its only, or its only direct, function, compare the relationship between the study of literature, history or philosophy and a graduate's future career as management consultant, solicitor or banker (or, indeed, teacher). Here there is no expectation that theoretical studies carry any direct 'pay-off'. They do not bring *knowledge* which can be *used* in the workplace. The idea is of course rather that, as elements of a liberal education, they transform the learner into one who is more flexible, more responsive, more alert to a variety of perspectives and so on. They constitute a kind of training in receptivity, in being open to a variety of perspectives and aware of the different kinds of language that are available to us. Such theory is 'contemplative' in that it involves a higher degree of attentiveness to the world and its subtleties than we generally achieve in our busy lives (cf. the section below on 'alertness' in practical wisdom).

This traditional picture is not without its problems, notably concerning the extent to which such capacities are transferable (as well as the issue of whether a liberal education amounts to little more than the badge of a cultural elite), but the general picture is sufficiently widely accepted to constitute the basis for much of the system of HE in the UK and elsewhere. Why has the function of 'doing theory' in the preparation of teachers not typically been viewed in a similar way? One answer might be that, in the form of 'the disciplines', educational theory grew too rapidly in the 1960s and 1970s, and with too little sophistication, to provide the kind of intrinsic interest I have indicated theory can hold. True, many who taught it found themselves required to master, and to teach, new disciplines in a very short space of time. At least as significant as this, though, seems to have been the readiness of 'the disciplines' to insist that they were 'relevant' and practically useful, and so to justify themselves in primarily or exclusively instrumental terms: as part of a 'form of rationality in which the calculation of outcomes takes pride of place' (Buchmann, 1990) and in which the discovering of effective means for predetermined ends is privileged over consideration of ends themselves, that is over questions such as what education is *for*.

I shall say more in the text section about the limitations of instrumental or technical reasoning. It would be mistaken to deny it a significant place in the connection between educational theory and classroom practice. Clearly there are many areas where such theory can cast light on practical problems and even suggest more-or-less direct solutions to them, although, interestingly, these areas change over time and with fashion. At the moment, for example, management theory is thought to illuminate school effectiveness and psychology is taken as the basis of techniques of 'assertive discipline'. My point in this chapter is that this is not the *only* role that theorising can play.

If the role of theory was not well-conceived in the disciplines-based approach, other and more recent accounts of what constitutes 'educational knowledge' and how it is to be acquired and taught are also often flawed. On the 'reflective practitioner' model, for example, particularly associated with Donald Schön, the teacher, experienced or trainee, moves backward and forward between action on the one hand, and analysis, interpretation and so on, on the other, drawing on ideas, books and bodies of what might be called 'systematic theory', on child development for instance, as is helpful from time to time. At its best the model emphasises that teaching involves a 'concern with aims and consequences, as well as with means and technical efficiency' (Pollard and Tann, 1987, p.5) and that teaching requires on the part of the practitioner judgement and an ethical stance as well as skills (and ch. 1 *passim*). There is a prevailing sense in the 'reflective practitioner' literature, however, that 'theory' is something to be drawn upon in an eclectic and ad hoc sort of way to improve practice (Pollard and Tann talk of 'insights from the disciplines'). Who could quarrel with that? Yet this begs a number of questions. How are the relevant parts of theory to be identified as the bodies of systematic theory itself become less and less widely known? How is theory itself to be developed if it is regarded essentially as a repository to be drawn on? How, in particular, could it possibly then be developed through a dialectical relationship with practice?

As Kemmis (1995) notes, the 'reflective practitioner' model often seems to presuppose 'a one-sided, rather rationalistic view of theorising, emphasising the power of ideas to guide or even direct action, rather than the way action and the circumstances of action also shape our ideas.' It seems too that this model is unlikely to sustain the teacher as a *person*, drawing on and enriching his or her wider being. Even in the avowedly anti-instrumentalist account that Pollard and Tann give there is a sense that the reflective practitioner only needs certain 'attitudes' bolted on to the inevitable 'skills'. Practice is reflected on from the basis of practice, to the neglect of any larger frame of reference, of 'theorising' in its broadest sense. Thus notions of reflective practice hold little promise of the kind of wider illumination, let alone of inspiration, that it is reasonable to look for in educational theory.

> *I enjoyed the excerpt we watched from Dead Poets' Society. The idea that education is about more than academic learning, that it's there to help you 'seize the day', is so attractive, and I found myself wishing I'd had a teacher like that for A-level when we were ploughing through Keats and listing all the techniques he used. Do I want to be that sort of teacher? I suppose we all want to be charismatic, but the film shows the danger – of turning out pupils in your own image. A kind of indoctrination, really* . . . (PGCE Secondary History student).

Technical Reason

Technical reason is sometimes called instrumental or scientific reason or rationality. It is concerned to find the best means to known and predetermined ends: to discover which medicine will more quickly bring down a temperature or what speed a car must run at to be most economical with petrol. In education we employ technical reason when we try to establish which laboratory procedures will minimise the risk of accidents or which kind of classroom organisation will enable us to hear each child read for a certain number of minutes each day (or week). Technical reason 'is concerned with the management of need and with prediction and control concerning future contingencies' (Nussbaum, 1986, p.95). It produces rules and procedures to codify the ways in which our desired ends may be reached, increasing our power to make universal rather than particular statements (about all relevantly similar illnesses causing high temperatures, and not just this individual case of fever), to teach others appropriate ways and means, to achieve a high degree of precision and to construct explanations that help us further to refine our procedures (cf. Nussbaum, 1986, pp.95–6).

As the preceding examples suggest, technical reason plays a large part in making our lives more tolerable. There is, as I already indicated, much 'teacher knowledge' which is indeed a matter of technical reason and can be taught as such, its universality and precision based on research of various kinds, its explanations taking the form of hypotheses which can be further tested. So impressive has been the success of technical reason in the areas to which it is appropriate – medical and scientific research, for example, and the development of technology, particularly information technology – that it constantly threatens to extend its influence to other fields where its suitability is more questionable. As Martha Nussbaum (1990, p.55) notes, 'the power of "scientific" pictures of practical rationality affects almost every area of human social life, through the influence of the social sciences and the more science-based parts of ethical theory on the formation of public policy.'

In education the influence of technical reason is widespread. One of its most characteristic signs is the prevalence of 'skills-speak': of the tendency to talk of all the capacities, abilities, qualities and virtues of the teacher (as of others outside formal education, such as parents and lovers) as 'skills' or, more recently, as 'competencies', and of teaching as the 'craft of the classroom'. This is *par excellence* the language of technical or instrumental rationality, for skills are what we use to bring about preordained ends: they have no say in the determination of those ends themselves. The skilled carpet-fitter fits the carpet as I ask, and is unlikely to counsel me to spend my money on a short break in Amsterdam instead. At the risk of appearing to damn by association, which is not my intention, the danger of reducing complex practices to sets of 'skills' and of according hegemony to technical reason can be seen in the case of the doctor working as a 'research physician' in a Nazi concentration camp. How could he allow his profession to be perverted? 'The answer was: by taking pride in his professional skills, irrespective of what purpose they were used for. Again and again this pride in his professional skill permeates his story of his own and other prisoners' sufferings' (Bettelheim, 1960, pp.261–2). More generally, it is now a familiar point that the evil done in those days consisted in large part of the 'banality' (Arendt, 1963) of those prepared merely to seek technical solutions to technical problems of train timetables or of the cheapest way to dissolve the chemicals for the gas chambers.

The domination of the technicist model of rationality is widespread now in education. It can be seen in the idea that quality in schooling can be *measured* (for the purpose of constructing league tables), perhaps with 'value-added' calculations of satisfyingly technical complexity. It can be seen in the way that the subject of English has been steadily reduced to the business of 'effective communication' (talk of 'effectiveness', like that of 'skills', is the clearest sign of the grip of technical reason. That a particular strategy is an effective means to a particular end says nothing about whether that particular end is worth pursuing). It can be seen in the rapid spread of competence models of learning, from GNVQs to training of various kinds, including the training of teachers, and it is very evident in the faith that information technology and 'learning packages', distance learning and so on will solve our problems at all levels of education. Above all it is there in the idea that teaching consists in the 'delivery' of a curriculum prespecified in detail.

The ascendance of technical and instrumental rationality is the product of the Enlightenment and the scientific revolution that both preceded and accompanied it. (It is now, however, a familiar point that science itself does not comfortably fit this paradigm: a point vigorously made in the work of Thomas Kuhn, eg, 1977, and one especially clear in such areas of science as quantum physics. See, eg, Gjertsen, 1989.) Critics of this version of rationality, such as Horkheimer and Adorno and, more recently, Jurgen Habermas, argue that the power of technical reason to predict and control, so far from improving people's lives and leading to 'progress', has rather brought about sophisticated forms of manipulation and enslavement. (An obvious example of this in education, and one frequently cited, is the way that new computer technology, by making possible the storage and retrieval of vast amounts of information, creates the demand for the supply of such information by headteachers, heads of university departments and others.)

Technical reason cannot meet our interest in understanding and communicating with each other – though it offers a burlesque of that in the Internet and other devices – or our interest in emancipating ourselves from dependence on our world (Habermas, 1974). It cannot do justice to the ethical dimension of our lives, our ability to reflect on ends and purposes as well as on means, to consider where we are going as well as how to get there. Worse than that, it brings about the marginalisation of the ethical, its relegation to the status of personal preference, 'values and attitudes', since the dimension which the sovereign mode of rationality cannot readily manage, organise and plan for clearly cannot be of major significance.

A corollary of this, and one of great significance for the way teaching and the preparation of teachers are conceived, is that technical reason threatens to eliminate the idea of *judgement*. (The idea of *judgement* is threatened with extinction by the widespread assumption that there is only knowledge – 'objective' or 'scientific' – on the one hand and inclination on the other. For some interesting remarks on the growth of this assumption during the last decade or so, see Gilmour, 1992, pp.208–9.) To see how this is so, consider the following example. An academic whose manuscript was turned down by a publisher asked what were their criteria for accepting and rejecting material. Although they had no set criteria of the sort nevertheless they replied, out of courtesy, indicating some general guidelines. This provoked another letter from the disappointed writer: *What were the criteria for having these particular criteria?* Now clearly this could go on indefinitely. The point is that in this, as in very many cases, there is no alternative but to have recourse to an act of judgement. Even when there are carefully laid-down rules, judgement is still required to determine which instance falls under which rule. Football authorities may 'tighten up the rules' on the tackle from behind, but the referee still has to judge whether what he sees counts as such a tackle. In many fields of human activity, from football to morality (in the context of the latter, see Larmore, 1987), and certainly including teaching, an excessive emphasis on rules, in the spirit of technical reason, has obscured the vital role of judgement. It is here, as well as in 'theorising' as I have discussed it, that I want to argue that higher education has a major role to play in the preparation of teachers.

Judgement and Practical Wisdom

Although I claim that technical reason enters significantly into teaching it would, I think, be widely accepted that classroom teaching is above all a constant series of acts of *practical judgement*. The teacher seldom consciously refers to rules, procedures or generalisations in day-to-day work with pupils, rather relying on what is sometimes described as 'native wit' or 'common sense'; but not so native that it did not need to be acquired or so common that we expect any reasonably well-educated member of the public to be able to take over at a moment's notice (so far, at any rate). My criticisms of technical reason and of skills-based approaches amount to the insistence that these are not the right terms in which to understand that large part of teaching which consists of acts of judgement. How then are we to develop an appropriate model in order better to articulate this major part of teaching and, in particular, to understand how the capacity for judgement may be improved, trained or educated?

There has recently been a renewal of interest in Aristotle's account of *phronesis* as a fruitful source for this purpose. *Phronesis* is variously translated as 'practical reasoning', 'practical judgement' or 'practical wisdom': although the idea of judgement is crucial, I prefer 'practical wisdom' for reasons that will become clear. Aristotle distinguishes *phronesis* from *techne*, which is, roughly, 'instrumental reason' with a 'scientific' flavour, of the kind exercised by a craftsperson who plans and makes a table. This being much like the technical rationality I discussed, he or she can, in principle, repeat the operation; there are procedures – rules of thumb at least – which can be taught to others; there is a degree of precision in what he or she does; and explanations can be given for doing it this way rather than that ('plane with the grain, otherwise it's likely to splinter'). *Phronesis* by contrast is characterised by flexibility and attentiveness to the details of the particular, and perhaps unique, case. Aristotle's word for this alertness, or 'situational appreciation' as some modern interpreters prefer, is *aisthesis*; it is reminiscent of the 'with-it-ness' sometimes said (eg, Kounin, 1970) to be a hallmark of the good teacher. There is sensitivity, a kind of attunement, to whatever is the subject of judgement, rather than the attempt to exercise mastery or domination over it. The thinking that occurs in *phronesis* does not occur before the event (although I express reservations about this point later): it is exercised in the course of experience itself and involves openness to further experience. To take an example: two pupils are throwing a rubber eraser to one another, to the apparent despair of the eraser's owner, who needs it to be able to finish his work. What exactly is happening here, and what ought the teacher to do? Are the throwers maliciously tormenting the third child, or is this little more than a game, perhaps even light relief during an otherwise intensive spell of work? Or is it a response to boredom, to a monotonous lesson? What is clear is that explanatory knowledge is not to the point here. There is no general principle, to the effect that children who throw rubbers do so because the lesson is monotonous, of which this can be identified as an instance. The teacher has to respond to these particular pupils, whom she knows, in this particular lesson. Furthermore the teacher's attentiveness must extend to her own reactions: perhaps for obscure reasons she is inclined to see this pair of boys as a bad lot while other teachers seem to find them attractively impish, or vice versa. Thus, *phronesis*, or practical wisdom as I shall from now on refer to it, has an ethical side to it which technical rationality lacks. Questions of character, of what kind of person the teacher is, are at issue here; it does not simply come down to what 'skills' she is exercising. Here there are no rules to follow.

An important distinction between practical wisdom and technical reason is that the latter produces goods, the ends to which the making is the means, which are specified by considerations external to the process of making. The table, for example, is determined by the needs of the customer, as it might be for a dining table rather than a coffee table (though the picture is complicated by the tendency of craft-workers sometimes to impose their own aesthetic vision). In practical wisdom, by contrast, the good to be realised is sought *through* the action and not as an independently specifiable aim. As Lasch (1984, p.253) puts it, 'the choice of means has to be governed by their conformity to standards of excellence designed to extend human capacities for self-understanding and self-mastery'. Aristotle's own prime example of this is politics, which cannot be indifferent to means: political ends can never justify corruption and chicanery, for the well-founded nation-state is characterised by honest, open and just dealings among its citizens as much as by the attainment of any particular ends such as security and low inflation. In teaching, similarly, we cannot imagine 'external' goals, however worthy, such as increasing children's reading ages, warranting all and every means, including bullying, excessive psychological pressure and naked bribery, of ensuring they are achieved. This is to say that certain goods are internal to the practice of teaching: that teaching by its very nature (as a *praxis* rather than a *poiesis*, to use another Aristotelian distinction largely co-terminous with that between *phronesis* and *techne*) goes about its business in a manner respectful of certain values and as much concerned to maintain that respect as to achieve those more external ends such as 'levering up' standards of numeracy or ensuring that children understand the dangers of glue-sniffing.

These internal goods include the integrity of the personal well-being of teachers themselves. As *phronimoi*, 'persons of practical wisdom', they cannot be regarded as mere operatives of techniques in which the real value and usefulness is held to lie. This is my reason for talking of 'practical wisdom' rather than of 'practical judgement': the former is true to the idea of an enduring quality of character rather than a series of disconnected actions, however well-judged each may be. The term *practical wisdom* is suggestive, and properly so on the Aristotelian account, of a state in which knowledge, judgement and feeling hold together and inform each other. If this kind of account is correct then teachers are justified in being concerned about their own conditions of service – in pursuing what it has become common to find dismissed as 'producer interests' – since these are part of the internal goods of teaching and are not merely the perks and privileges which a professional lobby includes among its prizes. Teachers demoralised by the worst kinds of 'line management', for instance, are not just to be thought of as struggling to do their jobs in the face of a handicap equivalent to indigestion or a hangover. Demoralisation impairs the practical wisdom which is at the heart of teaching.

> *We had a staff training day on Assertive Discipline, and almost rightaway I had the opportunity to put a bit of it into action. Twenty children stood up as I went into the room, five stayed in their seats. At Reddington I'd have blown up the five and got into a hassle with them, the lesson would've gone to pot and I'd have come out frazzled. Assertive Discipline says praise the twenty – and it works! Next time round they all stood up. I got to thinking: however much I'd* known *about Assertive Discipline at Reddington it would still have been hard not to pass on to the kids the pressure and negative feelings that were being dished out to me. At my new school I feel valued and supported, so I can be more positive with my pupils.* (Secondary teacher, Co. Durham)

Here the place of feelings in the teacher's 'situational appreciation', and the inadequacy of purely technical reason ('However much I'd *known* about Assertive Discipline') are well-illustrated, as is the vulnerability of practical wisdom to the pressures teachers experience. The 'market model' of education does extensive damage here by awarding validity only to those external ends which can be measured, ranked and advertised.

The Getting of Practical Wisdom

How, then, is the kind of practical wisdom of which I have been writing to be acquired? There are at least two obstacles in the way of any easy answer to this question. The first is that, since we are not dealing with a practice of technical reason, there are likely to be no simple *procedures* here, no possibility of reduction to a clear-cut 'method'. It is always easier to say what practical wisdom is *not* than what it *is*. The second is that, as Larmore (1987) notes, this is an area where much more work needs to be done. In the time since Aristotle philosophers have done little to develop his picture of practical wisdom; Larmore argues that they have themselves been mesmerised by technical rationality and the attraction of explicit decision procedures. (An instructive example is *Practical Reasoning*. The editor, Joseph Raz, finds it unnecessary to mention Aristotle in his 17-page introductory survey, and the contributors largely confine their interest in the Aristotelian account to his remarks on the practical syllogism – where

Aristotle himself, it seems, for once succumbs to the perennial temptations of technicism.) Only relatively recently have they begun to repair this omission (cf. MacIntyre, 1982; Gadamer, 1975; Dunne, 1993 and Larmore, 1987). It is, however, possible to develop the picture a little further here, even if what I write will be at best only suggestive. I shall follow Aristotle (and, up to a point, Dunne) in grouping my remarks around the headings of experience, character and alertness, which is my version of Aristotle's *aisthesis*.

Experience is, obviously enough, a necessary condition of practical wisdom. We do not develop the complex qualities of the good teacher by reading books alone or by doing nothing but listen to lectures. The force of this truth has often led the authority of experience to be exaggerated. Because experience is a necessary condition, it does not follow that it is a sufficient one. If that were the case then every teacher, like everyone else in all trades and professions, would be constantly improving. As Aristotle says, however, it is by experience that bad lyre players are produced as well as good ones; if experience was enough there would be no need of teachers. Experience on its own is no panacea because unless we are helped, and sometimes even directly shown, how to interpret what we see and to formulate the right response to it, we import ways of understanding and coping that are inappropriate to the new context. The experienced teacher sees the activity of the infant classroom differently from the beginner (or outsider), who perceives only chaos. It is notorious that young teachers faced with excessively difficult experiences 'to learn from' may develop 'survival skills' which quickly harden into routines inimical to stimulating and flexible teaching.

We are perhaps reluctant to think of people needing to be *helped* to experience because of a peculiarly Anglo-Saxon faith in (theory of, perhaps) empiricism: the idea that our senses will supply us with truth without the intervention of experts and authorities. Yet with every new experience both as children and as adults we turn constantly to those who are wiser and more knowledgeable than ourselves to help us grasp *what we are to make of this*. That is why young teachers need to have around them other people who are lively and responsive, who help them to see 'what can be made of' the world of education and the school.

> *When my tutor comes out she brings a fresh eye to my classroom and helps me to see things that I haven't noticed or sometimes to be honest haven't wanted to notice. And this year I'm really lucky with my teacher too: his first response to a problem tends to be 'that's interesting', and all I'd thought was oh God, look what I've done now!* (Third-year BEd student)

Much damage, incidentally, has been done by arguments associated particularly with the philosophers Ryle and Oakeshott, to the effect that 'practical knowledge exists only in use, is not reflective and cannot be formulated in rules' (Oakeshott, 1962, p.8). True, in many cases of intelligent action there is no 'ghost in the machine', to use Ryle's famous phrase, thinking *before* the action, but rather the intelligence is *in* the action.

Unfortunately this, taken in conjunction perhaps with Polanyi's notion of 'implicit knowledge' and some of Schön's remarks about 'professional artistry', is often used to suggest that teaching is somehow an instinctual business that we just 'pick up'. We may have 'know-how' more than we can put into words, and certainly much more than can be 'formulated in rules', but we must not lose sight of the fact that we do help each other to learn from experience in a great number of ways, largely verbal, often oblique (ie, not by trying to map out the 'know-how' in words and pass it on in that form) and allusive. This leaves open the possibility that the ability to help people acquire professional capacities from experience may be somewhat different from the ability which is the hallmark of the experienced practitioner in that profession.

By *character* I mean that practical wisdom is never only a matter of learning skills and acquiring competencies but is bound up with the kind of person you are (hence I have preferred to talk of 'capacities' above). It is not so much that practical wisdom *requires* certain qualities, even 'virtues', to be in place before it can develop on the basis of them, as that it partly *consists* in them. A degree of patience, receptivity, the courage to look at the world with open eyes, the willingness to consider both sides of an issue, are all dimensions of practical wisdom itself. These qualities have a cognitive element to which I return later; here I want to note that they, and so practical wisdom itself, have a strongly affective side. Technical reason may congratulate itself on being uncontaminated by human feelings (thus leaving feelings to rampage through its domain unacknowledged and unchecked), but practical wisdom works with and through them.

Since this book is unlikely to be read by Martians there is no need to catalogue the many ways in which teachers find their daily work emotionally demanding. Yet the Martians might not deduce this from much of the literature on teaching and learning to teach or from the general run of 'staff -development programmes' which, with the exception of the occasional session on 'stress-management skills', tend to be about new bits of curriculum to deliver and assess, about raising pupils' standards and satisfying the inspectors. Even the better books talk only of teachers' values, aims or attitudes, which sound safe and undisturbing things to have. Pollard and Tann (1987, p.8) cite 'wholeheartedness' as a key 'attitude' of the reflective practitioner, thus effectively dismissing ambivalent or contradictory feelings as something which no professional teacher ought to have.

Practical wisdom, by contrast, can perhaps only be developed 'when a state of not knowing can be borne long enough' for us to explore the pattern of our experience (Salzberger-Wittenberg *et al.*, 1983, p.58), when we have the capacity to live with 'uncertainties and doubts without irritable reaching after fact and reason' (the poet John Keats, quoted *ibid.*). We need the help of other people to bear our uncertainties and the emotions which we find painful. They help us if they can both acknowledge their own emotional experience of teaching and accept our own feelings about our work in such a way as to show that they are natural reactions and not signs of unusual and intolerable weakness. Compare the teacher (above) who was able to help a third-year student to see her problems as 'interesting' and so to examine and learn from them.

The general impoverishment of the language of learning that I mentioned at the start of this chapter is particularly damaging to the way we talk and think about the emotions, suggesting that they are mere surges of raw feeling that 'come over us', to be put aside and discounted as we make cool appraisals in the ideal state of calm rationality. The nature of *alertness* in practical wisdom, however, is such that, to the contrary, what we now tend to distinguish as knowledge and feeling must draw on each other. Our feelings help us pick out what is salient in a given situation: thus we are alert to the desperation and distress, rather than simple cynicism (or vice versa) of the child cheating in a test, and this colours our response. We have a *sympathetic* understanding of things in their own terms, of what they mean to the agents involved, instead of supposing we are grasping them as 'objective phenomena'. The alert teacher responds to the myriad interruptions and distractions of the classroom by experiencing them accurately, as it were listening to their 'true sounds', distinguishing what is *meant as* a challenge, what is a misguided attempt at friendliness, and so on. Her practical wisdom finds her attuned (cf. Taylor, 1985, p.142) to the children's world rather than simply seeking control over it.

> *The point is that without emotions we do not fully register the facts or record them with the sort of resonance and importance that only emotional involvement can sustain. It is as if we could see, but only flatly and inertly, as if our perceptions were strung together in our minds but not fully understood or embraced.* (Sherman, 1989, p.47)

We can see clearly now how the different kinds of knowing – theory, technical reason and practical wisdom – support and inform *and* permeate, each other. Psychological and other kinds of theory (*theory* here in the wide sense used in the first section, and including the use of novels, poetry and film) can help us enter the world of the child and understand something of what his or her behaviour means, and this can be of great practical benefit. Technical reason suggests valuable strategies, for example, for teaching a lesson in such a way as to minimise interruptions. Practical wisdom is a matter of experiencing what is going on accurately and sensitively, of becoming (maybe slowly, over time) the kind of person who finds these things absorbing and not merely discomfiting, and who as a consequence becomes still better able to experience them attentively. In this way practical wisdom involves aspects of what I described earlier as theory. Without the strategies of technical reason practical wisdom may be overwhelmed; without practical wisdom technical reason has nowhere to go, no end beyond satisfaction in its own accomplishment. Without theory, in the way I have described it, both become blunted, insensitive and impoverished.

Higher Education

What, then, can higher education contribute here to the development of practical wisdom? I have emphasised that acquiring it requires a special kind of help and support: help to be *alive* to our experience, rather than denying, rationalising or falsifying it, and to interpret the world of school and education and find ways of making sense of it without interpretations being *imposed* on us. And we need emotional support from people who are not themselves frightened of the world of feelings, whose own sensibility (another word we have nearly lost: the idea of 'emotional consciousness . . . quickness and acuteness of apprehension; *OED*) is a touchstone; who know something of the world that the learner, in this case the student teacher, is moving in and provide an example of how to live intelligently and satisfyingly in that world.

There is a tradition that sees all this as the function of the *mentor*: a trusted counsellor or guide, a more experienced person who takes a special interest in the development of another individual; a relationship in which tolerance of uncertainty is one of the chief things that stands to be learned, and which is 'marked by substantial emotional commitment by both partners' (Antal, 1993). The world of business and industry evinces great enthusiasm for mentoring, seeing it as one of the best ways to help people 'learn to learn', to cope with times of rapid, even unparalleled change. It is part of an increasing tendency for that world not only to invest in job-specific skills but to value a more general notion of education, of the development and personal growth of employees beyond areas of immediate practical utility (White Paper, DTI, (1994), p.40; Pedler, *et al.*, 1991), helping them to 'shape career goal and plans in a realistic way . . . [and] to expand the focus of management development beyond specific competencies and skills to promoting a balanced growth' on the part of the individual (Antal, 1993). Conceived in the same sort of way, the mentor begins to seem of great importance if teaching is to be learned as a matter of practical wisdom and not only as a matter of picking up the know-how that goes with the job; if beginners are to understand what educative teaching is *for* and how that relates to their sense of where they are themselves going in their lives.

The new partnerships between schools and universities institutionalise, at government prompting, the provision of 'mentoring' for trainee teachers. It is, however, worth looking closely at what is being done under this title. Two things emerge that need to be considered further. First, the most cursory survey of the new literature on mentoring in schools reveals that 'mentor' has largely become the label for the member of staff responsible for the induction of trainees: 'the mentor either personally undertakes, or arranges for colleagues to undertake, a number of training tasks with the student' (Wilkin, 1992, p.19). Although the older and richer notion of the mentor as previously sketched still appears here and there in accounts of good practice there is an unmistakable sense, revealed in particular by the quantities of bullet-points, lists, charts and diagrams, that the mentor in school is primarily a bureaucrat who ensures that procedures are followed, competencies acquired, regulations complied with. Second, and as a corollary, mentoring is becoming colonised by technical reason. The dimension of teaching that more than any other accepted uncertainty and the necessity of living with it is twisted into a mechanism for 'leaving nothing to chance'. What has been essentially a personal relationship offering encouragement, support, clarification and challenge is at risk of becoming an exercise of a radically different sort. Often, this has meant that excellent teachers, natural mentors in the original sense, have come to undervalue their own qualities as persons as they perceive the new regime making different demands of them.

Some responsibility here attaches to certain 'mentoring courses' put on by university departments of education which consist of little more than establishing who does what and who ticks what box under the new partnership schemes. The main responsibility, however, lies with government, for the thrust of its 'reforms' has been, as successfully as if this had been their principal aim, to transform what was once 'teacher education' into a bureaucratic minefield of competency lists, policy documents, partnership contracts, funding transfers and assessment criteria.

Higher education can do better than this. For universities, far from being doomed to be left floundering as the world of business and industry energetically reinvents ways of helping people 'learn to learn', have themselves a rich tradition of mentoring, though not usually called by that name, to draw on. The *tutorial relationship*, both as inspired by the tutorial system of Oxford and Cambridge and as developed by newer universities, is one in which the student learns a way of *being* – of being an historian, an adult, a reflective and self-critical sort of person, perhaps – rather than simply acquiring facts and skills. This relationship, in perhaps the most influential and carefully articulated idea of what a university should be – John Henry Newman's – is part of the essence of such a place, as 'an *Alma Mater*, knowing her children one by one, not a foundry, or a mint, or a treadmill' (Newman, 1852, I vi 8).

'Knowing Her Children One By One': as the future of higher education continues to be debated, in the UK and elsewhere, this aspect of university education ought not to be overlooked. The comparison with industry makes clear that it may be one of the most powerful ways available of promoting learning and change, and not an out-moded luxury to be jettisoned in the rush towards a future incoherently fantasised as a bazaar of computers, information super-highways and 'learning-packages'. The benefit of such new technology, I suggest, is precisely that it enables university tutors to escape from being typecast as primarily transmitters of knowledge, and frees them to work in ways that are more personal and responsive to the needs of individual students: in short, as mentors.

In the UK, that we have moved from 'elite' to 'mass' higher education is sometimes taken to imply that the sheer number of students now makes this personal dimension impossible and that this, together with other pressures, means that lecturers can be expected to do no more than deliver their lectures (or other learning-packages) efficiently before getting on with research and income-generation. We stand at a crucial juncture where we can choose either to accede to this expectation or to resist it. If we accede to it we shall have effectively collaborated in the reduction of the university lecturer to the point where it is hard to see why he or she should not largely disappear from the academy, to be replaced by computers, distance-learning materials, researchers, counsellors *and* managers; a splitting and separation of functions inimical to the idea of practical wisdom as a holding-together of the various things we *do* in the shape of who we *are*, a maintaining of a balance among our different activities and objectives in the light of our sense of how a human life should be lived. We shall have done no service to our students, whose sense of being abandoned among fragmented modules and distracted staff is becoming increasingly clear.

If the role of mentor is appropriate in general for university lecturers then it is especially so for those lecturers working with student teachers. Because the demands of the courses they follow go well beyond the 'purely academic' and because learning to teach touches us on so many personal levels, many (though certainly not all) education tutors are used to working in this sort of way. It would be a particular pity if the designation of school-based mentors was allowed to obscure the mentoring role of the university tutor, for this is distinctive in that the university is in a position to form an understanding of the adults (young and otherwise) whom it teachers, the expertise of the school being rather in the developmental needs of the child. This is (again) not to deny that many schoolteachers will have a particular sensitivity to the position of those entering the profession, at least as much so as many individual university tutors. But it is the university which should be familiar with 'useful maps of how adults change and develop' (a chapter title in Daloz, 1986: he refers to the maps drawn by writers such as Levinson, Kegan and Erikson), not as a substitute for alert and sensitive attention to the condition of individual students but as an invaluable stimulus to thinking about adults' needs in helpful ways, rich in suggestive language and metaphors. In this way the mentoring university complements the mentoring school, and is a source of practical wisdom that goes beyond narrow, cognitive or transmissional definitions of its function.

Conclusion

For teaching to be a profession with the status and standards which that implies it must be self-critical and reflective. In his re-examination of 'the idea of the university' Jaroslav Pelikan writes (1992, p.108):

> *To qualify as a 'profession', an occupation or activity must involve some tradition of critical philosophical reflection, and probably the existence of a body of scholarly literature in which such reflection has been developed and debated. But the corollary of that thesis is probably a definition of the university as the only possible setting in which such reflection on a profession, and therefore the training informed by such reflection, can be carried on in its full intellectual context.*

What I have tried to sketch in this chapter is elements of what that 'full intellectual context' might involve for the preparation of teachers: certainly something far broader than the narrow technicist notions now current, and broader too than the curiously stunted vision enshrined in the 'reflective practitioner' literature or the arid and instrumental 'disciplines of education' movement that preceded it. If they are to contribute richly to the training and education of the teaching profession universities need to change, as they always need to be changing, not only to respond to the 'changing needs of society' but to renew their critical mission to challenge the latest complacencies (and idiocies, half-truths and plain lies) and remind us of the diversity of voices and ideas, with their unexplored possibilities, beyond the dominant ones of the day.

There is nothing new in the idea that universities should play the part of the Socratic gadfly, providing the stimulus of radical questions and challenges, and be prepared to pay the cost of being brushed aside from time to time by those in pursuit of more obvious rewards and short-term gains. But we do seem in danger of forgetting that there is such a thing as practical wisdom, which universities can also foster, supporting students so they can draw on and value their experience, realise possibilities of personal growth and discover that 'connection between knowledge and the zest of life' which Whitehead, in his *Aims of Education*, identified as 'the very justification for a university' (quoted in Pelikan, 1992, p.103). That would indeed be to do something for the grown-ups.

References

Antal, AB (1993) 'Odysseus's legacy to management development', *European Management Journal*, **11**(4): 448–54.

Arendt, H (1963) *Eichmann in Jerusalem*. Harmondsworth: Penguin.

Bettelheim, B (1960) *The Informed Heart*. New York: The Free Press.

Buchmann, M (1990) 'How Practical Is Contemplation in Teaching?' in C Day, M Pope and P Denicolo (eds) *Insight into Teachers' Thinking and Practice*. London: Falmer Press.

Daloz, LA (1986) *Effective Teaching and Mentoring*. San Francisco, CA: Jossey-Bass.

Department of Trade and Industry (DTI) (1994) Competitiveness: Helping Business to Win. London: HMSO.

Dunne, J (1993) *Back to the Rough Ground: 'Phronesis' and 'Techne' in Modern Philosophy and in Aristotle*. Notre Dame, IN: University of Notre Dame Press.

Gadamer, H-G (1975) *Truth and Method*. London: Sheed & Ward.

Gilmour, I (1992) *Dancing with Dogma: Britain under Thatcherism*. London: Pocket Books.

Gjertsen, D (1989) *Science and Philosophy*. Harmondsworth: Penguin.

Habermas, J (1974) *Theory and Practice* (trans. J Viertel). London: Heinemann.

Kemmis, S (1995) Prologue to Wilfred Carr, *For Education: Towards Critical Educational Inquiry*. Milton Keynes: Open University Press.

Kounin, JS (1970) *Discipline and Group Management in Classrooms*. New York: Holt, Rinehart & Winston.

Kuhn, T (1977) *The Essential Tension*. Chicago, IL: University of Chicago Press.

Larmore, C (1987) *Patterns of Moral Complexity*. Cambridge: Cambridge University Press.

Lasch, C (1984) *The Minimal Self: Psychic Survival in Troubled Times*. London: Pan Books.

MacIntyre, A (1982) *After Virtue*. London: Duckworth.

Newman, JH (1852/1965) *The Idea of a University Defined and Illustrated*. London: Dent.

Nussbaum, M (1986) *The Fragility of Goodness*. Cambridge: Cambridge University Press.

Oakeshott, M (1962) *Rationalism in Politics and Other Essays*. London: Methuen.

Pedler, M, Burgoyne, J and Boydell, T (1991) *The Learning Company: A Strategy for Sustainable Development*. New York: McGraw-Hill.

Pelikan, J (1992) *The Idea of the University: A Reexamination*. London: Yale University Press.

Pollard, A and Tann, S (1987) *Reflective Teaching in the Primary School*. London: Cassell.

Raz, J (ed) (1978) *Practical Reasoning*. Oxford Readings in Philosophy series. Oxford: Oxford University Press.

Salzberger-Wittenberg, I *et al*. (1983) *The Emotional Experience of Teaching and Learning*. London: Routledge.

Sherman, N (1989) *The Fabric of Character: Aristotle's Theory of Virtue*. Oxford: Clarendon Press.

Smith, R (1992) 'Theory: An Entitlement to Understanding', *Cambridge Journal of Education*, **22**(3): 387–98.

Taylor, C (1985) *Philosophy and the Human Sciences: Philosophical Papers 2*. Cambridge: Cambridge University Press.

Wilkin, M (ed) (1992) *Mentoring in Schools*. London: Kogan Page.

INDEX OF PEOPLE AND PLACES